Under the Palace Portal

Under the Palace Portal

Native American Artists in Santa Fe

Karl A. Hoerig

UNIVERSITY OF NEW MEXICO PRESS

ALBUQUERQUE

©2003 by Karl A. Hoerig
First edition
All rights reserved.

LIBRARY OF CONGRESS CATALOGING-IN-PUBLICATION DATA

Hoerig, Karl A., 1970–
Under the palace portal : Native American artists in Santa Fe /
Karl A. Hoerig.— 1st ed.
p. cm.
Includes bibliographical references and index.
ISBN 0-8263-2910-1 (cloth : alk. paper)
1. Native American Vendors Program (Santa Fe, N.M.)—History.
2. Palace of the Governors (Santa Fe, N.M.)—History.
3. Pueblo art—New Mexico—Santa Fe.
4. Pueblo business enterprises—New Mexico—Santa Fe—History.
5. Culture and tourism—New Mexico—Santa Fe.
6. Tourism and art—New Mexico—Santa Fe.
7. Santa Fe (N.M.)—Social life and customs. I. Title.
E99.P9 H663 2003
381'.457455'089970789—dc21
2003011953

1   2   3   4   5   6   7   8   9

Design and typography Kathleen Sparkes
Text typography is Adobe Garamond 11.5/14
Display typography Garamond Condensed

Cover design Robyn Mundy

Printed and bound by Thomson-Shore, Inc.

Contents

Illustrations

To the people who make the Portal
part of their lives and in turn
make it come to life.

Acknowledgments

This book would not exist without the interest, involvement, and acceptance of the people of the Native American Vendors Program of the Palace of the Governors. Program participants have volunteered their time and knowledge to this project and to my education. Special thanks are due to everyone who has given videorecorded interviews for the Portal Program archive. Many individuals have read all or parts of earlier drafts of this work and have added important insights. Though it is impossible to identify all those who have contributed in one way or another, I thank everyone who makes the portal part of their lives for helping to make it such an important part of mine.

I cannot distinguish in any meaningful way between my life away from Santa Fe and my involvement with the program and with my friends there. A program committee member once told me that whether I liked it or not, I was part of the program. In fact, I can think of no greater honor. The friendships I have had the extraordinary fortune to make under the Palace portal are more important to me than any book or other project.

A large portion of this project is a result of the efforts of Sarah Laughlin, former Portal Program coordinator, who first thought of creating an archive of interviews with program participants and who has acted as an advocate, collaborator, and critic throughout the last seven years. Thomas Chávez, former director of the Palace of the Governors, also actively supported my work and has read and provided important comments on drafts of this book. Deborah Davis, Portal Program coordinator from 1998 until 2002, facilitated my continuing work with the program. The entire Palace of the Governors staff has assisted my research in various ways. Special thanks to Pamela Smith, Hazel Romero, Diana DeSantis, Charles Bennett, and Tomas Jaehn. For his gracious map-making efforts, John Laughlin, assisted by Sarah Laughlin and Kathleen Lyons, deserves recognition.

At the University of Arizona, I am indebted to my doctoral committee who worked closely with me for many years. My advisor, Ellen Basso, skillfully guided me through the graduate program in the Department of Anthropology. Nancy Parezo shared her immense knowledge of anthropology and the study of Native American art and created opportunities for me to interact with many important scholars in our field. Tsianina Lomawaima provided keen commentary and suggestions that have improved my research methodologies and my writing. David Killick provided a different perspective and fresh thinking during the latter stages of my writing.

Chris, Lynn, Allyson, and Nathaniel Werhane have given me a home base in Santa Fe and have made me a part of their family. John and Zelda Polaski and everyone at Trail Dust Adventures and Eastside Radiator provided me with an extremely flexible workplace, allowing my absence for months at a time and also ensuring that my car made the frequent trips between Tucson and Santa Fe.

Evelyn Schlatter and others at the University of New Mexico Press have shown enthusiasm and patience in seeing this project to print. Nelson H. H. Graburn gave the manuscript a careful reading and through his comments improved this book. Sheila Berg's copyediting has considerably tightened the prose.

The research of which this book is a product was supported by a series of small grants from the Comins and Spicer Funds and a significant grant from the Stanley Grant Scholarship Fund through the University of Arizona Department of Anthropology. A University of Arizona Graduate College Final Project Grant also supported a portion of this work. Funds provided to the Portal Program by the Museum of New Mexico Foundation purchased some of the videotapes used in this project, and the museum sponsored the purchase of video equipment that allowed high-quality recording.

My parents and family have actively supported my continuing education. My wife, Nancy J. Davis, has provided moral, emotional, and economic support and has been my greatest supporter and most thoughtful critic. She accepts my frequent and extended absences and gives me a reason to come home. She helps me to see that what I do is worthwhile.

Prologue

What follows is the story of Santa Fe, New Mexico's most popular tourist attraction and the people who make it happen. The Native American Vendors Program of the Palace of the Governors in Santa Fe, known by many as the Portal Program, or more simply, the Portal, supports a marketplace where hundreds of Native American artists sell their work to millions of visitors each year. Because of the program's high profile, it is familiar to almost everyone who has visited the city. Images of the portal and the program's vendors appear on postcards, T-shirts, and in tourist literature. All of the tour buses that drive visitors past the "important" places in Santa Fe stop along Palace Avenue in front of the portal. But few outside of the program understand its complexity, the rules participants abide by, or the efforts and sacrifices made by the vendors to maintain their program. The tour bus guides sometimes provide incomplete or inaccurate information to their passengers; rare references to the Portal in academic writing reflect incomplete knowledge of the program;[1] even Museum of New Mexico staff acknowledge a limited understanding of the structure and operation of the Portal Program.[2] My primary goal in writing this book is to promote greater understanding of the program and its importance.

As is inevitable when engaged in a project such as this, I have frequently been asked what my work is about. In seeking to define it, I have generally hedged by identifying it as a mixture of genres. It is a history, documented both by written materials and, more important, by the words and memories of the people who have created and continue to re-create the program. It is also an ethnography of sorts, documented by formal and informal interviews, observation, interaction, and collaboration with program participants and meant to provide a more complex understanding of how the program operates and what it means at the end of the twentieth century and at the beginning of the twenty-first.

This is a time of great possibility for Native people. Varying assimilationist and isolationist policies of the U.S. government and the broader Euro-American society during the twentieth century aimed alternately to force Indian people to forsake important family, tribal, and cultural connections in order to attempt to integrate into American society or to marginalize them on reservations where they could maintain traditional ties but were subject to extremely limited access to resources. Native people have steadfastly refused to accept this artificial separation between tradition and integration and have firmly asserted their rights as indigenous people and as members of global society. They have clearly demonstrated that it is possible to live in both worlds, without compromising "tradition" or "culture" to do it.

In a recent essay, Marshall Sahlins (1999:vi–vii) expressed quite clearly what has been a surprise to anthropologists over the course of the twentieth century: indigenous cultures have not disappeared. Sahlins argues that hunters and gatherers, for example, though eulogized in 1966 at the well-known "Man the Hunter" conference, are still hunting and gathering at the beginning of the twenty-first century. Indigenous people have steadfastly proven earlier social scientists wrong as they continue to live culturally distinct, meaningful lives. The use of modern technology, active involvement in the money economy, the pursuit of university degrees, or living hundreds or even thousands of miles away from one's home community does not necessarily mean loss of one's indigenous culture.

From Native American artists developing Web sites and selling their work through Internet auctions to the use of "distance learning" technologies to teach indigenous languages, Indian people are celebrating the value and inseparability of their lives "at home" and in the wider national and global society. This book is about the ways in which one group of Native American artists in New Mexico engage in this complicated world every day. At the same time it recognizes that this integration of worlds is not new and that indigenous people have always maintained their agency in the face of tremendous adversity. The Native American Vendors Program exists because Native people made it, developed it, and continue to maintain it.

This book also reflects the changes that have occurred in the practice of anthropology during the last twenty-five years. I began the study of anthropology at a time when the discipline was working its way out of what George E. Marcus and Michael M. J. Fischer (1986) called a "crisis of representation." The metatheories that had long driven anthropological understanding had been declared dead, and ethnographers were questioning the fundamental validity of their profession. It was a time of realization of what now seem to be fundamental truths—for example, that self-reflexivity is a critical part of ethnography, that no ethnographic writing can capture the whole reality of social experience, that ethnography is (true) fiction (Clifford 1986:6–7).

In the last quarter century, ethnographic research has shifted from the study of isolated "others" to focused examinations of elements of peoples' lives in a complex and disjunctive world system. Marcus has identified "multi-sited ethnography" as a strategy for exploring the intricacies and interconnections of life in contemporary societies. Multi-sited ethnography, he says, "moves out from the single sites and local situations of conventional ethnographic research designs to examine the circulation of cultural meanings, objects, and identities in diffuse time-space" (Marcus 1998:79).

I have tried to keep in mind both the value of intensive, single-sited ethnographic research and the realities of the disjunctures of contemporary life. Though concentrating on a single site, the daily market held under the portal of the Palace of the Governors, I have had to consider a number of realities that are not actually situated under the portal, what Marcus (1998:91) calls "'off-stage' knowledge." What happens under the portal is influenced by what happens at "home" (both in the Pueblo villages and on the reservations and at people's homes in Santa Fe, Albuquerque, and other cities); by the status of Native Americans vis-à-vis the federal government (and more specifically, how this has played out in the courts); by what happens in the unique bureaucratic world of the Museum of New Mexico; and by what happens in the world of national and international tourism and in the broader market for Native American arts.

As an undergraduate at the University of Texas, I took a course from Stephen Feld in which he talked about reading his book, *Sound and Sentiment*, to the Kaluli people of Papua New Guinea, about whom he had written. In the second edition of the book (1990), he includes a discussion of that experience. By the time I entered graduate school, it had become a truism that the subjects of ethnographic writing were also members of the audience.[3] I cannot imagine it any other way. This work is about a program and the people who participate in it, but more important to me, it is for the people who make up the program.

Methodology

My "fieldwork" has been rather nontraditional, but it reflects the changing nature of funding, ethnographic subject matter, and interaction among the academic anthropological community and the people we work with. I have been involved with the Portal Program since summer 1995, when I first met with members of the Palace of the Governors administration and staff (in particular, Sarah Laughlin, former Portal Program coordinator) and with the program's administrative committee. During the seven years that have transpired since that time, I have maintained contact with program participants and museum staff. Though I have not lived full-time in Santa Fe during this period, the relative proximity of Santa Fe to Tucson (about 525 miles) has allowed me to be present at the portal regularly. A series of small research grants supported extended stays in Santa Fe during the summers of 1997 and 1998 and for a shorter time in 1999 and regular one- to two-week visits at other times of the year, beginning with preliminary two-week visits in the summers of 1995 and 1996 and continuing through the present. The extended period of involvement has proven invaluable in coming to know the program and the people.

When I came to the Portal Program in 1995, I planned to study the interaction among tourists and artists, to see how and what cultural knowledge was exchanged. I pitched the idea to the program's administrative committee, who politely told me they were not interested in research of that sort. During that visit, I saw enough of the program to know that it was a remarkable institution. In early 1996 Sarah Laughlin began to develop the idea of creating an archive of videotaped interviews with program participants. The idea found widespread support among the participants, but neither Sarah nor members of the program had the time, expertise, or sense of urgency to go very far with the project. I recognized the value of the idea, including the possibility that I might contribute to the program by helping with the project. I met again with the program committee, and we agreed to pursue the archive and that I should develop my doctoral dissertation as a history and description of the Portal, using the collected interviews as a primary data set.

I took a video production course through Access Tucson, the local community access cable television organization, and in consultation with the program committee developed a basic set of questions to be used in the semistructured, open-ended interviews. We began taping interviews in earnest during spring 1997 on a consumer-level VHS camera. In June a funding windfall at the museum allowed us to acquire a hand-held Sony Hi8 video camera, on which the majority of interviews have been recorded. To date interviews have been recorded with twenty-nine individuals involved with the program, ranging from a half-hour to more than three hours in length. Copies of these recordings are housed in the Portal Program office.

In addition to the recorded interviews, I have conducted a number of untaped interviews of varying formality. Equally important for gaining an understanding of the daily working of the program, I have spent hundreds of hours under the portal during all seasons of the year. I have also served as a laborer, an errand boy, and a photographer of artists' work and of program events.

To gain a historical understanding of the program's development, I conducted archival research at the Museum of New Mexico Fray Angelico Chávez History Library, at the New Mexico State Records Center and Archives, and in the Portal Program's logbooks. As a long-standing but largely unquestioned Santa Fe institution, the Portal Program has been mentioned in a number of secondary histories of the city and is regularly if superficially noted in travel guides and magazine and newspaper articles. The most striking feature of these published accounts is the way in which the program is naturalized as part of the Santa Fe scene. Simply put, it is generally accepted that Indian artists have always been under the Palace portal.

I am the author of this work only in the sense that I have put together words to try to provide an accurate description and explanation of the Native American Vendors Program to others who know less about it than I (though, of course, the shortcomings of this work are solely my responsibility). The people who have shared their experiences under the portal are the true bearers of knowledge and are the ones who give value to this work. A more accurate assessment of my role would be that of compiler, editor, or even abridger of what has been taught to me.

Notes on the Text

A significant portion of the text is drawn from the collection of interviews conducted as part of this project. Transcriptions of these interviews are set as extracts. The speaker in each instance is identified by name and tribal group of origin, as requested by the speaker, or by standardized tribal name (or in the case of nonvendors, by association with the program). Some interviewees have asked not to be identified by name and have been given a pseudonym, designated by an asterisk (*). For clarity, the transcripts have been edited to remove false starts and nonmeaningful "you knows," "uhs," and other extraneous interjections. At the request of and through consultation with the individuals quoted, language has been standardized to clarify meanings. In all instances, every effort has been made to preserve the speech styles of interviewees. Editorial interpolations are placed in square brackets ([ ]). Ellipses (. . .) denote the omission of a word, phrase, or line. Where nonconsecutive portions of an interview are placed together, the divide is marked by a double forward slash (//). Interviewers' questions or comments are enclosed in curly braces ({}). The interviewer is identified by initials (KH for the author, SL for Sarah Laughlin).

O N E

Introduction

As the bells of Saint Francis Cathedral chime 7:00 A.M. each day on the Santa Fe plaza, the heart of New Mexico's capital begins to come to life. The shops, galleries, and museums that occupy most of the downtown area will not open for at least two hours, but already there is a bustle of activity along the north side of the plaza. Singly and in small groups, Native American artists walk along the portal, or porch, that fronts the Palace of the Governors, home of the Museum of New Mexico's history museum. Each artist drops a brightly colored cloth, a foam kneeling pad, or a carpet square at a spot along the sidewalk in front of one of the sixty-four numbered spaces that line the wall of the Palace. As the minutes pass cars, trucks, and vans slowly pull up to the curb and other artists emerge and place their cloths along the portal.

Each of the artists has come to the plaza from their homes in the Pueblo villages, on the Indian reservations, or in Albuquerque or Santa Fe for the opportunity to sell the artwork they and their family members have produced as participants in the Native American Vendors Program of the Palace of the Governors. The Portal Program is the most visited program of the Museum of New Mexico and is a central part of Santa Fe's tourism industry.

The more than two million tourists who visit Santa Fe each year make the Portal Program possible, but it is much more than just a market for Native American tourist arts.[1] Growing out of the nearly four-hundred-year history of Santa Fe, the portal market is grounded in centuries of interaction among people from different cultures. It is important to the city in bringing visitors to the plaza area and critically important in the economies of hundreds of Native American families and their communities. The Portal Program is also a central focus of the Native American arts and crafts market in the southwestern United States and plays an important role in promoting Native American arts and in shaping trends in the arts themselves.

As befits its location on the front porch of a state institution, the Portal Program is a threshold for interaction on many levels. Sponsored by the Museum of New Mexico, it is a threshold between Native American and non-Native people. Starting in the 1920s, the museum began to host Native American arts and crafts markets to instruct visitors on what constituted "good" (in the eyes of the events' organizers) Indian art and to encourage Native American artists to produce that kind of art instead of hastily made, cheap curios. Over time, the educational emphases of the program have changed. Museum administrators now emphasize the educational value of the program as residing in the interaction between non-Native visitors and the Native American vendors. Most commonly, visitors learn about the materials and techniques used in the production of Native American jewelry, pottery, and other art forms sold under the portal. Some vendors spend a great deal of time talking to visitors (and potential customers) about their art and about themselves and their communities. On a more basic level, visitors who are unfamiliar with the lives of contemporary Native American people learn a great deal from interacting with the Portal Program participants; they begin to identify Native Americans as individuals rather than as stereotypes or categories and recognize some of the realities of contemporary Native American life. As Sarah Laughlin put it, "[T]here's lots of information available about the crafts, and the history, and the culture, but what isn't [available], the most important educational thing, is just like, 'Oh my God, we're all in the same stew!'"[2]

But the educational nature of the program goes far beyond what visitors learn about Indian people and the stones, materials, and techniques used in their arts. The Portal Program is educational for vendors too, as it serves as a threshold of interaction among participants with diverse life experiences and from different cultural backgrounds. Native people from urban backgrounds enter the program and learn much from their fellow vendors. Likewise, vendors who have lived their entire lives in Pueblo communities and on reservations learn about the experiences of urban Native people. Young artists who enter the program are gently guided and advised in the development of their art forms by their elders. This mentoring often moves beyond the limits of materials and techniques, and younger vendors are encouraged to learn more about their cultural histories, traditions, and languages. On a more abstract level, the possibility of making a living selling art under the portal not only supports the production of Native American art but also allows artists to live in their home communities and uphold traditional responsibilities that often demand significant time and money. Thus the Portal Program allows New Mexico Native people to maintain their cultural traditions in ways that no other work environment could.

People from Santo Domingo, Jemez, Santa Clara, and all of the other pueblos come together on a daily basis with Navajo and other non-Puebloan people. Though the program is generally limited to members of New Mexico's recognized Native American communities, Native people from other areas across the United States who have family connections to New Mexico tribes or who have attended the Institute of American Indian Arts have been admitted to the program, greatly increasing its cultural diversity. Some vendors have been technicians, administrators, truck drivers, educators, or managers who have turned or returned to traditional arts for their livelihoods. Others have made the production of arts and crafts their life's work. Some are young artists just entering the art "scene." Some will leave the program to go to college and on to other careers. Vendors come from very different and sometimes mutually antagonistic cultural and personal backgrounds to create, on a daily basis, a new kind of Native American community.

The Portal is a threshold between Native American people and the state of New Mexico. Its very existence depends on a continuing dialogue between and continuing support from both the state museum (and its Board of Regents) and the body of vendors. The Museum of New Mexico continues to define and to defend the program. Without the museum's support, the program would not exist. But at the same time, the program could not exist without the dedication and efforts of the program participants. The vendors and especially the ten-member administrative committee, elected annually by the program membership, ensure that the program continues to operate according to the high standards established by the vendors and the museum. Formal rules and procedures that direct the program are evidence of its place within the bureaucracy of a Western cultural institution; a commitment to giving all interested parties equal voice and to sincere efforts to reach unanimous consensus on issues affecting the program reflect a Native American way of doing things. The Portal Program is an example of cross-cultural cooperation and of how state institutions and indigenous peoples can work together to create programs that are mutually beneficial to participants, the institution, and visitors.

Finally, the Portal is a threshold for dialogue about what constitutes Native American arts and crafts. Questions of craft versus art are played out every day under the portal in the interactions between producers and consumers. Issues of tradition and authenticity sometimes clash with the desires of artists to expand their modes of expression. Participants must regularly negotiate between producing what tourists want to buy and creating what they themselves see as art, between participating in an ethnic arts and crafts market and fully expressing themselves as creators and innovators. At the same time artists must constantly walk the often thin line between making art rooted in Native American traditions and preserving and protecting those traditions that have often been compromised by both Native and non-Native people.

The Native American Arts and Crafts Market

With annual estimated retail value in the United States of $1 billion (Shiffman 1998), to say nothing of extensive trade in Europe, Japan, and elsewhere, the Native American arts and crafts market has a significant impact not only on the individuals, families, and communities that make up Native America but also on the economy of the United States and especially on the regional economy of the Southwest. At Zuni Pueblo in western New Mexico, for example, as much as 70 percent of the population produce arts and crafts (Shiffman 1998; see also Mills 1995; Ostler 1991). Closer to Santa Fe, almost 10 percent of the population of Santo Domingo Pueblo are registered as Portal Program vendors (more than 300 out of a 1993 enrollment of 4,050 [Tiller 1996:464]). Hundreds more sell their work elsewhere in Santa Fe and in Albuquerque or produce pieces that are wholesaled to shops, galleries, and other distributors. In addition to the huge value of the arts bought and sold, the economic impact of the market for hotels, restaurants, and others in the tourism industry is immeasurable.

Though a few artists in nearly every Native community in North America sell their work from their homes or shops, the vast majority of consumers never travel to the reservations or reserves. As a result, with the exceptions of the Southwestern Association for Indian Arts' annual Indian Market in Santa Fe, the Gallup Ceremonial, the Eight Northern Pueblos Artist and Craftsman Show, and annual shows at the Heard Museum in Phoenix and similar smaller Native American arts and crafts shows held across the United States and in other countries—when the artists go to the consumers—purchasers of Native American art rarely have the opportunity to interact with the artists who make the objects they purchase and collect.[3]

A unique exception is the Portal Program, which allows access to Native America in a setting that is readily accessible and not as foreign or socially intimidating as a visit to a Pueblo community or reservation might seem. Consumers of Native American art have the opportunity under the portal to purchase directly from the artists or family members of the artists who have made the pieces they buy, thus lending greater meaning to the objects they take home.

As Native American arts have increased in popularity and marketability, the sale of machine-made and imported non-Indian-made pieces and the representation of low-quality and artificial materials as genuine has increased dramatically. Federal and state attempts to control the fraudulent sales of imitation Indian arts have been largely ineffective. Since the first federal regulations against the counterfeiting of Indian arts and crafts were enacted in 1935, there have been no convictions (Arrillaga 2000; Parsley 1993:491–92; *USA Today,* April 8, 1998, p. 2A). The Indian Arts and Crafts Act of 1990 was an attempt to strengthen anticounterfeiting laws, providing for fines of up to $1 million and fifteen-year prison terms for violators (Parsley 1993:487). Unfortunately, lack of funding and the absence of full-time investigators have rendered the legislation largely unenforceable (Shiffman 1998). New Mexico passed state laws against the counterfeiting of Indian art in 1973, but enforcement has likewise suffered from inadequate funding. In 1998, $150,000 was appropriated from the New Mexico state budget for enforcement, and some Native American artists—most notably Isleta sculptor Andy Abeita—have begun to help train law enforcement agencies in the detection of counterfeit Indian art. Still, as much as 40 to 60 percent of the pieces sold as Native American arts are thought to be fake (Shiffman 1998).

The Portal Program is an exception here too. One of the goals of the museum is to provide a marketplace where tourists can be confident that they are purchasing authentic handmade Native American arts and crafts. As George Ewing, former director of the Museum of New Mexico, explained, "Museums always, with their sales activities[,] . . . are dependent upon quality. You've got to assure everyone that what you're selling in there [is] of a good quality" (interview, 1998). To ensure this, program rules require vendors to sell only items made by themselves or by members of their households. Techniques that can be used for mass production are prohibited, and vendors must sign their pieces with a maker's mark. On jewelry, this hallmark must be placed directly under any stones, eliminating the possibility of stamping pieces after they have been made. Similarly, signatures must be inscribed on pottery before it is fired. One of the duties of the program's administrative committee is to conduct daily checks of the art for sale under the portal to ensure that program rules are followed. Violations are recorded, and items that do not meet program standards cannot be sold. Significant or habitual violations of program rules can lead to suspension from the program. The vast majority of program vendors are strong advocates of both the program rules and the state and federal legislation aimed at protecting Native American art. Though not perfect, the enforcement of the Portal Program rules goes a long way toward upholding state and federal regulations and ensuring that customers get what they pay for: art pieces handmade by the families of the vendors who sell them.

The Portal Program

At the time of this writing, about one thousand Native American artists are registered participants in the Portal Program. Members of Santo Domingo Pueblo make up about one-third of the program; Diné (Navajo) people comprise another one-third. The remaining third includes vendors from nearly all of the other Pueblo villages and tribal groups of New Mexico along with a small number of Hopi people and enrolled members of Native American tribal groups outside New Mexico. To generalize about the vendors is to point out the diversity that exists among them. In addition to coming from many different cultural backgrounds, the vendors have diverse educational, employment, and life histories. Vendors' ages range from the minimum of eighteen to well over eighty, with young people under eighteen often helping in household production or producing their own art to be sold under the portal by their parents or grandparents. On any given day, about an equal number of women and men come to sell.

The households that they represent likewise illustrate the diversity of Native American life experiences. A 1991 modification of the program rules defines households as "those persons residing in the same house, who are related by blood or marriage, and who qualify as members of New Mexican Indian tribes or pueblos" (Museum of New Mexico 1991:3; see also Appendix A), but acknowledges the complexity of the issue by allowing the director of the Palace of the Governors to make "minor exceptions" to the rule. Most households

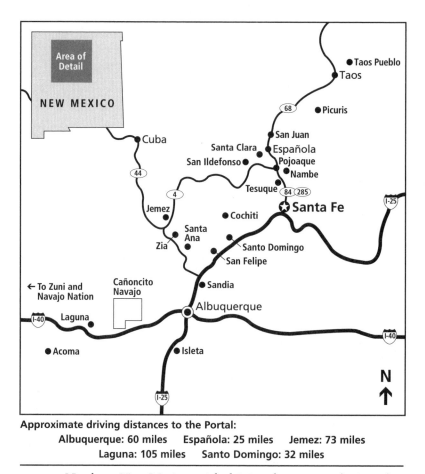

Approximate driving distances to the Portal:
Albuquerque: 60 miles   Española: 25 miles   Jemez: 73 miles
Laguna: 105 miles   Santo Domingo: 32 miles

MAP I: *Northern New Mexico, with driving distances to the Portal from the home communities of vendors.*

are made up of nuclear and extended families. In some of these households one member, most often the wife-mother, is the regular salesperson, leaving the other family members at home to produce most of the work. Some households are made up of siblings, and others include single individuals who do all of the artwork and selling themselves. Participants whose domestic partners are non-Indian also have to do both the production and selling of their art themselves. Occasionally households are made up of unrelated friends who join together to share expenses; however, the limitation of two artists to one cloth usually is economically difficult and such convenience households are short-lived. In some instances, vendors choose not to share households with other members of their families because of the limitations presented by the household rule. Not infrequently, elder vendors who can no longer work will be allowed to sell for their children or grandchildren, and when vendors suffer from significant illnesses or injuries other family members are permitted to temporarily sell those artists' work until they are able to return to the portal.

The ten-vendor volunteer administrative committee, which directs the daily operation of the program, is assisted by a full-time museum staff member who serves as program coordinator and liaison between the vendors and the museum administration. It is the committee that makes the program possible. They are responsible for making sure the program runs smoothly and that the program rules are followed. The committee also takes responsibility for organizing special events such as program potluck dinners during the holidays, an annual Christmas children's show, and fund-raising. Though funding from the state and especially from the Museum of New Mexico Foundation has increased in recent years, it is still limited. A significant percentage of moneys used for advertising and other program activities comes from the committee's sale of soft drinks and other items and occasional events such as frito pie or frybread sales.

The Palace portal itself stretches some 259 feet along Palace Avenue, occupying the entire northern side of the Santa Fe plaza. Along the south wall of the Palace, the portal is divided into sixty-four numbered spaces, each twelve bricks wide and six feet deep. The bancos (benches) built inside the bastions on each end of the portal hold another two spaces each, and two more spaces are marked along the curb, one on each end of the porch, just inside the bastions. The first space to the west of the main entrance to the Palace (space 34) is reserved for the duty officer of the day. No other spaces are reserved, but starting at 7:00 A.M. vendors may mark desired spaces by placing a cloth or other marker on the sidewalk. Most vendors use the same marker each day, and other vendors can pick who they would like to sit next to for the day through recognition of these markers. If at 8:00 A.M. there are not more vendors than spaces available, each vendor can occupy his or her marked space and begin to set up his or her "cloth" for the day.

When more than seventy vendors arrive at the portal before 8:00 A.M., a lottery is held to select spaces for the day. During the summer tourist season, on weekends year-round, and especially around major holidays it is not unusual for up to one hundred fifty vendors to come to sell under the portal. On these days with a "draw," the committee member who is on duty lays out a set of poker chips numbered to represent the sixty-nine spaces available. Other committee members count the prospective vendors, who line up along either side of the portal, facing the center. Blank chips are added to the numbered ones to equal the total number of vendors waiting to draw, and the number of chips is verified by a noncommittee vendor to ensure the accuracy and honesty of the draw. The chips are then placed in a bag, and each vendor is given the opportunity in turn to pull a chip from it. Those who draw numbered chips register their space numbers with the committee and begin to set up. Those who "blank" can sign up on a waiting list, find a generous and luckier associate willing to share space, or go home and try again another day. Current rules permit all but ten of the seventy spaces to be shared, the nonsharing spaces being odd-shaped or small because of variations in the contours of the Palace wall. As many as one hundred thirty vendors could sell on any given day, but not all vendors like to share, and more typically fewer than one hundred will be set up at any one time. On the busiest holiday weekends, the director of the Palace may authorize the opening of an additional twenty-two spaces on the west side of the Palace, which gives that many more vendors the opportunity to sell.

All vendors must have their cloths completely set up by 10:00 A.M. and after that time cannot be away from their cloths for more than one hour at a time. After the 8:00 A.M. draw, some vendors will go to breakfast at one of the local restaurants; others will set up and begin selling. Some set up and then leave to run errands or to go home to polish pieces of jewelry or do other work until they have to be back at their spaces. When away from their spaces, vendors are required to "cover up" their cloths so that visitors will know that the pieces are not available for sale during their absence. Many vendors use the same cloth used to mark their places before 8:00 A.M. as their "cover up" cloth. The prime selling time is from about 10:00 A.M. to midafternoon. On most days some vendors leave between 3:00 and 4:00 P.M. so that they can pick up their children or grandchildren from school, visit the jewelry supply store, or go home to work on their art. Some vendors come in the afternoon to take spaces vacated by those who leave early, but by 5:00 P.M. the portal begins to empty except for those few vendors who sometimes stay until dusk.

To become authorized participants in the program, artists must complete application materials, supply a certificate of Indian birth or other proof of tribal membership in a New Mexico tribe, identify a unique maker's mark, and demonstrate their arts for the program committee. Demonstrations are performed at the potential vendors' homes or workshops, which can require significant travel for committee members. Because of the demands on the time and energy of the committee members to observe demonstrations and because of the custom of having at least two observers at each "demo," former committee members and the program coordinator sometimes assist, and even I have sometimes served as a second observer of demonstrations. Potential vendors must show their ability to make all of the objects they intend to sell and demonstrate all of the steps involved in making each object. Vendors who want to add new media or techniques to their cloths must demonstrate their proficiency in each new art form or method. Vendors selling items that they have not demonstrated are asked by the committee to remove offending pieces from their cloths and are subject to sanctions. The demonstrations and the regular review of the artists' work help to maintain the integrity of the program.

In keeping with the aims of the Portal Program, rules regarding materials and techniques are stricter than those of most Native American arts and crafts shows. White metal sold on the portal must be sterling silver (92.5 percent silver) or fine (99 percent pure) silver. Coin silver and silver-plated materials are prohibited. With a few exceptions, stones used by jewelers must not be dyed or laboratory manufactured. Precarved or predrilled stone or shell pieces are not allowed, but preshaped cabochons (stones cut ready for setting) may be used in the making of jewelry. Stabilized turquoise, stone that is infused with a clear resin to strengthen it, is allowed and is used by most turquoise artists, though some silverworkers use only natural turquoise in their pieces. Reconstituted turquoise (also called "block" turquoise, or more simply, "plastic"), stone that is pulverized and then mixed with resin and re-formed, is prohibited, as is color-shot (dyed) turquoise. Potters must form their own pieces from earth clays collected on their reservations, and pieces must be fired "outside" using wood fires. Kiln-firing is not allowed. Sandpaintings can only be made with natural, undyed materials. All pieces must be handmade; machine stamping, cutting, or forming is not allowed.[4]

Unlike juried shows, the demonstrations, inspections, and rules are not for the purpose of limiting participation to artists whose work meets some criteria of aesthetic quality. In this way the program is very inclusive, as it allows artists and craftspeople of all levels of skill, experience, and artistic vision to participate. Unlike most shops and galleries, which are directed at a limited clientele, the portal is visited by a vast range of consumers, from vacationers seeking souvenirs to serious collectors. While most artists produce pieces with a range of value, and most pieces under the portal are sold for less than $100, artists who produce only low-priced pieces and those who produce few pieces under $100 are all able to support themselves through portal sales. The program is designed to maintain honesty in representation but more important to protect the Native American artists and craftspeople who make up the program. While income for Native American artists is decreasing as imitation work floods the market (Shiffman 1998), the Portal Program provides a place where artists can sell their work to a clientele that appreciates its value.

In discussions of the Native American Vendors Program, issues of authenticity, quality, and what characteristics make objects Native

American art surface again and again. The opportunity to buy "real Indian art" from Native American artists is what brings visitors to the portal, and these visitors make participation in the program possible for vendors. But the Portal Program is about much more than these things. It is about multicultural interactions. It is about state institutions and indigenous people working together. It is about the experiences of Native American people in a local, national, and world economy and society.

Touristic Front Regions and Real Life

In his now-classic book, *The Tourist: A New Theory of the Leisure Class* ([1976] 1999), Dean MacCannell adapts Erving Goffman's performance theory of social interaction to the touristic experience and enterprise. He theorizes the existence of "front" and "back" regions in tourist settings. "Front" regions are those places set up for touristic experience, the spaces where visitors can view staged indigenous cultural displays; "back" regions are the spaces of "real" life, where local actors really live (and prepare for acting in the "front" regions) and where tourists seek to gain access to "authentic" experiences. He makes the important point that there exists a continuum between front and back and that even back regions can be shaped and "cleaned up" for touristic visitation (MacCannell [1976] 1999:101–2).

Tourism theorists disagree on the goals of tourists in regard to front and back regions. MacCannell's argument is in large part a reaction to Daniel Boorstin's (1961) assertion that tourists are satisfied with or indeed even desire artificial experiences or "pseudo-events" rather than seek authenticity (which is the goal of a more sophisticated, intellectual figure, the "traveler"). MacCannell's counterpoint is to deny as artificial the distinction between tourist and traveler and to assert that both groups seek authentic experience but that neither really ever gains that experience. Others (e.g., van den Berghe 1994) take a more balanced view, recognizing that tourists exhibit a variety of expectations, desires, and tolerances, ranging from those who are quite content to view the world from the safe confines of the tour bus (the front region) to those who are not satisfied with anything less than to observe Native people as they go about their "authentic" lives (in, to some degree, back regions).

Whatever their ideas regarding the desires of tourists, there has been general agreement by scholars that on varying levels touristic settings are somehow false or imitation, not real life. MacCannell ([1976] 1999) presents the concept of "staged authenticity," wherein the events that tourists witness are made by the touristic hosts to have the appearance of real life. Ranging from staged "traditional" dances performed in hotel ballrooms to glimpses into peoples' homes, there is a measure of artifice in all touristic experiences. More recently some theorists have criticized the concept of staged authenticity, arguing that in varying ways all cultures are "staged" and that the supposed inauthenticity of the tourist setting is fundamentally no different from the constructed authenticity of all cultures (Crick 1989; Urry 1990).

Both the theory of staged authenticity and its critiques suggest that because touristic front regions are constructed, they are therefore false on a fundamental level. Because they are staged examples of "real" life, these settings are given a sort of Disney World aura; because the cultural expressions that are found in the front region (or in the cleaned-up back regions) are staged, they are somehow not true life experiences for the indigenous host-actors, just as they are not "real" experiences of indigenous life for the tourist visitors. This is, I think, a result of the conflation of the experience of tourists with the experience of the subjects of tourism. Tourism is a "sacred journey," a period of abnormal or sacred time and experience away from the profane time of ordinary life (Graburn 1977). Tourism is a state of liminality (Turner [1969] 1995), in which tourists are removed from their ordinary experiences.

Because of the extraordinary nature of the touristic experience, the spaces through which tourists travel and the nontourists they meet there are also thought to be in some way unreal. For example, in discussing a successful ethnic tourism locale, Pierre van den Berghe (1994:150) distinguishes between the real and the touristic and emphasizes the necessity of the image of reality: "Still, nine-tenths of the town [San Cristóbal, Mexico], and most obviously, the sprawling produce market, are quite visibly and convincingly real, in the sense that they would be there, unchanged, with or without tourists." Thus locales such as Santa Fe that cater to tourists become inauthentic as they begin to suffer from "museumization," "Disney-landization," and "boutiquization" (van den Berghe 1994:149). Similarly, Jeremy Boissevain makes a distinction between "ordinary" life and life during the tourist season for residents of European coastal towns:

> Those who live and work in popular seaside destinations must work extremely hard during the summer months. Once the season is over, they are able to recover from the summer onslaught and resume the more tranquil rhythm of their ordinary lives until the following high season. (1996:9)

Recently some scholars have begun to critique this notion of the artificiality of the touristic setting for the subjects of tourism. In her discussion of Torajan funeral rituals in South Sulawesi, Indonesia, Kathleen M. Adams (1997) argues that although the Torajan people change some aspects of their rituals to accommodate visitors and tourists, the funerals continue to be vitally important events in Torajan society. Christopher Tilley (1997) comes to a similar conclusion about the "Small Nambas" dance performance put on for tourists by Wala islanders of Malekula, Vanuatu. The show was created from traditional dances taught to the group's chief by his father and grandfather. However, some of the details of the dancing ground construction and other elements of the performance have been informed by an ethnography of nearby islands published in 1942 (J. Layard's *Stone Men of Malekula*) and information from a regional cultural center and its former director (Tilley 1997:79–80). Most tourists seem thrilled with the opportunity to witness the performance, though some self-identified "travelers" (see Boorstin 1961) were appalled at the inauthenticity of the constructed show: "'We have not seen anything like that before. A Disneyland in Vanuatu.

We did not come for that'" (Tilley 1997:79). Tilley argues that rather than a spurious invention of culture, the Small Nambas show is based on two fundamental aspects of the Wala islanders' (real or authentic) culture. The incorporation of cultural elements from different sources and the selling of that "bricolage" to others are cultural practices much used in the past and now simply adapted to the realities of global tourism (Tilley 1997:84). The Small Nambas are thus not creating an inauthentic cultural performance but are engaging in authentic cultural practices.

The point that I wish to make in contributing to the critique of staged authenticity is a more basic one. Not only do cultural performances in touristic settings have meaning and authenticity for those who perform them, but engaging in the business of tourism is also real and authentic experience for indigenous people. Just as working at Disney World (or performing in the Small Nambas show) is a real job and part of real life for employees, so too is engaging in the commerce of tourism real life for the indigenous people who do so. What might be constructed authenticity for tourists is also a part of the authentic lives of the people who are the subjects of ethnic tourism.

As I discuss in chapter 2, Santa Fe is a quintessential example of staged or constructed authenticity (see especially Lippard 1999; Rothman 1998; Wilson 1997): from the intentional development of a particular style of architecture and the enforcement of that style through city building codes to the encouragement of tourism through the promotion of a particular tricultural atmosphere in the city (of which the Portal Program is a significant part), the Santa Fe that became a tourist destination in the twentieth century has been intentionally shaped to become that tourist destination. While one can debate whether lodging in a hotel constructed of cinder blocks but appearing to be made of adobe provides a more authentic experience for Santa Fe visitors, the fact of the matter is that living and working in Santa Fe is real life for those who do it. One of the points of this work is to demonstrate that the Portal Program is an important, vital part of Native American artists' economic, social, and cultural lives.

Agency

An issue related to the realness of life experiences for peoples who are the subjects of ethnic tourism is the question of agency. While earlier tourism researchers have emphasized the loss of agency experienced by indigenous people at the hands of state tourism officials and developers (e.g., Erisman 1983; Greenwood 1977; Urbanowicz 1989; van den Berghe 1980, 1994), others have recognized the ways in which Native people have been able to direct and shape ethnic tourism to their benefit (e.g., Adams 1997; Lippard 1999; McKean 1977; Swain 1977; Tilley 1997). Often indigenous people have little control over the national and international promotion of tourism, which is dominated by state governments (Adams 1997; Greenwood 1977), influential individuals in the communities (Reiter 1977), outside tourism promoters (including the publishers of tourism guidebooks; see Tilley 1997), or a combination of the above. In such settings, however, the people who are the objects of tourism still have the significant power to decide what sorts of images of themselves tourists will see (Tilley 1997:84–85).

In other settings, such as the Portal and the Native American communities from which Portal participants come, indigenous people retain significant control over the forces of tourism, deciding what elements of their culture and how much of themselves to open up to the touristic gaze. As Lucy R. Lippard (1999:65–68) points out, the Pueblo villages around Santa Fe have developed differing policies regarding tourist visits. Jemez Pueblo, for example, generally maintains a "closed village" policy (Lippard 1999:65). Other villages close to outsiders during important ceremonial events by placing manned roadblocks on incoming roads and turning away those who are not village residents.

Even when tourists are allowed to witness dances and other events (such as the Santo Domingo corn dances and feast day; see chap. 5), it is clear that the activities are not performed for tourists but rather that limited touristic activity is tolerated. The August 4 corn dances at Santo Domingo, with a thousand or more participants dressed in traditional mantas and kilts dancing on the village plaza, would be a highly sought photo opportunity for tourists. The people of Santo Domingo, however, have chosen to prohibit photography and other forms of recording in the village (as have the people of numerous other Native communities throughout the Southwest and in other parts of the country and world). The dances are held by and for the people of the village because they are important to the people of the village. Tourists are invited to view the dances because of the generosity of the people, not because the people have anything to gain from the tourist presence.[5]

As I argue throughout this work, the Native American artists who make up the Portal Program are fully in control of the interaction that takes place between them and their tourist visitors. This is readily evident in the decision not to produce a "staged authenticity" under the portal. For example, though some vendors and others associated with the program have suggested that the vendors should dress in "traditional" clothing,[6] there are no rules to that effect and in general vendors wear the same kinds of clothing as portal visitors. Portal participants have consciously decided not to conform to some sort of created, "authentic" image of Indianness but rather to wear the clothing they would wear in any other everyday setting. While other Native American people in tourist settings have chosen to don buckskin clothing and feathered headdresses to conform to a generalized image of the American Indian (see, e.g., Finger 1991:161–63), Portal Program participants have steadfastly refused to change their appearance to meet tourist expectations, even though they recognize the potential attraction to customers that costumes would provide.[7]

Juanita Atencio, Santo Domingo

When I was a child there was this one time [when] this lady from back East walked up to a Santo Domingo man sitting next to me and asked him if he was an Indian. [He] said, "I am an Indian." [She responded,] "Where's your feathers?" And the man replied and told the tourists, "I said that I was an Indian, I didn't say that I was a chicken!"

Portal participants are not selling themselves or their cultures but rather are creatively using elements of their cultures to their advantage. As discussed in greater detail in chapter 7, there is sometimes a thin line between what tourists desire and what participants are able or willing to give, but always it is the participants who determine the exchange. The decision by indigenous people to engage in the business of ethnic tourism is to accept encroachment from outsiders, but it does not necessarily signal a loss of agency.

I turn now to the history and the story of the Portal Program. Chapter 2 provides an overview of the history of the Palace of the Governors and its role as a locus of interaction between Native American people and Europeans and Euro-Americans, leading to the development of a Native American arts and crafts market under the Palace portal. Chapter 3 turns to the more recent history of the Portal Program as it has grown in importance and become an official program of the Museum of New Mexico. Chapters 4 through 6 approach the program from different perspectives—the Portal as workplace, as community, and as museum program—in an effort to explore the complexity of the institution. Finally, I discuss the production of art under the portal, an issue that addresses connections between the program and the broader Native American art market, between participants and their tourist customers, and between artists and their cultural traditions. Trails throughout lead to explorations into what the Portal Program is and what it means to participants, to the Native American arts and crafts market, and to the experiences of contemporary Native American people.

T W O

Early History

The Palace of the Governors is celebrated as the oldest public build-ing in the United States, a distinction that is advertised on a wooden plaque at the main entrance. During its nearly four-century history, the building and its environs have served a number of purposes. In addition to providing housing and office space for Spanish, Mexican, and U.S. officials, the building was occupied by Pueblo people from 1680 to 1693, has housed chapels, post offices, jails, courtrooms, libraries, private law offices, the New Mexico legislature, the Histor-ical Society of New Mexico, the School of American Research, and since 1909 the Museum of New Mexico (for short histories of the Palace, see Shishkin 1972; Snow 1974; Twitchell 1924).

Much as the uses of the building (or more properly, buildings) have varied greatly, so has the physical structure. The evolution of the structures is of significant interest and importance to the archae-ology and architectural history of Santa Fe, but for a social history and ethnography, what matters more is how the Palace has been and continues to be socially constructed as a historic site. Its construc-tion of high-maintenance adobe bricks, a state owner unwilling or unable to commit significant resources to its preservation (be it Spain, Mexico, the United States, or the state of New Mexico), varied architectural trends and different uses have worked against but a small portion of the structure being actually "original" to the early seventeenth century. Nevertheless, its designation as a National Historic Landmark and reputation as the most ancient of public buildings plays a significant role in many people's perceptions of the building and the events that take place there. Among the many things that the Palace and its surroundings have been, the Palace, the Palace portal, and the Santa Fe plaza have been a principal locus for cross-cultural interaction for nearly four hundred years.

The construction of the complex of buildings known as the Casas Reales, the surviving part of which is the Palace of the Governors, began in 1610 under the direction of don Pedro de Peralta, the second official Spanish governor of New Mexico. Peralta was named governor in 1609 to replace don Juan de Oñate, who had resigned his governorship in 1607 coincidentally with the king's attempt to remove him from office (Hackett 1923:214–15; Twitchell 1963:25). Among Peralta's instructions from the viceroy were orders to relocate the capital of New Mexico from Oñate's site of San Gabriel, near San Juan Pueblo, to a more accessible location farther south and more central to the native Pueblo population of the province (Bloom 1929; Hordes 1990:5).

In choosing the site and laying the plans for the *villa* of Santa Fe, Peralta loosely followed the regulations of the Laws of the Indies. Specific ordinances relating to city planning in New Spain were dictated by King Philip II of Spain in 1573 in the *Reales Ordenanzas* (Hordes 1990:4; translated text of the ordinances can be found in Crouch, Garr, and Mundigo 1982:6–19). The site chosen for Santa Fe, at the edge of the foothills of the Sangre de Cristo Mountains along the Santa Fe River, was deemed to have adequate water, readily available wood for construction and fuel, and at an altitude that was neither so high as to be inhospitable nor so low as to be unhealthy. Furthermore, while the site of the capital was more or less central to the Pueblos of the northern Rio Grande drainage, there were no currently inhabited indigenous villages in the immediate vicinity of the new town. Peralta's instructions were insistent that Indian people should not be harmed by Spanish settlement but also stated that settlements should be located near enough to Native populations that the latter might be converted to Catholicism.

Following these ordinances as well as Spanish and Native American custom, an open plaza was located in the center of the new town. The plaza was bounded on the north by the Palace of the Governors and other structures constituting the Casas Reales.[1] By rule, the plaza was to be one and one-half times as long as it was wide, with a minimum dimension of 200 feet by 300 feet. This configuration was thought by the Crown to be best suited for fiestas, especially those that included the use of horses (Crouch, Garr, and Mundigo 1982:13; Hordes 1990:5; Sze and Spears 1988:5). Though there is disagreement about exactly how large the original plaza in Santa Fe was (Tigges 1990), it is generally agreed that the plaza was likely at least twice the size it is today, extending to the east as far as the site of Saint Francis Cathedral and south perhaps to the Rio Chiquito (present-day Water Street) (Sze and Spears 1988:5).

In addition to the use of the plaza for fiestas, during the early years of settlement, it undoubtedly served as a gathering place for the residents of Santa Fe. The plaza was also used as a location for public censure: the fragmentary data from the seventeenth century contains a report of one Ana María Romero being punished—for calling a prominent woman a whore—by being paraded around the plaza on a horse, naked from the waist up (Hordes 1990:16). The plaza may have also served as a field for the mustering of troops and may have been used for growing crops and grazing livestock (Hordes 1990:16). As a central public place the plaza certainly served as a marketplace for bartering and trade among the Hispano and Native American people of the area from the time of the villa's founding.

Just as the plazas of the Pueblo villages are used by Native people for ceremonial dances, the Santa Fe plaza was also used for this purpose. Though the Catholic clergy were vehemently opposed to the expression of indigenous religion, as early as 1660 the Spanish governor don Bernardo López de Mendizábal made a room in the Palace available for Indian people to use in preparation for dances, and Pueblo people performed "*catzina*" (Katsina) dances in the plaza (Shishkin 1972:7). While this performance most likely was allowed by the Governor to strengthen ties with the Pueblo people and to spite religious authorities—indeed, the governor and his wife would later be tried in the Inquisition (Scholes 1937:17)—in later years Pueblo people would be invited to Santa Fe to dance for the entertainment and edification of residents and, finally, tourists. In 1822 dancers from Tesuque, San Felipe, and Pecos Pueblos came to Santa Fe to contribute to the celebration of Mexican independence from Spain, much to the delight of the celebrants (Bloom 1913:142–44, quoted in Twitchell 1963:181; James [1846] 1962:143–44). With the re-creation of the Santa Fe Fiesta starting in 1911, Indian dances on the plaza made up a significant part of the festival's appeal for tourists (Bernstein 1993b:49).

During the Spanish period of New Mexico's history, the relationship between the Spanish colonists and the indigenous people of the area was at best ambiguous. The rival interests of the Church, whose goal was to Christianize and thus save the souls of Indian people, and the secular, military government and colonists, whose goals were to occupy and pacify the region, made for complicated relations (Kessell 1987; Scholes 1937:6). Both the Church and the secular government made regular use of Indian labor, which only added to the tensions among the colonists and between the colonists and the Native people. Pueblo laborers were undoubtedly required to work on the construction of the Palace and other governmental buildings starting in 1610 (Scholes 1937:24; Snow 1974:4). Sometimes the laborers were paid in money, supplies, or provisions, but often they were not so much as given food (Espinosa 1942:145–46; Shishkin n.d.:79).[2] Throughout the Spanish period, the Pueblos were required to make tribute to the Crown through labor on governmental buildings. As late as 1819 there is a report of the people of Isleta providing gypsum for windows for the Palace (Shishkin 1972:23).[3] While the clergy worked tirelessly and often brutally to abolish indigenous religion, secular authorities would sometimes urge religious expression to counter the Church's efforts. At the same time, the military governors often imposed their heavy-handed authority on the Indian people, as was the case in 1675 when forty-seven "Indian sorcerers and idolaters" were charged with killing ten Spanish by means of witchcraft. The supposed witches were imprisoned in the Palace, and four were hanged. Eventually a party of some seventy Pueblos entered the Palace and forcibly rescued the remaining prisoners (Hackett 1942:1:xxii, 2:300–301; Shishkin 1972:8–9).

The Palace and the plaza would become the site of last defense by the Spanish colonists during the Pueblo Revolt of 1680. On August 10, 1680, after more than eighty years of increasing Spanish population in New Mexico, increasing demands for the lands and labor of the Indian people, and increasing efforts to abolish indigenous religious practices, the residents of the Pueblos arose en masse to kill or drive out the Spanish from New Mexico. Within three days all of the Spanish colonists and missionaries in northern New Mexico had either been killed or had retreated to the Casas Reales in Santa Fe under the protection of Governor Antonio de Otermín (Hackett 1942:1:liv–lxi). Otermín himself, perhaps with some suspicion of impending strife, had fortified the dilapidated Casas Reales earlier in the year, finishing a scant eight days before the rebellion (Hackett 1942:1:207–8). On August 15 a large group of Pueblo warriors laid siege to the city and the Palace. In the following days there were a number of skirmishes in which the Pueblos lost many of their men while the Spanish suffered few casualties. However, the Pueblo fighters were able to sack and burn most of the houses and other structures of the villa and cut off the water supply to the Palace. The Spanish, suffering greatly from lack of water and realizing the futility of trying to survive an extended siege, made one last pitched effort to defeat the Pueblo attackers. This August 20 counteroffensive apparently took the besiegers by surprise and as many as three hundred were killed. Though this battle ended the siege, on the next day Governor Otermín divided the remaining provisions from his hacienda among the one thousand surviving Spanish colonists and led the party on their retreat from New Mexico (Hackett 1942:1:liv–lxvii).

After the retreat of the Spanish settlers, the victorious Pueblos almost immediately took over the Palace and Casas Reales and what little else remained of the villa of Santa Fe.[4] This was very much a political act. The conversion of the villa of Santa Fe into a Pueblo village marked the determination of the Pueblo people to reclaim their homeland and return to the way of life they had known before the Spanish arrived in New Mexico. During the more than thirteen years in which the Pueblo people were able to keep the Spanish out of New Mexico, the Palace and the Casas Reales were converted into large and well-fortified Pueblo apartment dwellings that were occupied primarily by Tano people from Galistéo (Schroeder 1979:247–248; Twitchell 1963:122, 125). A 1694 description of Santa Fe reports four "large communal dwellings" (Espinosa 1940:96), and there may have been as many as five (Snow 1974:9). The apartment buildings were multistoried, with many sections three stories and some four (Twitchell 1963:122, 138). Fifteen hundred Pueblo people lived in the converted structures, and the plaza was divided in two, with a kiva constructed in each section (Hordes 1990:10). This division reflects the dual social and ceremonial organization among the Rio Grande Pueblo peoples.

It is not known exactly how the building that is now known as the Palace relates to the pre-Revolt Casas Reales or to the Revolt-period pueblo. Cordelia Snow has argued that before the Revolt the Casas Reales surrounded the present plaza area, placing the building (or buildings) where the Palace is located today in the back part of the Casas Reales (C. Snow to T. Chávez, July 4, 1987, Collections Archives). Archaeological excavations have uncovered a significant number of pre-Revolt architectural features in parts of the Palace, including a diagonally patterned adobe brick floor that extends beyond the south wall. Such finely finished floors have only been found at a few other Spanish colonial sites in New Mexico, which suggests a building of some importance (Snow 1993:17; C. Snow, pers. com., 2000). Part of the historically known Palace was included in the Revolt-period pueblo. During excavations in the west end of the Palace in 1974, archaeologists found nine Revolt-period food storage pits in an area that had been outside the building during the period of occupation (but which is now inside the Palace) (Snow 1974:16). Inside the building, there is evidence of spaces partitioned into typical pueblo-style rooms, previous doors and windows filled in with adobe, and pueblo-style fireplaces added (Arnold 1984:40; see also Seifert 1979). The Puebloan residents of the Palace also constructed a system of trenches that brought running water into the building's living quarters (Arnold 1984:40).

After escaping down the Rio Grande past the southernmost of the pueblos, the retreating Spanish colonists finally stopped in the vicinity of contemporary El Paso, Texas, where they settled awaiting an opportunity to return to northern New Mexico. Otermín and each successive governor of New Mexico attempted to return to Santa Fe, but during the next twelve years all such efforts failed (Twitchell 1963:83). In 1691 Diego de Vargas Zapata Lujan Ponce de Leon was named governor of New Mexico, and like his predecessors he planned an excursion into the northern provinces of New Mexico.

During the twelve years that had passed since the Revolt, the revolutionary zeal that had drawn virtually all of the Pueblos together against the Spanish had waned. Pueblo villages have historically been, and largely continue to be, autonomous political units led by local political and religious leaders. The cooperation that brought about the successful removal of the Spanish was unprecedented, and mechanisms to maintain it did not exist. The leaders sought to institutionalize the solidarity of the Revolt, but they were unsuccessful. Lacking the unity of purpose that had allowed them to remove the Spanish colonists and missionaries, each village or group of villages was left to its own defenses. Vargas, marching up the Rio Grande with a small group of soldiers and priests in late summer 1692, decided to use persuasion rather than violence to reconquer the provinces of New Mexico. He returned to Santa Fe, where he negotiated a peace with the Native residents. He reported to the viceroy that he was allowed to reclaim the villa in the name of the Crown without bloodshed (Simmons 1977:74; Twitchell 1963:89–96). Vargas then proceeded to visit twelve of the remaining Pueblo villages, where he claimed that he performed ceremonies of returning the Cross and the Spanish flag while the clergy baptized a number of the Pueblo people (Kessell and Hendricks 1992:357–490; Twitchell 1963:98–119).

Thinking that he had resubjugated New Mexico, Vargas returned to El Paso to begin planning the recolonization of the northern provinces. In October 1693 Vargas set out for Santa Fe with as many as eight hundred colonists (Twitchell 1963:121). While the Native residents of Santa Fe allowed Vargas and his colonists to camp in the area of the villa, they were not inclined to surrender the Palace or the Casas Reales to the *reconquistadores*. Though Vargas had promised that the Spanish would not attempt to remove the Tano people from their homes, by late December 1693 the Spanish colonists were desperate. Twenty-two children had already died as a result of the harsh weather and poor living conditions, and the settlers were ready to give up (Kessell, Hendricks, and Dodge 1995:374). Vargas finally relented to their demands and ordered the Tano people to vacate the villa. The Tanos refused, and a pitched battle ensued. The Spanish were eventually victorious, retaking the Palace and other buildings on December 30, 1693, with the considerable help of one hundred forty men from Pecos Pueblo (Kessell, Hendricks, and Dodge 1995:529–33). Many of the Tanoans escaped, but some seventy people were captured and executed in the plaza and four hundred women and children were enslaved and given to various Spanish colonists as servants (Kessell, Hendricks, and Dodge 1995:533–36; Twitchell 1963:126).[5] The reconquest of New Mexico continued through the next year, and many of the pueblos were abandoned as the residents fled to the mountains or went to live in Hopi, Zuni, and Navajo communities. Through regular use of "fire and sword" Vargas and his troops were able to force most of the Pueblo people back to their villages where they could serve as productive vassals to the Crown. Finally, by January 1695, Vargas was able to report to the viceroy of New Spain, the Conde de Galve, that he had defeated all of the Pueblos in the kingdom of New Mexico (Kessell, Hendricks, and Dodge 1998:584).

In spite of Vargas's reported reduction of all the Pueblos, conditions remained anything but peaceful in New Mexico for the next two years. The Spanish settlers, who had been subsisting largely on food stores pillaged from abandoned pueblos, suffered severely from hunger and disease (Kessell, Hendricks, and Dodge 1998:641–69). The Pueblo people likewise were suffering—from shortages of food, displacement caused by warfare with the Spanish, and increasing demands by the Spanish government and Church for their labor and other resources. In June 1696 people from the Tano, Tewa, Northern

Tiwa, Jemez, and some Keres villages joined together to attempt once again to remove the Spanish colonists from New Mexico. Lacking the strength and the unity the Pueblos had enjoyed in 1680, the insurgents had limited success, killing twenty-six religious and settlers. Vargas reacted quickly; he killed almost one hundred insurgents and captured forty-eight (Kessell, Hendricks, and Dodge 1998:723–24). The rebellion had the effect of forcing the viceroyalty of New Spain to provide additional support to the Spanish colonists in New Mexico and brought an end to serious attempts by the Pueblo people to remove the Spanish settlers.

With the forceful taking of the villa of Santa Fe by Vargas, the Spanish government reestablished its seat in the Palace of the Governors and began to remodel the structures to meet Spanish preferences. However, through the early part of the eighteenth century the building was allowed to deteriorate considerably (Hordes 1990:16; Shishkin 1972:17; Snow 1974:9). By 1731 the Palace had deteriorated to such an extent that Governor Juan Domingo de Bustamante claimed to have had to build new Casas Reales at his own expense (Adams and Chávez 1956:22). With the return of the Spanish government, Native people once again had to come to the Palace to conduct official business with the dominant state. The residents of the Pueblo villages developed a tenuous alliance with the Spanish government and were made Spanish subjects in 1820 (Simmons 1990:213). However, strife between the Spanish and the Pueblos, on the one hand, and other Native American groups, on the other, increased during the eighteenth century. Throughout the remainder of the Spanish period the Crown was almost constantly in conflict with Apache, Navajo, Ute, and Comanche peoples who gained much of their subsistence from raiding Pueblo and Spanish settlements for livestock and agricultural produce. A reflection of this strife and of the attitudes of the Spanish colonials toward these Native groups could be found in the Palace, where the governor's office was said to have been decorated in war trophies in the form of scalps and ears taken from slain indigenous people (Twitchell 1924:26).[6]

In 1821 Mexico gained its independence from the collapsing Spanish empire and New Mexico became a province of the new

nation. While conflict with raiding Native American groups continued, with the notable exception of the Comanches, the Pueblo and
Hispanic people of New Mexico maintained their tenuous alliance.
Because of the distance from Mexico City and the difficulty of travel
between Santa Fe and central Mexico, news of the revolution and
Mexico's independence from Spain arrived several months after the
events. In spite of this distance, both temporal and physical, the residents of Santa Fe were happy to celebrate Agustín de Iturbide's
September 27, 1821, entrance into Mexico City on learning of it on
December 26 (Bloom 1913:140; Twitchell 1963:179). The events of
the independence celebration indicate the ties that existed between
the Hispano and Pueblo people. On January 6, 1822, after a pro-
cession around town and the singing of hymns at the *parroquia*
(parish church), the celebrants went to the plaza "where a gay dance
by the Tesuque Indians awaited them" (Bloom 1913:144). Tesuque
was not the only pueblo to participate in the festivities. Thomas
James, an American trader who came to New Mexico with a Spanish
passport at the end of 1821, reported, "A large company of men and
women from San Felipe, an Indian town forty miles south of Santa
Fé, marched into the city, displaying the best formed persons I had
yet seen in the country" ([1846] 1962:143). The people of San
Felipe, dressed in fine clothes and valuable coral, turquoise, silver,
and gold jewelry,

> danced very gracefully upon the public square to the sound of
> a drum and the singing of the older members of their band.
> In this exercise they displayed great skill and dexterity. When
> intermingled in apparently hopeless confusion in a very compli-
> cated figure, so that the dance seemed on the point of breaking
> up, suddenly, at the tap of the drum, each found his partner
> and each couple their place, without the least disorder and in
> admirable harmony. (143–44)

Also present at the celebration were people from Pecos Pueblo, who
came to town disguised in bull and bear skins, apparently causing
great confusion among the celebrants on the plaza (143–44).

Santa Fe and the rest of New Mexico was occupied by General Stephen Watts Kearny and the Army of the West in 1846 during the early stages of the Mexican-American War (Singletary 1960:58). On their arrival in Santa Fe, Kearny and his troops took possession of the Palace of the Governors. With the ratification of the Treaty of Guadalupe Hidalgo in 1848, the war came to an end and New Mexico was annexed to the United States (Singletary 1960:160–61). The Palace was occupied by the governor and the legislative assembly of the new U.S. territory, continuing the traditional uses of the building. In addition, on his appointment as Indian Agent for New Mexico in 1849, James S. Calhoun set up an office for Indian Affairs in the western end of the Palace (Anderson 1944:100). Calhoun was also appointed the first U.S. governor of New Mexico in 1850, a position he occupied concurrently with his job as Indian Agent (Anderson 1944:100; Loyola 1939:144–46). Through at least the first half of the 1850s the Indian Agent's office remained in the Palace, and Native people continued to maintain relations with the dominant government there. During this time, a large room was kept vacant for the use of visiting Indian people where, according to W. W. H. Davis ([1857] 1982:172), the visitors were fed by the government.[7]

The office of Indian Agent was eventually moved elsewhere as the various parts of the Palace were turned over to other public and private uses through the remainder of the nineteenth century. In 1881 the Historical Society of New Mexico was granted use of a few unoccupied rooms in the east end of the Palace, and with the transfer of ownership of the Palace from the federal government to the territory of New Mexico in 1898, the Palace became the Historical Society's permanent home (Anderson 1944:117). By act of the territorial government in 1909 the Museum of New Mexico was established, with responsibility for repairing and maintaining the Palace as its home (Shishkin 1972:50). The transition of the Palace from seat of government to historical and cultural institution marked an important change that would bring about new relations among Native Americans, the government, and the public.

The Portal

The 1573 *Reales Ordinanzas* called for portales to be added to buildings around the plaza and along the principal streets, "for these are
of considerable convenience to the merchants who generally gather
there" (quoted in Crouch, Garr, and Mundigo 1982:14). As antici-
pated in the ordinances, the space under the Palace portal would
become an active marketplace for the growing villa of Santa Fe. It
has been argued that the Palace may not originally have had a portal
(see Historic Santa Fe Foundation 1972:15), and a town plan drawn
by Lieutenant Joseph de Urrutia in 1766 does not specifically indicate portales on the buildings around the plaza (Wilson 1997:32).[8]
However, a plan of the Presidio of Santa Fe dating to 1791 includes
a portal facing the plaza (reproduced in Simmons 1990, following
p. 50; Wilson 1997:33–34).[9]

By the time significant numbers of Anglo-Americans began to
visit and write about Santa Fe, portales were common features on
the Palace and other buildings around the central part of the city. In
1831 Albert Pike reported "a mud covered portico supported by
rough pine pillars" (quoted in Anderson 1944:98). Josiah Gregg
([1844] 1967:137), who first visited Santa Fe in 1831, likewise
reported "*portales* or *corredores* of the rudest possible description"
fronting the Palace and other buildings around the plaza. Other
visitors in the mid-nineteenth century commented on the portal in
front of the Palace, universally declaring this and all portales around
the city to be roughly made but exceedingly serviceable (Allison
1914:177; Davis [1857] 1982:165; Taylor [1847] 1936:146; see
also Shishkin 1972:31).

Like the Palace itself, the front portal has gone through many
architectural manifestations. The earliest portales in Santa Fe were
likely simple porches attached to buildings, usually supported by
unworked log pillars like those reported by Albert Pike in 1831. By
the mid-1850s the Palace portal had been replaced by a Territorial-
style porch with squared wooden pillars (Wilson 1997:60–61). In an
1867 description of the public buildings of the territory of New
Mexico prepared by Governor Robert B. Mitchell, the portal is
described as "a plain portal or porch, shed roof, supported by hewn

posts seventeen feet high and standing ten feet apart[,] ... unpaved and unfloored" (H.R. Ex. Doc. No. 33, 40th Cong., 2d sess., appended to Anderson 1944:121). Sometime after this report was made, a "neat sand walk" was laid under the portal (Shishkin 1972:42). In 1877 U.S. marshal John Sherman renovated the portion of the portal in front of his offices at the western end of the Palace, adding a plank sidewalk and Greek Revival moldings and cornice. By this time the portal and the front of the Palace exhibited no less than three facades, leading the editors of the *Santa Fe New Mexican* to call for federal appropriations to unify them (La Farge 1959:94–95). Territorial secretary William Ritch received funding from the Treasury Department that along with private donations allowed for the entire portal to be refinished in the Greek Revival style (Wilson 1997:61). This shift in architectural appearance for the Palace and other buildings around the plaza reflected a desire by city leaders to change the appearance of Santa Fe, to make it seem more like a progressive, American city. This change required a move away from the Hispanic and Native American architecture and imagery of the city and the territory. Though city leaders tried to be progressive, they could not entirely remove the realities of New Mexican life from the plaza. For example, a new wooden sidewalk that was placed under the Palace portal in 1890 was almost immediately occupied by "ubiquitous" burros that apparently enjoyed sleeping on the cool new walkway (Shishkin 1972:46).

By the end of the nineteenth century, businessmen and civic leaders began to realize that tourism could be the economic salvation of Santa Fe and that tourists were interested in the Native American and Hispanic past of the region. The Southwest began being popularized in the 1880s through the works of the journalist and author Charles Lummis and through the advertising efforts of the Atchison, Topeka and Santa Fe Railroad, which reached New Mexico in 1880 (Kenneson 1978:261; Twitchell 1963:397). These proponents of the Southwest recognized the value of the indigenous and Hispanic cultures as promotional tools and began to encourage tourists to come experience the cultural diversity of the Southwest for themselves.

Santa Fe business and governmental leaders were at first hesitant to promote non-Anglo cultures. During the entire territorial period, civic leaders of Santa Fe and New Mexico generally had worked hard to present an image of the territory as progressive, as culturally similar to the rest of the United States, as ready for statehood. This demanded the exclusion of Hispanic and Native American imagery from the city center, and city leaders continued to try to make Santa Fe an (Anglo) American city.

The year 1912 finally brought statehood for New Mexico. The same year the Santa Fe City Planning Board was created, in part to turn around the city's thirty-year economic slump (Wilson 1997:121). Among the members of the board were Edgar Lee Hewett, director of the Museum of New Mexico and School of American Archaeology (later the School of American Research), and Sylvanus Morley, an archaeologist and museum staff member. Part of the City Beautiful movement, the planning board produced a comprehensive city plan that included encouragement for the use of a unified style of architecture. "Santa Fe style" celebrated the Native American and Hispanic adobe architecture that had been shunned during the territorial period and was meant to distinguish New Mexican architecture from the "mission style" popular in California (Wilson 1997:123–24). The style was defined following a photographic survey of the city conducted by Morley and museum photographer and archaeologist Jesse Nusbaum that included scores of historic buildings. This survey resulted in an exhibition at the museum entitled *New-Old Santa Fe*. The celebration of earlier architectural styles and the exhibition showcasing them were explicitly aimed at increasing tourism in Santa Fe. A solicitation flyer proclaimed one of the purposes of the exhibition: "To advertise the unique and unrivalled possibilities of the city as 'THE TOURIST CENTER OF THE SOUTHWEST'"(cited in Sheppard 1988:75; emphasis in original).

The "Pueblo Revival style," as this reinterpretation of earlier architectural features has also been called, found its first important manifestation in a reconstruction of the Palace portal. Based on a corbel found embedded in the Palace wall and on Urrutia's 1766

FIGURE I: *View of the Palace portal from the Santa Fe plaza, ca. 1998. The architectural style has remained unchanged from the 1913 renovation. Photo by the author.*

city plan that showed rooms extending from the front of the Palace on either end, Nusbaum designed a new massive portal meant to reflect how the original Spanish colonial portal might have looked (Twitchell 1924:34; Wilson 1997:125). The result was the portal as it appears today. With massive log pillars topped by large zapata capitals, a tall parapet pierced by heavy viga ends, and large bastions at each end of the Palace, the new (-old?) portal significantly changed the facade of the Palace of the Governors and boldly proclaimed Pueblo Revival as the Santa Fe style. Though criticized for not being an accurate reproduction of Spanish colonial architecture (see Boyd 1974:38; Bunting 1970:15; Wilson 1981:xvii, 1997:126), the new portal clearly reflects the shift toward the celebration of indigenous culture that was occurring during the early part of the twentieth century.

Pueblo Revival as the style of choice for the plaza area was reinforced with the construction of the Museum of Fine Arts in 1916–17 on the northwest corner of the plaza. This new museum building, designed by Isaac Hamilton Rapp, was modeled on the seventeenth-century mission church San Esteban at Acoma Pueblo. The design of the museum is a refinement of the New Mexico Building designed by Rapp for the 1915 California-Pacific International Exposition in San Diego, which in turn was modified from a warehouse of Rapp's design in Morley, Colorado (Sheppard 1988:79–88). The plaza's destiny as a Native American–oriented tourist destination was sealed with the construction of the puebloesque La Fonda Hotel, a Rapp design built on the southeast corner of the plaza in 1920 (Sheppard 1988:94–97). This shift in architectural style reflected the changing attitudes among the Santa Fe elite that would support the development of a Native American arts and crafts market under the Palace portal, as did the actual plan of the new portal. While Nusbaum and the other museum staff members who helped him to design the new portal chose to anchor it with massive structures at each end, they chose not to make the projections from the Palace closed rooms— as they had been when such projections existed in the past (see Davis [1857] 1982:169)—but rather as open walkways, to facilitate the flow of pedestrians entering from the Washington and Lincoln Avenue sides of the Palace (Wilson 1981:131–32, 1997:126). This layout enables the relatively smooth flow of pedestrian traffic, even on summer days when as many as forty-five hundred people pass along the portal. The south-facing orientation allows winter sun to warm the porch, making it habitable on all but the harshest winter days. In summer, the roof shades the portal from the intense high desert sun. Though the Palace portal was almost certainly not intentionally built this way for this specific purpose, the southern orientation is key to allowing a year-round market.

The Genesis of the Portal Market

During the early years of Spanish colonization, commerce was limited. With the exception of the governmental buildings to the north and the church structures to the east, most of the buildings around the plaza were the private residences of prominent citizens (Historic

Santa Fe Foundation 1972:13). In fact, very little permanent space was afforded to commercial activities during the early years of Spanish settlement at Santa Fe (Crouch, Garr, and Mundigo 1982:78). Though there were few shops until the nineteenth century, it seems likely that open-air bartering existed on some scale during the first two centuries after Santa Fe's founding. There was apparently a significant amount of trading going on within the Palace itself during some governors' administrations. The same Governor Bernardo López de Mendizábal who in the 1660s encouraged Pueblo people to dance in the plaza also traded the "sugar, chocolate, shoes, hats, and European textiles" that he imported to New Mexico for "*mantas*, hides, piñon, salt, livestock, and other local goods that could be resold at a profit in New Spain" (Shishkin n.d.:14–15).

Mexican independence from Spain in 1821 brought about the opening of the Santa Fe Trail, a major trade route from Missouri to Santa Fe and continuing south to Chihuahua, that made Santa Fe a center for commerce between the northern portions of Mexico and what were then the western portions of the United States. Mexican officials were eager to expand trade relations with merchants from the United States and to decrease New Mexico's relative isolation. The decades after independence brought an economic boom to Santa Fe as American traders began to bring goods overland. By the 1840s there were a number of shops fronting the plaza (Crouch, Garr, and Mundigo 1982:78), and the plaza and its surrounding portales contained an active marketplace. Perhaps the earliest report of a market under the portales around the plaza comes from the recollections of don Demetrio Perez, who remembered,

> The butchers who killed sheep placed the meat on perches which
> they placed under the shade of the cottonwoods planted in front
> of the Old Palace; on the west side, under the spacious porch of
> the Palace, the bakers were installed together with the fruit vendors
> and others who sold their diverse kinds of food for the people
> who depended on the market for their supply, for at that time
> [the 1840s] there was no public building for the sale of such
> articles. (Read 1927:93)

Elias Brevoort, who visited Santa Fe in 1850, also places the market in the vicinity of the Palace portal: "The market consisted of people seated on the northwest corner of the plaza with baskets" (Brevoort 1884, quoted in Crouch, Gunn, and Mundigo 1982:79). By the mid-1850s the market under the portal of the Palace was well established. W. W. H. Davis, who was in New Mexico between 1853 and 1856 as U.S. Attorney, writes:

> In passing under the portal to the western end of the palace, we encounter the market on our way, where the country people sell the meats, fruits, and vegetables they bring to town. The supply is scanty enough, and hardly sufficient to meet the limited demand of Santa Fé. It consists principally of mutton, an occasional porker, red peppers, beans, onions, milk, bread, cheese, and, during the proper season, grapes, wild plums, and wild berries. In the winter, Indians and others bring in, almost daily, fine venison and wild turkeys, and now and then the carcass of a large bear is exposed for sale, all of which are shot in the mountains a few miles from the town. The various articles are brought in on burros, or carried on the backs of the Pueblo Indians; and it is often the case that one of them will come several miles with less than a dollar's worth of marketing. The meats are hung upon a line made fast to two posts of the portal, while the vegetables are put on little mats or pieces of board on the ground, beside which the vender will sit and wait for customers with a patience that seems to rival Job; and if they do not sell out to-day, they are sure to return with the same stock to-morrow. (Davis [1857] 1982:172–73)

In addition to produce and game, Pueblo artisans may have also sold utilitarian pottery and basketry, which Davis ([1857] 1982:47) reports was in great demand.

Marian Sloan Russell, who first came to Santa Fe in 1854 at the age of nine, remembered a much more substantial market:

> The market place in Santa Fé was a wonder. In open air booths lay piles of food stuffs. Heaps of red and green peppers vied with heaps

of red and blue corn and heaps of golden melons. There were
colorful rugs woven by the hands of the Mexicans and deep-
fringed shawls, gay with embroidery. There were massive Indian
jars filled to the brim with Mexican beans. There were strings of
prayer beads from old Mexico, beads worn smooth and shiny to a
patina by many praying hands. Mexican turquoise in heavy settings
of silver. Silver was then cheaper than tin. Here was to be found
exquisite Mexican drawn work and intricate Indian bead work.

In deep, old hand-carved frames were pictures, mottoes,
wreaths of flowers all cunningly fashioned of human hair, red,
black, brown, and yellow. There were beaded moccasins and
chamois coats, leather trousers, silver trimmed saddles, spurs
and knapsacks; great hand-carved chests and cupboards, Indian
baskets and jars without number. So many things that were fine
and splendid; so many things that were rude and clumsy, the
Santa Fé market afforded.

If one were in quest of a pair of Indian moccasins he might
hunt among booths until he was dizzy, only at last to come to a
heap of footwear of every size, shape and quality and in such
abundance as to make him forget what he came for. (1954:55–56)

Although it is not clear whether Russell's account of Santa Fe in the
1850s was embellished by memory or is a reflection of later experiences (Russell continued to visit Santa Fe throughout her life), Santa
Fe continued to grow as a regional trade center until the railroad
bypassed the city in the 1880s.

The market under the Palace portal continued as a multicultural venue for the next one hundred years. As late as the mid-1900s
Hispano vendors came to the plaza and portal to sell various goods.
For example, Thomas E. Chávez (1997), former director of the
Palace of the Governors, tells of an uncle who sold bubble gum
under the portal. More typically, vendors brought such things as
firewood, produce, and livestock. Orlando Romero, former director
of the Museum of New Mexico History Library, came to Santa Fe
with his uncles to sell goat kids in front of the Palace as late as the
1950s (Romero 1997). During the post–World War II era, however,

the use of the plaza and portal by non-Indian vendors largely came to an end.

There were several reasons for the decline of the multicultural market. First, as more rural people moved into wage jobs and away from subsistence agriculture and ranching, the economic importance of agricultural markets decreased. Equally significant was a shift in the use of the plaza area. While the plaza was the center of political, social, and economic life from the seventeenth through the latter part of the nineteenth century, by the 1900s the face of the plaza was beginning to change as Santa Fe catered to tourism. With the growth of tourism in the twentieth century came an emphasis on Native American over Hispanic culture, and the promotion of Native American culture became a key activity for businesses and cultural institutions around the plaza. Though never eliminated, Hispanic arts became secondary to Native American arts in popularity, and the picturesque image of Santa Fe created by Anglo cultural leaders did not include Hispano artists selling their work around the plaza.

During the last quarter of the nineteenth century, Mexican filigree jewelry was the most popular souvenir item in Santa Fe, and its production was an important industry. This Hispanic-originated craft dominated the market in Santa Fe until about 1915, when its popularity waned nationally (Wilson 1981:109).[10] Since that time Hispanic arts and crafts, while continuing to have a limited but fairly steady appeal, have never enjoyed the same popularity that Native American work has found in the twentieth century. An attempt made in the 1930s by Leonora Curtin to develop a marketplace for Hispanic arts in downtown Santa Fe is indicative of the limited viability of this market: the Native Market, as the combination workshop-market was called, was popular enough to be a regular stop for tour companies but was never self-sufficient. When Curtin stopped underwriting the market, it was forced to close (Nestor 1978).[11]

The limited popularity of traditional Hispanic arts is at least in part a reflection of the priority placed on Native American culture over that of Hispanic America in New Mexico (see Kenneson 1978). This emphasis is in turn a product of institutionalized racism against Hispanic peoples and a devaluation, by many Anglos, of

Hispanic cultural products. Although there was some scholarly interest in traditional Hispanic arts in New Mexico, particularly by Mary Austin and Frank Applegate (McCrossen 1931:456; Rothman 1998:105–6), it never achieved the popular appeal that Native American art did. Eastern artists, writers, and social activists who came to New Mexico in the first half of the twentieth century, such as Elizabeth and Martha White, Margretta Dietrich, Gertrude Ely, Oliver La Farge, Willa Cather, Mary Cabot Wheelwright, and Ernest Thompson Seton, made the preservation and promotion of Native American cultures their cause (see Mullin 1993; Parezo and Hoerig 1999). The scholarly popularization of Native American culture coincided with the promotion of Native American arts and crafts by the Santa Fe Railroad, the Fred Harvey Company, and various traders and curio dealers. By the 1920s the editors of the *Santa Fe New Mexican* were advocating Native American land rights by writing against the Bursum bill, legislation aimed at giving title of Pueblo lands to non-Indians. They urged support of Native American communities and their arts and crafts, so that Santa Fe could continue to grow as "the focus and beneficiary of the [Native American arts and crafts] movement" (September 20, 1922, cited in La Farge 1959:275).

Though Santa Fe was increasingly becoming a center for Native American arts and crafts, during the early decades of the twentieth century the artists themselves were kept largely in the shadows. Native American artists and craftspeople had begun selling directly to tourists at their home pueblos and at train stations as early as the 1880s, but regular access to the Santa Fe plaza and the Palace portal did not come until the 1930s. In part this was due to transportation difficulties. Travel to Santa Fe from most of the pueblos required a full day—or more—by horse-drawn wagon. Artisans would periodically bring wagon-loads of pottery or other work to town where they would sell shop to shop or wholesale their pieces to traders (Bernstein 1993b:85), a practice that continues today. In a typical day, however, they probably would not have been able to sell enough pieces directly to tourists to justify the time and effort of a trip to Santa Fe.

Transportation has continued to be an important issue for vendors under the portal. By the 1950s there was enough daily traffic from the villages to Santa Fe that vendors without cars were usually able to catch rides to town. Juanita Atencio (1996) tells of waiting for rides at Santo Domingo: "I used to stand by the bridge at home and whenever somebody drove by if I had my jewelry in front of me they knew that I was coming to Santa Fe." With increasingly reliable transportation, artists from more distant pueblos and communities such as Jemez and Laguna have been able to sell regularly at the portal. But because of the considerable distances many vendors must travel, there continues to be great emphasis on having reliable cars and a number of vendors continue to depend on others for daily transportation to Santa Fe.

During the early twentieth century, transportation was not the only factor keeping Native American artists from selling their work directly to tourists in Santa Fe. Though their cultures were celebrated by Euro-American artists and authors and the popularity of their crafts was growing by leaps and bounds, Native people themselves often were not welcome in Santa Fe. In recalling the 1930s, Maria Chabot told Bruce Bernstein: "[T]hey [Native American artists] came to town when they knew they were acceptable in town" (quoted in Bernstein 1993a:53). In the mid-1930s the Museum of New Mexico did not afford Native American artists the use of its limited restroom facilities, even though it supported the New Mexico Association on Indian Affairs in inviting the artists to sell under the Palace portal. The vendors had to use the facilities at a gas station that stood on the corner of Palace and Washington Avenues (Bernstein 1993a:53).[12]

Fiestas and Indian Fairs

The portal began to become a popular place for Native American artists to sell their work during the annual Santa Fe Fiesta. Set around a reenactment of Diego de Vargas's supposed reconquest of New Mexico in 1692 and claiming descent from a 1712 proclamation calling for an annual fiesta in Vargas's honor, the first Santa Fe Fiesta was held in 1911 (Chávez 1953; Chávez 1985). Held in 1912, it was not celebrated again until 1919, when the festival was moved from July to September. The program that year was expanded to celebrate the different periods of New Mexico's history, with days dedicated to the three cultures that have been reified as Santa Fe's "tricultural" heritage: Native American, Hispano, and Anglo (see Chávez 1985:12–13; Grimes 1992:187; Walter 1920; see also Lippard 1999 for a more critical view of New Mexican triculturalism). In 1919 the daily themes of the fiesta were "Before Santa Fe Was," "Antigua," and "Moderna" (The Fiesta of Santa Fe 1919; *El Palacio* 1919:100). By 1922 the themes had been modified to "Indian Day," "De Vargas Day," and "Santa Fe Trail Day" (Official Souvenir Program 1922). The primary role played by Native people in the Fiesta presentations, besides surrendering to the character of Vargas in the reconquest pageant (Bernstein 1993b:57), was the performance of ritual dances for Fiesta spectators. In her review of the 1921 Fiesta, Dorothy McAllister (1921:79) wrote positively about the Indian dances: "Far outclassing the dances of last year were those presented this year, and in which the Zunis, the Santa Claras, the Tesuques, the San Ildefonsos, the Jemes [*sic*] and the Cochitis, took part."[13] During the 1919 Fiesta, some Indian people sold their work under the portal, while others sold pottery and paintings on the steps and along the east side of the Fine Arts Museum, across Lincoln Avenue from the Palace (Bernstein 1993b:52; *El Palacio* 1919:106; Walter 1920:20). In 1920 the front of the Palace, including the portal, was fenced in so that admission could be charged for the events (Will Shuster, cited in La Farge 1959:391). The fences kept vendors from selling under the portal, but a significant number of Native American artists displayed their goods near the Fine Arts Museum, as a photograph of vendors with Edgar Lee Hewett documents (MNM Neg. No. 52582).

The staff of the Museum of New Mexico and the School of American Research was interested in promoting Native American arts and in ensuring that the artists be fairly compensated for their work. They also wanted to encourage Native artists, and in particular, potters, to produce pieces that they felt met their interpretation of the technical and aesthetic standards of prehistoric or at least precurio trade work. To that end, starting in 1912 museum director Hewett and curator Kenneth Chapman invited the San Ildefonso potter Maria Martinez and her sisters to demonstrate the various steps of pottery making for summer school classes at the Palace (Burton 1975:59). Though Maria and her husband, Julian Martinez, did not develop the innovative black-on-black decorative technique that made them world famous until 1918 (Berlo and Phillips 1998:59), by the early 1900s she was already an acclaimed traditional potter and the museum staff sought to promote the technical mastery she exhibited.

Recognizing that Native artists were paid little for their work by area merchants, in about 1922 the museum staff began to allow potters to store their work in the patio of the American School of Research building (Burton 1975:62). The venture was so successful that the curator of arts, Bertha Van Stone, was reported to have sold $900 worth of pottery in August 1922 for one potter.[14] While beneficial for the artists, the noncommissioned sales proved too much for the museum staff to handle. The prohibitive amount of time spent selling pottery combined with protests of unfair trade from local dealers quickly convinced the museum staff to discontinue the practice.

However, the museum remained committed to the promotion of Indian arts. In 1922 Chapman organized the First Annual Southwest Indian Fair and Arts and Crafts Exhibition to coincide with the Fiesta (Bernstein 1993a:17; Official Souvenir Program 1922). This was the first time that Native American arts and crafts were officially made part of the Fiesta. For this first fair, which would eventually become the annual Santa Fe Indian Market, Indian artists along with Indian school representatives, Indian agents, and traders were invited by the fair organizers to collect Indian-made articles to send to Santa Fe so that the objects could be judged and sold. The objects were displayed in the National Guard Armory building north of the Palace, where in the course of three days several thousand paid the fifty-cent admission to see the show.

Rose Dougan, an Indiana resident who spent time in Santa Fe and developed an interest in Indian arts, was an early advocate of the show and established a fund to provide $85 a year in prize money for the best examples of several categories of artwork (*El Palacio* 1922a:81).[15] With additional monetary contributions from the chamber of commerce and other groups, prizes were awarded in more than forty categories. The majority were in pottery but also included basketry, weaving, clothing, and agricultural products and the "best baby." The cash prizes had the intended effect of promoting competition in the production of pieces meeting the Anglo judges' standards, as the prizes in many cases equaled or exceeded the price obtained for the sale of the objects.

Most of the art objects entered in the competition were sold during the fair. By 1925, in fact, sales were so good that some visitors complained that most of the pottery had been sold on the first morning, though all objects remained on exhibit through the end of the show (*El Palacio* 1925:94). The pieces were kept on display after they had been sold so that more visitors and artists could see the work, and this continues to be a standard organizational procedure followed by many museums that sponsor shows today. The selling was done by the fair committee, which added 10 percent to the minimum prices requested by the artists to cover expenses. The artists' shares were distributed after the conclusion of the fair (Burton 1975:62; Dietrich 1952, cited in Bernstein 1993a:18). Though the artists were removed from the business of the market, the fair organizers included many of them as demonstrators. Because of the difficulties of transportation and the distance from Santa Fe of many of the pueblos, Fiesta organizers provided transportation to town for some of the Native American participants and set up an "Indian encampment" at the edge of town, providing tents, food, cooking facilities, and hay for horses. At the first fair, Indian artists worked under a canopy at the entrance to the Armory, demonstrating sand painting, silverwork, pottery making, weaving, and beadwork. In addition to the craft demonstrations, inside a kitchen range was set up where "Indian girls demonstrated their skill in cooking" (*El Palacio* 1922c:93). In 1925 demonstrators were located in the patio of the Palace, and the "Indian Encampment" was moved to a location adjacent to the museum buildings so that it was included as part of the Indian fair (*El Palacio* 1925:94–95).

The stated purpose of the early Indian Fairs was education. Organizers and supporters were interested in showing the public what they thought was "good" art, but mostly their concern was to guide and support the Indian artists. In 1922 the organizers wrote:

> The objects of the exhibition are the encouragement of native arts and crafts among the Indians; to revive old arts, and to keep the arts of each tribe and pueblo as distinct as possible; the establishment and locating of markets for all Indian products, the securing of reasonable prices; authenticity of all handicraft offered for sale and protection to the Indian in all his business dealings with traders and buyers. (Official Souvenir Program 1922)

These objectives were reiterated annually for a number of years in the announcement of the fair and publication of the premium list (*El Palacio* 1923a:23; 1924:109; 1926:204). In addition to trying to maintain their views of cultural integrity by encouraging artists to work only in their own tribe's traditional styles, organizers were concerned that outside influences would contaminate indigenous designs. In an effort to promote what they perceived as authentic Indian arts, the fair organizers discouraged "non-Indian" designs such as flags and lodge emblems in weavings and other works and nontraditional pottery forms (*El Palacio* 1923a:23).

For Chapman, Hewett, and the other activists involved in the Indian Fair, authenticity in Indian art was closely linked to prehistory.[16] After the first show *El Palacio* (1922c:93) reported, "Not all of the exhibits measured up to the high artistic ideals of the primitive designs but much of the material shown was of great excellence and gave promise that the future would see development along the lines that the leaders of the movement are urging." Archaeologically recovered materials were seen by Indian arts activists of the time as being the ideal toward which contemporary Native American artists should aspire, and their work was judged accordingly. In a 1915 article entitled "The Survival of an Ancient Art," for example, Olive Wilson extolled the virtues of prehistoric pottery and urged the contemporary use of prehistoric designs:

Museums collect and display specimens of the handiwork of the cliff people, the forefathers of the present Pueblo Indians, where one may see the forms and designs of the past, beautiful, varied, full of meaning, presenting to the mind of the student a wealth of symbolism that brings a constantly deepening desire to examine, to study, and if possible to learn the real mind of the race that produced these things. So it is when they follow the old paths, using with knowledge the old symbolic designs, that the pottery makers of the present reach the highest possibilities of their craft. (Wilson 1915:24–29)

Under the directorship of the avid but informally trained archaeologist Hewett, the main research initiatives of the museum concerned the archaeology of the Pajarito Plateau. Nonacademic advocates were also very interested in archaeology. The artist Gustave Baumann, who for a time occupied studio space in the Palace, remembered "times when the artists forgot their business and went completely archaeological." "We learned all the familiar terms and became quite expert in identifying potsherds as belonging to this or that period" (Baumann 1989:125–26; see also Chauvenet 1983:122; Mullin 1993:129). The goal was to encourage Native artists to use a design system that was free from European influence (Bernstein 1993b:104). Revival wares such as those produced by the Tewa potters Hewett and Chapman worked with and the Sikyatki Revival pottery of Nampeyo at the Hopi First Mesa were very popular, and today potters continue to use design elements drawn from prehistoric pieces.[17]

After the second Indian Fair, *El Palacio* (1923b:100) proclaimed that "the Santa Fe Fiesta and the Second Annual Indian Fair...were more expressive of the culture of the aboriginal inhabitants of the Southwest than any event thus far recorded."[18] Indian artists had begun to tailor their works in response to the fair judges' preferences. This statement in the museum's publication may also be an effort to endow the Santa Fe fair with authority as the bellwether venue for determining quality and authenticity in Indian art. Significant competition existed between traders and academics and activists for control of Indian arts development.

A second but no less important goal of the fairs was to promote the sale of Indian arts, and they proved profitable for the participating artists (though not for the fair organizers; the event never quite broke even). The 1923 program contained a clearly articulated explanation of the economic development aims of the fair:

> It was not curiosity on the part of the Santa Fe public, nor a mere desire to attract more tourists hitherwards, that prompted the Fiesta management a year ago to incorporate an Indian arts and handicrafts exhibit as an integral part of its general scheme. The main idea was to impress the Indian mind with the fact that these things, when properly brought before the public, are of far greater value than farm products or a salaried job in carpentry, painting, etc. Almost anybody with a modicum of common sense can raise melons and hoe corn, but only an artist to the manner born can turn out Indian handicraft. So why make a cheap blacksmith out of a boy who can paint a picture that will attract the attention of the whole nation? Above all, by giving him a fair return for his work in this line, make the Indian realize that his arts and handicrafts are wanted, and that people are willing to pay enough for them to make it worth the Indians' while to engage in this line of endeavor. When this is done the question of how to prevent these lines of artistic enterprise from disappearing from the earth will probably be solved. Money talks, and even an Indian has to have a meal-ticket. So show him where he can market his articles at a fair price, and then, other things being equal, he will come on with the output. If he doesn't, we are going to have a serious case against him. This is the main idea underlying the Fair part of the Santa Fe Fiesta. (Official Souvenir Program 1923)

By the 1920s activists were beginning to see arts and crafts production as an important part of Native American economic survival (Schrader 1983:3–4). The Office of Indian Affairs (later the Bureau of Indian Affairs [BIA]) supported the fair for this reason. An unattributed letter from the Office of Indian Affairs to Ralph Emerson Twitchell states:

I have always felt that the Indians of this country could be made producers and become an economic asset to the country, as well as being developed into first-class, self-supporting citizens of the republic. We appreciate the interest being shown in the Indians of New Mexico by this "First Annual Exhibition of Indian Arts and Crafts under the Auspices of the Museum of New Mexico." (*El Palacio* 1922b:148)

However, while supporting economic development, the Office was skeptical of efforts such as the Indian Fair that promoted traditional culture. For decades representatives of the federal government had been working very hard through boarding schools and training programs to make Indian people into the farmers, carpenters, and blacksmiths that the fair promoters belittled (for discussions of BIA schools, see Hyer 1990; Lomawaima 1994). Federal officials went so far as to "advise" pueblo governors on which ceremonials their people would be allowed to leave home to attend and to threaten to arrest any Indian people who disobeyed (Chauvenet 1983:192; C. J. Crandall to Edgar L. Hewett, July 23, 1925, Hewett Collection, History Library). It was not until the passage of the Indian Arts and Crafts Act of 1935, which was designed to promote the market for Native American arts, that federal policy recognized the growing economic importance of Indian arts (Cohen 1982:151; for text of the Arts and Crafts Act, see Schrader 1983:appendix). The passage of the act also reflected a shift in attitudes among federal administrators. While late-nineteenth- and early-twentieth-century federal policy had been geared toward assimilation of Indian peoples into the dominant Euro-American society, by the 1930s that policy had changed to one that accepted cultural difference but at the price of continued marginalization of Indian people (Hoxie 1984:187).

In spite of the Fair organizers' paternalistic attitudes, it is clear that from the very beginning the Native American artists clearly understood and were able to manipulate the market to their benefit. An anecdote related by Henrietta K. Burton illustrates this point:

In 1925 Antonita [Roybal, of San Ildefonso] brought an unusually good pot to the fair exhibit. It was soft, satiny, and of a dull red. The red clay had been mixed with a light material, and the pot was not highly polished. She informed Mr. Chapman that she wanted twelve dollars for it. That, with a ten percent commission, which the fair charged the Indians for selling their products, would make the selling figure thirteen dollars and twenty cents, a price then unheard of. It proved to be the prize-winning pot. After the awards had been made, the pieces, according to custom, were placed on sale. This one was marked thirteen dollars and twenty cents. Mr. Chapman felt that only through experience would Antonita learn what buyers would or would not pay. No sooner had the price been set than another member of the staff asked, "What does this mean, putting such a price? Mark it reasonably; there are certain limits." Mr. Chapman's reply was, "How are they to learn?" In fifteen minutes the pot and ribbon were sold for thirteen dollars and twenty cents. (1975:62)

In 1927 a corporation was formed by the Santa Fe Chamber of Commerce to manage the Fiesta, and Edgar Lee Hewett was able to terminate the Museum of New Mexico's official involvement in the Fiesta and the Indian Fair. Hewett felt that the annual event took too much of his time, and at sixty-two he wanted to commit more of his time to writing. Though the museum was no longer officially linked to the events, Kenneth Chapman organized the Indian Fair Committee to continue the annual event. While part of the fair was held in the Saint Francis Church parish hall in 1927 (*El Palacio* 1927:343), in 1928 the fair returned to the museum grounds, where it would continue to be held annually through 1931. While the annual Indian Fair had not kept Native American vendors from selling some of their wares on the plaza during Fiesta—in fact, some sold articles that had been rejected by the show's jury (Dietrich 1952, quoted in Bernstein 1993a:18)—in 1931 the fair moved to the Palace portal. In a major shift from previous years, for this final Southwest Indian Fair the committee ceased to provide transportation, camping gear, kitchen facilities, or food for the vendors

(Bernstein 1993a:49). For the first time, Native American participants in the fair sold directly to their customers under the portal,
marking the first museum-sanctioned Native American arts and
crafts market under the portal proper.

Because of a lack of funding during the Great Depression and
because organizers wanted more people in the Pueblo villages to see
the work that was produced for the fairs, between 1932 and 1935
no annual Indian fairs were held in Santa Fe. Instead, under the
sponsorship of the Southwest Indian Fair Committee, which in 1934
became part of the New Mexico Association on Indian Affairs
(NMAIA),[19] local fairs were held at a number of pueblos (Bernstein
1993a:50–51). In spite of this hiatus, the stage had been set for the
development of the portal market as a museum program. Through
the Museum of New Mexico's sponsorship of the first Indian Fairs,
under Hewett and Chapman especially, the museum set the precedent for its support and encouragement of Native American arts and
crafts as an educational component of its mission. While Native
American artists had used the Palace portal as a marketplace during
Fiesta since its inception, the staging of the 1931 Southwest Indian
Fair under the portal affirmed the museum's support of the market
and its location under the Palace portal.

In 1936 the NMAIA decided to bring the fair back to Santa Fe
so that a larger segment of the non-Indian public could benefit
from seeing "good" Native American work. The plan for the 1936
fair was developed by Maria Chabot, a young writer who had been
hired by the NMAIA to develop a series of articles for *New Mexico
Magazine* on Indian arts and crafts (Bernstein 1993b:192–93).[20]
Chabot, who had been impressed by markets held in Mexican villages, suggested that the organization sponsor a weekly Saturday
market under the Palace portal, highlighting a different pueblo each
week. On each market day, transportation was to be provided for
artists from the featured pueblo and their work was to be judged, with
prizes awarded for the best pieces. While Chabot intended to have
Native Americans serve as judges, the artists that she asked refused to
judge each other's work and non-Indian judges had to be recruited
(Bernstein 1993b:195). Seven markets were scheduled for 1936,

FIGURE 2: *Vendors under the Palace portal, mid-1930s. Photo by T. Harmon Parkhurst. Courtesy Museum of New Mexico, Neg. No. 69973.*

beginning on July 11 (Bernstein 1993a:54; Chabot n.d.). Artists from San Ildefonso and Tesuque were invited the first week, and in the following weeks prizes were awarded to artists from Santa Clara, Nambe, San Juan, Santo Domingo, Cochiti, Acoma, Laguna, Zia, and Jemez (Bernstein 1993b:199–200; Chabot n.d.). Each week artists from previously invited pueblos returned to sell more of their work. The markets were hugely successful, with about one hundred fifty vendors participating each week. The final scheduled market for the year was held on August 22, but the program had proven so successful that artists came the next weekend as well. The Santa Fe Fiesta was held the first weekend of September, and for the first time since 1931 the Fiesta Council asked the Native American artists to set up under the portal for what became the ninth and final market of the season (Bernstein 1993a:54; Chabot n.d.).

No Saturday markets were held in 1937, because the NMAIA could not find enough volunteers to organize and run the events (Bernstein 1993b:202). However, the organization sponsored events in 1938 and 1939. The markets continued to be successful. In 1938 Kenneth Chapman reported that an average of 150 exhibitors came each week, with more than 300 attending on Fiesta weekend. He also estimated that more than 8,000 visitors attended the series of markets, buying some $2,500 worth of art and craft pieces (quoted in Bernstein 1993b:202–3). The majority of work was presumably purchased by tourists and Santa Fe residents. Local dealers who were consulted by the NMAIA before the staging of the markets were generally in favor of the events and thought that they might be able to purchase remaining pieces for lower prices at the end of the day (Meeting Minutes, June 11, 1936, SWAIA Records). The NMAIA-sponsored Saturday markets demonstrated the validity of the portal as a marketplace for Native American artists and provided the opportunity for artists to support their families through the production and sales of their work.

The 1938 and 1939 markets reaffirmed the portal as a Native American marketplace, and vendors continued to come to Santa Fe to sell under the portal on a regular basis (Bernstein 1993b:203). While Museum of New Mexico and NMAIA sponsorship made the first markets possible, it was the continuing interest of Native American artists and vendors and the markets' economic viability that made them successful. After the 1936 season, the now legendary San Ildefonso potter Maria Martinez told Maria Chabot that the money earned over the summer had allowed eight women to bring water to their houses (Bernstein 1993b:199). This was just the sort of economic opportunity that was needed by the people of the pueblos in the 1930s and 1940s as the traditional agriculture-based economy became less viable. A limited land base and restricted access to irrigation water, combined with growing populations, made subsistence agriculture difficult for many, and finding other means of support became crucial. By the 1930s arts and crafts production began to play a more important part in Puebloan economic life. In 1930 about 16 percent of total income for the Pueblos of the upper Rio Grande region in New Mexico came from arts and crafts, and during the depression years between 12 and 25 percent of Navajo income was derived from arts and crafts sales (Schrader 1983:44–45). At San Ildefonso, the village that dominated the revival of Tewa pottery in the 1920s, more than 50 percent of total income ($9,900 of $19,061.08) in 1933 came from pottery sales (Wade 1976:91). The opportunity to sell directly to tourists under the Palace portal was an important part of the development of the market, and Native American artists took advantage of it.

The NMAIA ceased its sponsorship of the weekly markets after 1939, and its members instead concentrated their efforts on the busiest weekend of the year, Fiesta. During the 1940s and 1950s, Fiesta weekend was such a popular time to sell under the portal that vendors would arrive at 3:30 the first morning of Fiesta and keep their spaces by sleeping on the sidewalk (Bernstein 1993b:215). The problem was resolved in 1959 when the NMAIA began to assign spaces to vendors but would be revisited in the 1970s and 1980s when the portal became a popular daily market.

Throughout the 1940s and especially after the end of World War II, more and more Native American artists began to sell under the portal on summer weekends and other periods of high tourism, even though the NMAIA and the Museum of New Mexico sponsored the

Native American market only during Fiesta. Documentation of the market under the portal during the period between 1940 and the early 1970s is limited, but that which exists is informative.

In 1941 the Santa Clara painter Pablita Velarde found the portal market significant enough to document it in a painting ("Pueblo Craftsmen, Palace of the Governors," reproduced in Berlo and Phillips 1998:218). In 1944 the anthropologist Ruth Underhill wrote about the weekly Saturday markets sponsored by the NMAIA:

> On Saturday mornings in summer the portico before the old governor's palace is gay with their bright shirts and shawls. White tourists pick their way among pots in shiny black or red, pottery animals, drums, bows, and arrows or string of colored corn, bright as jewels. No traveler returns to his home State without talking about the Indian market at Santa Fe. (Underhill 1979:129)

Bertha P. Dutton, then curator of ethnology at the Museum of New Mexico, gave the following description of the portal in 1948:

> Visitors who are fortunate enough to be in Santa Fe during the summer months and over Labor Day, will find the Indian markets held on Saturdays and at Fiesta time, under the portal of the Palace of the Governors, a picturesque spectacle.... Early in the morning on market days, the Indians, carrying their wares wrapped in pieces of calico or packed into paper cartons, come into town and arrange themselves for the day. Their backs to the wall, they sit either on the sidewalk or on low stools.... In front of them, the Indians spread their pottery, drums—both full-size and toy, dressed dolls, jewelry, baskets, moccasins, tanned goat skins, paintings, beaded trinkets, textiles, and unpredictable articles. (Dutton 1948:56)

Dutton (1948:41) also suggested to tourists that the portal was a good place to learn the stylistic differences in pottery from different pueblos. Institutions such as the Museum of New Mexico, the Arizona State Museum, and the Museum of Northern Arizona, which have long been important resources for scholars and others interested

FIGURE 3: *Vendors under the portal, ca. 1950. Courtesy Museum of New Mexico, Neg. No. 10597.*

in Native American art, were not added to her list of places to learn about pueblo pottery until later editions of *Indians of the Southwest* (see Dutton 1958:51).

In 1956 the New Mexico historian Paul Horgan commented on vendors under the portal during Fiesta and the tourists who tried to teach them salesmanship, illustrating common stereotypes of Native Americans and tourists alike:

> Older Indians were not lost altogether. Where she sat in the portal
> of the palace, selling her little rows of painted clay dishes and
> necklaces of dyed corn, an old Indian woman was addressed by a

prosperous Texan who knew the kind of salesmanship that had produced his affluence.

"Now lissen," he said to her while she kept her sober face unchanged, "you goan have to *smahl* if you goan sell anythin today, you know that?" (Horgan 1956:323)

The portal market was becoming a timeless element of the Santa Fe atmosphere. An article published in *New Mexico Magazine* in 1963 suggested that Indian people had been selling under the portal since the Palace was constructed (James 1963:23).[21] A photo was published by the same magazine in 1967 showing the spaces along the wall of the portal filled, with vendors also set up between the columns near the curb (Powers 1967:25), and in 1969 yet another article made reference to "the eternal Indian vendors under the old portal of the Palace of the Governors" (Calloway 1969:23).

By the middle part of the twentieth century the market under the portal was beginning to look like the Portal Program as it would be formalized in the 1970s and 1980s. The portal market had grown from an occasional market, held only a few times a year, to a marketplace that was regularly attended by a growing number of Native American artists and vendors. At the same time, the portal became part of the allure of Santa Fe: while the Pueblo Revival style of architecture catalogued by museum staff members Sylvanus Morley and Jesse Nusbaum and adapted by architect Isaac Hamilton Rapp became the distinguishing characteristic of the "City Different," Native American vendors under the Palace portal became the symbol of Santa Fe as one of the world's greatest tourist destinations and art meccas.

THREE

From Portal Market to Portal Program

As the portal markets grew from occasional affairs to daily events during the middle twentieth century, the number of vendors began to grow and more Native American communities were represented. During the early 1900s, vendors at the portal were mostly from Tesuque Pueblo, the pueblo closest to Santa Fe (Bernstein 1993b: 184). During the Indian Fair years of the 1920s and 1930s, vendors from other pueblos began to frequent the portal, with potters and other artists from the Tewa pueblos north of Santa Fe predominating. That San Ildefonso and Tesuque were the first pueblos featured in the 1936 markets was not an accident: San Ildefonso, led by Maria and Julian Martinez, had become the leading pottery producer, and Tesuque continued to be a large contributor to the Native American arts and crafts market. After World War II, more vendors began to come from Santo Domingo Pueblo. One of the largest and most conservative of the New Mexico pueblos, Santo Domingo gained a commanding presence on the portal, much to the chagrin of the Tewa vendors.[1] By the 1960s a majority of vendors were from Santo Domingo (see James 1963:23). Santo Domingo artists are world renowned for their turquoise and shell (heishi) jewelry, and the increasing number of Santo Domingo vendors brought more jewelry to the portal. By the 1960s jewelry was beginning to rival pottery as the most prevalent art form available under the portal. Increasing tourist demand for jewelry in the 1970s encouraged more vendors to bring jewelry to the portal, and it became the dominant art form. The composition of vendors shifted again in the 1970s, as more Navajos and people from pueblos more remote from Santa Fe began to sell under the portal.

During the period before the mid-1970s, the Portal was not strictly organized as a program either by the Museum of New Mexico or by the vendors. The NMAIA (later, SWAIA) had made some attempts to regulate the portal marketplace, but the organization concentrated primarily on the Fiesta weekend market. Though unregulated, the portal became known as a good place to find "real Indian folk art" (James 1963:23). A key to successful folk, ethnic, and indigenous art markets is that the goods sold are perceived by consumers as authentic (Littrell, Anderson, and Brown 1993), and authenticity continues to be a major issue in the Native American art market and in other ethnic art markets (see Mobley-Martinez 1997; Ryan and Crotts 1997; Shiffman 1998; *USA Today,* April 8, 1998).

Imitation "Indian" jewelry was being made at least as early as 1910 (Adair 1944:27), and in 1929 New Mexico was the first state to implement an Indian arts and crafts act to protect against imitation work and fraudulent marketing practices (Evans-Pritchard 1990:19; NMSA 1929:chap. 33). Early attempts to protect the market were spearheaded by advocates trying to protect Indian craftspeople or by Indian traders looking to protect their livelihoods (Evans-Pritchard 1990:27–39). A significant problem was the advent of machine-made jewelry that could be sold for much less than comparable handmade pieces. Around 1926 Maurice M. Maisel's Maisel Trading Post Company in Albuquerque began to employ Indian workers to operate machinery mass-producing "Indian" jewelry (Schrader 1983:53–54). In 1931 a group of traders who were being undersold by Maisel organized the United Indian Traders Association and complained to the Federal Trade Commission that by selling machine-made jewelry as Indian made, Maisel was engaging in unfair trade practices (Evans-Pritchard 1990:28). Maisel was eventually ordered to cease using the term "Indian made" to describe his jewelry unless he also stated that the pieces were machine processed (Schrader 1983:56). He refused to follow the order but in 1935 was finally ordered by the Tenth Circuit Court of Appeals to comply with a significantly weakened order that allowed him to use the vague phrase "press cut and domed blanks" to describe the machine processing of his jewelry.

The reason the traders challenged Maisel was not consumer protection but rather the protection of their own livelihoods and those of the Indian artists and craftspeople they bought pieces from. Likewise, the federal government was concerned more with supporting Indian artists than protecting the buyers of Indian art; as Secretary of the Interior Harold Ickes told the United Indian Traders Association, "We will not tolerate any misrepresentation which will injure our Indian craftsmen" (*Gallup Independent,* October 24, 1933, quoted in Schrader 1983:56). The federal Indian Arts and Crafts Board Act of 1935 was enacted to "promote the economic welfare of the Indian tribes and the Indian wards of the Government through the development of Indian arts and crafts and the expansion of the market for the products of Indian art and craftsmanship," with consumer protection a secondary consideration (text of act reproduced in Schrader 1983:299–302). The marketing of arts and crafts was seen by governmental representatives as an important part of Native American economic advancement and a way to decrease the financial responsibilities of the federal government to the Indian tribes (Prucha 1984:932–34).

In Santa Fe, the organizers of the first Indian Fairs in the 1920s shared the same concern for protecting producers rather than consumers. It was only after World War II that greater emphasis began to be placed on educating the purchasers of Indian art. With the increasing sophistication of Indian art consumers, finding reputable sources became a greater concern.[2]

Before the mid-1970s the portal market had no formal "rules"; rather, it was just a good place for tourists to buy arts and crafts and a good place for Native American vendors to sell.

George Ewing, former director, Museum of New Mexico
Well, it was pretty casual. It was the kind of thing that sort of ran itself. The primary supervisory document, I would say, was the

New Mexico Indian Arts and Crafts Act, which stipulated the conditions for considering things to be Indian. They had to be hand-made by American Indians, and so everybody was under a certain amount of surveillance, to be sure, that they were conforming to that Act.... And in point of fact, it was something that had simply gotten started, and had continued on without any real formalizing of policy or anything on the part of the Board of Regents. The Board of Regents was involved with it, of course, and certainly approved of the way that it was being operated and really knew about it.

Dorothy Chavez, Santo Domingo:
At that time [in the 1960s] when I was here we didn't have to get a certain amount of space, we chose whatever space we wanted and just put out any size cloth we wanted, small or large or extra large, whatever, and we also sold for each other then. If we wanted to take a break we didn't have to cover up; we would just [ask] our neighbors or our friends who were sitting next to us if they could watch our stuff and when we came back something would be sold. And that was nice because we were helping each other sell either way.

Juanita Atencio, Santo Domingo:
We used to, if somebody was sitting next to you, say, "Can you watch my stuff?" We used to sell for each other! If I was gone, if this person or tourist came along and wanted that one, they could sell it for you. The person sitting next to you could sell it for you. And when you came back they'd give you the money. Because we more or less knew the prices for all the items with our neighbors next to us. So we used to do that. If my neighbor was gone for lunch and if somebody came back, because some, especially the ones with potteries, they would mark their prices on the bottom of the pottery. So you know how much it is. So if this person wanted to buy it then I'd go and sell it for her and then put the money under the cloth, and give it to them when they came back.

When I was coming up as a child I used to bring some stuff up for my uncle, my mom's brother, or my grandmother, I would bring some of her stuff and sell it for her. We would sell for all the family members on one cloth. But now you have to sell things that are made within your family or things that you make yourself. Which is okay, and I agree with that, but when I first came back there were quite a few things that I couldn't get used to as I am right now. And when I was coming up we didn't have to draw, there were no numbered spots....We would get up here about 8:00, well 8:00, 8:30, and there would still be spaces open.... And then there were no limited spaces, you [could] take up whatever [space] you thought you needed. There was no twelve block [spaces] here. No, if you wanted to take twice as much, you took it. Or if you wanted to take up a whole space and then maybe share it with somebody that didn't get a space, but to tell the truth, it never filled up like it does now. There's always spaces open, you know, maybe on the ends. But there's always some space. Even if you got up here late, like if you couldn't catch a ride you might get up here by twelve o'clock, there would still be a space and you would set up. And it didn't fill up like it does now. Because there was no Navajos. (Laughter)

The last statement reflects the tensions that exist between Pueblo and Diné (Navajo) people but also leads to a discussion of the cross-cultural trading of arts and crafts that has occurred for centuries (see Parezo 1990). Although no Navajo people sold regularly under the portal before the 1970s, their work was widely available from Pueblo vendors who traded their own work for Navajo silver.

Juanita Atencio, Santo Domingo

{SL: And what did the Navajo want from you?}

Necklaces. Turquoise necklaces. Mostly *jaclas* [Diné: "ear string"] because that was their traditional necklaces.... You'll hardly ever see the traditional necklaces that the Navajos, the older Navajos, used to [want] when they were trading. They used to like the nuggets on shells with a jacla hanging down as a set.

Or mostly they loved the jaclas, which is their traditional [jewelry], what they used mostly.

There were no age restrictions for vendors, and children and teenagers would often help to support the family through selling at the portal in addition to helping with the manufacture of pieces. Often children would come with a parent or other family member; sometimes they would come alone.

Alfonso Tenorio, Santo Domingo

{KH: So your mom came to the portal when you were a lot younger.}

Oh yeah, I sat with her when I was about six. We used to come together, just to keep her company, or whatever she wants, I go get: Cokes, whatever, lunch. I'd go get stuff for her. // I was about twelve when I was first selling by myself. There was no age limit yet, until two girls took off the whole day and left all their jewelry is when they started doing that. // I even, after school [and on] weekends, I used to sell over here. Then Monday morning, go back to school. In the summertime I used to come over here.

Dorothy Chavez, Santo Domingo

I do have a daughter that started to sell here for me when she was just ten years old. And to me she was just a little girl then, but she was already interested, and she does help me do vending here. Her name's D., and she's good at selling too, but she has her own thing to do now, but she still comes to help me sell sometimes on the weekends.... She was only like ten years old when she started selling here and one of the vendors was the one that started me off with her, because I had just had my last baby then, back in 1970.... She said, "Because you're having a tough time taking care of your little one, why don't you let D. come with me to Santa Fe, I always need somebody to come with." By that time they were not really fighting for spaces, but it was getting scarce to get a space out there because a lot more people were coming in at the time. So she would pick up my daughter and say, "She can sleep. I can help her set up and she can just be with me." So they would just pick out that space

22 we have now which has that area in there where there's a lot of room, and if my daughter got sleepy she would just put her down on the floor and she would watch our stuff for us. And we have records of all the jewelry that she sold back then, and she sold for two years for me and that's how she got very interested too in doing jewelry.

The Portal Program as it exists at the end of the twentieth century is not just a multicultural community of Native American people from diverse cultural groups. It also includes non-Indian people who help to make up the social fabric of the Portal community. In addition to museum staff, other local residents and businesspeople take part in daily life on and around the portal. This interconnectedness with the larger social milieu of Santa Fe is part of what makes the Portal Program such an important local institution. Program participants have fond recollections of nonvendor community members in the 1950s and 1960s.

Juanita Atencio, Santo Domingo

Oh there was a man that lived down Palace Street, and I don't know what's there now but it's a two-story building going this way on the left-hand side. There used to be a couple that lived there. They were an elderly, middle sixties couple and the man used to bake cookies I guess every morning and he used to come up and go under the portal and start giving out cookies to little kids like us, you know, oatmeal cookies or peanut butter cookies or I don't know what other cookies he made but there were some other cookies that were good. [They] had nuts in them, but I don't know what ingredients he used, but we used to love getting cookies from him. He would go all the way up and then whatever he had left he would go back [and] give everybody seconds. To the little kids. We used to love waiting for him. Or sometimes he would come over and take a few of us down to his place for some soup. It was always good, because sometimes I came up without even any money, you know my parents didn't have any money, so I would just come up here and my mother would tell me, "Whatever you sell go ahead

and get something to eat." So sometimes I came up here without
a penny. So if you're hungry, you know, that was very nice of
him, even a cookie would really fill you up, you know. Curb
your appetite. (Laughter)

{SL: Were there other people you saw every day other than
the man who brought cookies?}

There was this one man, he was a Hispanic man called
Manuel. He used to fetch everybody coffee. You give him the
money, he'd go get coffee, you give him a tip. I don't know if
he had a job or not, but he used to be around the plaza, or if
you want to go to the bathroom he'd sit in for you, watch your
stuff. You know, just watch them and then he, you'd tell him
the prices for your items and when you came back he'll probably
say, "I sold this for you." And then he would take fifty cents or
a dollar tip, something like that, to keep him happy. I guess that's
how he was making his living. But I noticed years later that I
didn't see him anymore and somebody said that he had passed
away, he had gotten sick and died. But he seemed like a nice
man. Someone that you can trust, with your jewelry, if you
go for lunch or whatever he would sit there for you and watch
your stuff.

While vendors do not note many changes over the years in the
visitors who come to Santa Fe, they have seen significant changes in
the downtown environment as more and more downtown businesses
have begun to cater directly to the tourist market.

Dorothy Chavez, Santo Domingo

[The] stores near the surrounding area used to be helpful a lot
when instead of all the jewelry stores, the galleries, and all those
stores we had clothing stores or five and ten stores, drugstores,
and you name it. Those places like that all moved away and they
were very nearby, where we could stay right here and get our things
in town and then head on home instead of now we have to stop at
the mall, we have to stop at different places if we need something.
Jewel-Osco, grocery store, you name it.[3]

Crafting a Program

Through the 1970s and 1980s the portal became more crowded as vendors started to take advantage of the marketplace. These decades were marked by increasing tensions among vendors competing for limited space as well as by increased organization and formalized support for the market as an official program of the Museum of New Mexico. In 1972 the Museum of New Mexico Board of Regents (MNMBOR) affirmed an Indians-only policy for sales under the Palace portal and prohibited sales elsewhere on museum grounds (MNMBOR minutes, May 18, 1972). The MNMBOR was concerned that the museum grounds around the plaza (including the sidewalk areas around the Museum of Fine Arts in addition to the portal) had become an open marketplace in which the museum had no control over the types or quality of goods sold. The MNMBOR's affirmation of the Indian-only portal market set the stage for the museum's direct involvement in the portal market for the first time since the 1930s (MNMBOR minutes, May 18, 1972).

By this time the vendors recognized that the popularity of the market was growing so rapidly that they would have to regulate it. In 1974 a committee of vendors led by Tony Tortalita, an artist from Santo Domingo who has served as a leader both in the Portal Program and in his village for many years, came together and developed a basic set of rules governing sales under the portal (pers. com. 1999). These rules for the Portal Program would be adopted by the museum in 1976 when it sought oversight of the program.

Though contrary to museum policy, through the first half of the 1970s non-Indian artists and vendors had continued to sell a wide variety of arts and crafts and other items on the sidewalks around the Museum of Fine Arts, on the northwest corner of the plaza across Lincoln Avenue from the Palace of the Governors. Because of threats of reverse-discrimination lawsuits, museum director George Ewing allowed the non-Indian vendors to continue their sales activities in spite of the museum's desire to control sales on museum grounds and the problems that arose with increasing numbers of vendors. In an effort to justify eliminating the non-Indian vendors from the museum grounds, Ewing contacted the New Mexico Attorney General's office for legal assistance. In February 1976 Jill Z. Cooper, then assistant attorney general, found legal justification for the museum's Indian-only policy for sales under the portal: the Civil Rights Acts of 1964 and 1972 support preferential treatment for Indian people engaged in "Indian-related" industries on and near reservations (MNMBOR file, memo from George Ewing, February 2, 1976; 42 U.S.C. § 2000e–2(i)).[4] Backed by this legal finding, the museum removed all but Native American vendors selling under the portal from the museum grounds.

In response to losing a lucrative place to sell, some of the non-Indian vendors began to set up next to the Native American vendors under the portal. The most aggressive of these non-Indian vendors were Paul and Sara Livingston, Anglo immigrants from New York who had begun making Indian-style jewelry in an attempt to profit from the booming popularity of Indian arts and crafts (Evans-Pritchard 1990:67).[5] After being removed from the Museum of Fine Arts property, the Livingstons and a few other non-Indians attempted to sell their goods under the portal. On numerous occasions, museum officials enlisted the aid of the state police to remove the non-Indians, who would return the next day. The conflicts between the non-Native vendors, on one hand, and the museum and the Native American vendors under the portal, on the other, led to a series of lawsuits and complaints to the New Mexico Human Rights Commission that stretched over more than a decade. The museum and the program eventually prevailed in these suits; in the process an informal market became the Portal Program.

While questions over the legality of the Indian-only portal market were contested in court, tensions remained high between Native and non-Native vendors under the portal (*Santa Fe New Mexican*, February 24, 1978). The Native American vendors had long considered the portal an exclusive Native American marketplace and were closely allied with the museum in its efforts to maintain it as such. As cases were litigated, the non-Native vendors occasionally won temporary injunctions allowing them to sell under the portal. The Native American vendors did their best to limit their opposition to these intrusions into their marketing space to nonviolent protest.

Grace Ann Herrera (Diné [Navajo]) tells of trying to occupy as much space as possible with her own cloth to limit the space under the portal available to the non-Indian vendors (pers. com. 1999). Others set up signs on their cloths, warning tourists that not all the vendors on the portal were Indians (see *Santa Fe New Mexican*, March 26, 1977). When tourists purchased jewelry from the non-Indians, Native American vendors would inform them that they had purchased inauthentic goods. On one occasion, a Canadian tourist attempted to return a necklace to Paul Livingston on learning that it was not Native-made; Livingston refused to take it back (Evans-Pritchard 1990:67; note from D. Christie, March 18, 1978, Portal Log).

In 1977 the Livingstons, supported by the American Civil Liberties Union, filed a reverse-discrimination lawsuit against George Ewing, director of the Museum of New Mexico, the museum Board of Regents, and the mayor, police chief, and city council of Santa Fe. The Livingstons argued that their right to equal protection under the law, guaranteed by the Fourteenth Amendment to the U.S. Constitution, was violated by the museum's Indian-only policy. In what would be a precedent-setting decision supporting museums' rights to determine their own programming, the U.S. District Court for the District of New Mexico granted the summary judgment motion of Jill Z. Cooper, assistant attorney general of New Mexico, counsel for the defense. The court agreed with the defendants that the museum had the right to support and encourage the production and sale of traditional Native American arts and crafts as a cultural program of the museum and therefore that the museum was not engaging in reverse discrimination against the Livingstons.

The Livingstons appealed the decision, and the case went to the Tenth Circuit United States Court of Appeals in Denver. For the appeal, a group of vendors led by program committee chair Dennis Anderson, from Cochiti Pueblo, petitioned the court to enter the legal fray. The court determined that because the vendors had a considerable stake in the outcome of the lawsuit, they were allowed to enter on the side of the defense as Intervenors-Appellees. Supported by a brief for amicus curiae submitted by the All Indian Pueblo Council, Inc., Michael P. Gross, attorney for the vendors, argued that the museum's Indian-only policy was valid because the vendors could be considered employees of the museum. Under 42 U.S.C. § 2000e(b) and § 2000e–2(i), the acts first used by the museum to justify its portal policy of 1976, businesses operating on or near Indian reservations are exempt from the Equal Employment Opportunity Act of 1972 in that such businesses can preferentially hire Indian people.

The museum and its attorney were not interested in identifying the portal vendors as museum employees because the museum neither considered the vendors employees nor wanted to classify them as such. The museum preferred to recognize program participants as independent businesspeople, and it did not want the added responsibilities or administrative burden that legal employment of the vendors could entail. Furthermore, they wanted to reaffirm the validity of the argument that the museum had the right to determine the participation in and content of its programs (Ewing 1998).

The appeals court upheld the district court's decision in favor of the museum, this time affirming the vendors' argument that the relationship between the museum and the vendors constituted an employment practice and that the limitation of the program to Native Americans was supported by the Preference Statute, 42 U.S.C. § 2000e–2(i). Though basing its decision on the employment issue, the court further found that the museum was protecting "a valuable state interest, that of acquiring, preserving and exhibiting historical, archeological and ethnological interests in fine arts" (Livingston v. Ewing, 601 F.2d 1110, *1114 [1979]), therefore upholding the museum's freedom to decide the content and participation in its program.

The appeals court also upheld the trial court's finding that "It is thought that only Indians can make Indian goods and, therefore, that it is in the public interest to allow the Indians to do it" (Livingston v. Ewing, 601 F.2d 1110, *1112 [1979]). Though seemingly an obvious statement, this finding speaks to an issue that has been and continues to be of concern in the Native American arts and crafts market: authenticity. Dierdre Evans-Pritchard (1990:63) argues that the key issue underlying Paul Livingston's legal battle against the museum was authenticity. Livingston argued that there was no real difference between the Indian-style jewelry he and his wife made and the jewelry being made and sold by Indian people and that the attribute that makes Indian jewelry authentic (i.e., the fact that it is made by Indian artists) is an invisible attribute (Evans-Pritchard 1990:74). While this may be true, for Indian artists and for consumers of Indian arts this invisible attribute is critically important: for the Native American arts and crafts market to be a viable ethnic arts market, the objects being sold as Native American arts must be made by Native American people.[6] Federal and state laws regarding Native American arts and crafts have long focused on this issue: New Mexico enacted the first state Indian Arts and Crafts Act in 1929, and the federal government followed with the creation of the Indian Arts and Crafts Board in 1935 (Schrader 1983). As I discuss below, concerns about ensuring that items sold under the portal are authentic, handmade, Native American art and craft objects have played an important part in the development of the program's rules and regulations.

The U.S. Supreme Court refused to hear a further appeal by the Livingstons in their suit against the museum (Evans-Pritchard 1990:63). Paul Livingston made some further attempts through the state courts to negate the museum's policy on statutory grounds but again was ultimately unsuccessful (see 98 N.M. 685; 652 P.2d 235 [1982]). Livingston and another non-Indian vendor, Brian Joyce,[7] each made claims of civil rights violations to the New Mexico Human Rights Commission, but these claims were dismissed. Livingston eventually attended law school at the University of New Mexico, was admitted to the New Mexico state bar, and resurfaced on the plaza several years later when he instigated yet another lawsuit against the program and the museum, this time as plaintiff's attorney for a vendor at odds with the program.[8]

The immediate impact on the portal of the Livingstons' legal challenges was seen in the first sets of rules that defined and regulated the portal market. The first policy statement was adopted by the MNMBOR in February 1976 as the board sought to eliminate the growing numbers of non-Indian vendors occupying the museum's sidewalks. In addition to affirming the policy of prohibiting sales elsewhere on museum grounds, the resolution stated, "Permission to use the area under the portal is granted to the Indians with the express understanding that the Indians themselves are solely responsible for the fair and orderly regulation of the use of that space" (MNMBOR minutes, February 18, 1976). This statement was followed in July 1976 by a set of nine rules regulating the Portal Program that were adopted from the rules the vendors themselves had established two years earlier. These rules set limits on space size (four feet), established setup time (7:00 A.M.), and gave the Committee of Indian Craftsmen, a group of six vendors, authority to assign spaces to vendors under the portal, to enforce the rules, and to correct rules violations. This first set of rules also required that all items be handmade by Indians and restricted vendors from selling items for stores or wholesalers. Though not officially stated, vendors were allowed to buy goods from other Indian artists and resell the items under the portal. The final rule "suggested" that vendors park their cars in public lots instead of at the metered spaces around the museum, an issue that continues occasionally to be debated by vendors, museum administrators, and nearby shop owners today.

By expressly giving responsibility for the operation and regulation of the portal market to the Indian vendors, the museum administration and Board of Regents acknowledged that the vendors were best qualified to run the program. They had informally maintained the market for decades prior to the formal creation of the program and continued to protect their interests by keeping the program as orderly as possible. Furthermore, the museum was understaffed and unable to commit staff time to the program.

George Ewing, former director, Museum of New Mexico
[W]e were awfully thin on staff, we didn't have the facility to go out and really didn't want to take on responsibility for running it, we wanted the Indians to, and they did. So two things took place: The Board of Regents got involved in establishing their position much more formally and also we called the Indians together, Mike Weber [then head of the Museum of New Mexico history division] did, and said, "Okay, you guys, now this is your market and you have to run it and be responsible for it." And they did,

they established their committees and they had their meetings periodically, there was a set procedure for them, and how they handled any disputes that come up, and since that time they have, as far as I know, continued to operate it in a fair and equitable manner. So that's the basis of that, the two things: the museum had to get everything formalized there, but also the Indians had to take some responsibility for it too. Tony Tortalita, who is now [in 1998] the governor of Santo Domingo, was the principal figure out there.

The museum and the MNMBOR officially gave their support to the program, but it continued to be *outside* of the museum, not just physically, but also in terms of programming, staff, and for the most part administration. Integrating the Portal Program into the museum is a continuing process.

A Booming Market

The lucrative market for Native American jewelry that arose in the 1970s and encouraged non-Indians such as the Livingstons to make Indian-style jewelry has been characterized by longtime dealer Al Packard as a "jewelry explosion" (quoted in Bernstein 1999:63). This explosion also brought increasing numbers of Native American vendors to the portal. By the late 1970s and early 1980s, spaces were at a premium and sales were very good.

Stella Platero, Diné (Navajo)
People would just come. I mean, there wasn't even enough room! There were all kind of [tourists] pushing from here to the end. Because I remember it: they would stand and lean trying to get to your space. They were looking over a good look sideways, and they would actually point at your stuff, they [would] say, "I want that one, that one." I mean three, four pieces at a time!

As the daily demand for room under the portal increased, vendors began to come earlier in the morning to claim spaces. Soon vendors began sleeping under the portal to save their preferred spaces,

FIGURE 4: *Under the portal in the 1970s. Increasing numbers of visitors brought more vendors. Photo by Arthur Taylor. Courtesy of the Museum of New Mexico, Neg. No. 112135.*

as they had in the 1940s and 1950s on Fiesta weekends. Cheryl Arviso (Diné [Navajo]), who as a young child came to the portal with her mother, Lori Hesuse, remembers sleeping in the car with her mother and sister on summer nights so that they could hold a place to sell the next day. One vendor who came each morning only to find all the spaces under the portal occupied decided to see for herself what was happening.

Stella Platero, Diné (Navajo)
Then, I was always left out. I remember me and one lady we parked here on the side, so we could get our space. Sure enough people were here at twelve midnight, putting their cloth down. That's when I started [to] think that it [was] too much, if people were sleeping [under the portal]. You were tired! (Laughs)

When the museum and Portal committee no longer allowed vendors to sleep under the portal to save their spaces, they had to come very early so that they could rush to the portal at the official starting time (7:00 A.M., then 8:00). Cheryl Arviso would occasionally be asked to carry several vendors' cloths to the portal because she was young, small, and fast and could get to the spaces before other vendors could.

Marvin Slim, Diné (Navajo)
I remember that too. Spending the night out here, early in the morning, a lot of people [would] just line up across the street and run across to get a space.

The increase in demand for spaces also led to increased tensions among the vendors under the portal. Even without the disruptions caused by the Livingston lawsuits and the occasional injunctions that allowed non-Indians to sell under the portal, tempers sometimes flared.

Marvin Slim, Diné (Navajo)
Yeah, that's kind of crazy. And they used to get your cloth, they would throw it in the trash can [if] they didn't like you; get your cloth and they would throw it in the street. That's why there was

a lot of fights out here; they used to get the cloths and just throw them in the street. You'd come by [and] you'd find a cloth in the street. It was awful, there used to be a lot of fights out here.

{KH: This is a way that the rules have helped things, huh?}

Oh yeah, because [of] a lot of things, everybody has scars, battle scars, you know.

Sarah Martinez,* Santo Domingo

Well, when I first started selling here.... God, it was just a mess every morning. There were arguments, and "I was here first!" and Oh! Well, when I first started I remember the first couple of years, when I first started you could come selling on a Saturday and still get a space, a good space, you know, you could still get a good space. Now you have to be here at eight o'clock or you don't get one at all. And I remember people would be fighting about how many blocks you're supposed to have, and the spaces weren't marked, and "I was here first," and then after a while it started to get personal! Oh, and it was awful! And I even remember myself arguing with some of the people out there. But when I first started selling out here, I remember that the committee was starting to get formed, and there were a lot of things that had to be ironed out, you know a lot of people were griping about a lot of things, all the rules and stuff like that, and I think there were more people at the annual meeting than there are now.

The committee and the museum administration had to step in and attempt to regulate the program that was growing by leaps and bounds. Progress came by trial and error; a number of the vendors had been coming to the portal for many years, but they had never had to deal with such large numbers of vendors. Often the committee and vendors had to learn from mistakes. A well-remembered example is "Dorothy's race."

Dorothy Chavez, Santo Domingo

Well, at one time we couldn't figure out, this was just the start of what we were trying to do for the program. And we tried many ways to get people to assign spaces and at that time they were letting us use the spaces across the portal there on the curb. We were using all those spaces then because there were a lot of people by then and it was during the tourist season. So in the morning, this is one of the jokes that Tom always makes with me—Tom Chávez—in the morning one time I happened to be on duty that day and I didn't know what to do. When I got here there was a flock of people out in the front and they already had their spaces, put their cloths where they were going to sit for the day. But we also had a lot of people over and I go, "Oh my God, what do I do?" So I went across the street, which they used to do, they used to stand across the street over there at the park in the mornings to wait for eight o'clock to come so they could come across. And I was the only person here that day on the committee; [I had] no help. And I was lost, I didn't know what to do. So I went across (laughs) and I made the biggest mistake (laughs), by having everybody just take whatever spaces they could. So that was a race across the street. (Laughter)

{SL: It turned into a stampede.}

Yes. Everybody took whatever spaces they could get and there were some people that didn't get a space, and boy it was a big mess that day. So that's the race across the street. (Laughter)

The development of the rules in the late 1970s and early 1980s demonstrates how the vendors, the program committee, and the museum staff searched for ways to organize the program in a fair and equitable manner, to maintain the economic benefits of the program for vendors and preserve the spirit of the market while at the same time protecting the integrity of the Portal as a museum program. It was imperative to the museum and to most of the vendors that the program maintain standards of quality agreed upon by the vendors and the museum administration and that the program not become a "flea market." In 1977 the original nine rules adopted the year before were expanded to fourteen. Included in the new rules were a minimum age requirement (eighteen), a suggestion that small children not be brought to the Portal, and a request from the committee "for cooperation from all the vendors and a friendly spirit in sharing spaces with each other" (Program Rules, May 23, 1977). During these first two years of regulation, the language of the rules shows a real deference to the vendors: points were "suggested" or "asked" of the vendors rather than dictated.

A pair of memos released in October 1978 by George Ewing illuminate other concerns. The first memo, which was issued soon after the conclusion of the first Livingston lawsuit that allowed the museum to restrict the Portal Program to Native Americans, had two points. The first point was that all Native Americans, regardless of tribal origin (though presumably limited to tribal groups in the United States), were permitted to sell under the portal so long as they could provide "appropriate records" demonstrating their enrollment in a recognized tribal group. Though the majority of vendors came from the Southwest, a few Native Americans from other regions of the United States also sold under the portal. As vendor numbers continued to climb, the program eventually had to be restricted mainly to members of tribes and villages with historic ties to New Mexico. The second point affirmed that all vendors were independent businesspeople and that neither the museum nor anyone associated with the museum would set prices for items to be sold (memo, Ewing to vendors, October 10, 1978, Portal Log).

The second memo, sent out four days after the first, addressed what would be a more complicated issue. The purpose of the memo was to establish the authority of the program committee to manage the market under the portal. Before the museum took a greater role in the portal market, vendors generally relied on their tribal governments, especially the Pueblo governors, to assist in resolving any disputes that could not be readily and informally managed by the vendors themselves. The Pueblo governors took (and continue to take) an active interest in acting as advisors and advocates for their people, and the portal was seen largely as an extension of the Pueblo communities. Thus even after the museum began organizing the market as a museum program and an administrative committee for the program had been created, vendors still looked to their governors to resolve problems.

The Livingston lawsuit made clear that the museum would have to take an active part in supervising the Portal Program if it was going to maintain control of the activities occurring on its property. Ewing's memos were an attempt to reinforce the museum's position as owner and operator of the Portal as well as to establish a new chain of command for the administration of the program: the Portal committee would be responsible for coordinating the daily operation of the program and for resolving any disputes that might arise. The museum staff, in the person of the director of the Palace, would handle any problems that the committee could not resolve.

Over the years the museum and the Pueblo governments have negotiated their respective roles in the program. The pueblos' leaders continue to maintain an active interest in the Portal and advise their village members regarding issues that arise under the portal but are not involved in the operations or administration of the program. The museum keeps the governors informed of major issues and invites them to attend the Portal Program's annual meeting. The governor of Santo Domingo attends the meeting almost every year, and occasionally representatives from the other pueblos attend.

Within the program, the committee has taken the lead in managing the portal, with the museum staff serving to back up the committee's decisions. When vendors are penalized for violating program rules—sanctions usually consist of suspension from the program for a period of a few days but may be as long as six months for repeat violations—the committee generally recommends penalties that are enforced by the director of the Palace. The most common rules violations include missing or mismarked trademarks or the use of prohibited materials and result in limited penalties. Severer rules violations such as fighting and public intoxication are much rarer but result in stiffer penalties. The fact that suspension from the program can have an impact on the incomes of entire households is never far from the committee members' thoughts, and sanctions are not imposed without careful deliberation. Appeals of decisions and penalties are heard by the director of the Palace and finally by the director of the Museum of New Mexico.

In 1979 the language of the rules began to reflect the growing formality and organization of the program. This came about in response to the legal challenges and to the growing number of vendors who wanted to use the program's limited space. For the first time, the rules outlined offenses that would lead to automatic suspension from the program: being intoxicated and harassing other vendors or tourists and fighting under the portal. For other violations, vendors would be given two warnings before being suspended for the third violation of a rule. The first raw material restrictions were implemented in 1979 as well, with German silver being prohibited except for use in findings.[9] The regulation of the materials and techniques that can be used in the manufacturing process for items sold under the portal represents attempts by the museum and the vendors to maintain a level of traditionality and authenticity in the program and to provide an outlet where traditionally manufactured work can be profitably sold (see Appendix).

Beyond these regulations, the Portal is unusual as an ethnic tourism destination in that there is virtually no pressure from within the program or from the museum to maintain "traditional" or "authentic" clothing or appearance under the portal. As I noted in chapter 1, I believe that this reflects a decision on the part of the vendors not to engage in this sort of "staged" authenticity. Rather than create an idealized image of the American Indian, the vendors choose to represent themselves as they are: contemporary Native American people.

The most significant exception to this trend away from regulating "traditional" appearance is the restriction of credit card machines, televisions, and radios from the portal, rules that were first implemented in 1979. In later years the restrictions were expanded to include "tape recorders and players, binoculars, cellular phones, cameras . . . and other modern appliances or equipment not essential to participation in the Portal Program" (see Appendix). These rules are generally accepted by program participants, even if they sometimes express dissatisfaction with some of them. Though a majority of vendors support the credit card ban, many do accept credit cards at shows or other venues, where such sales often make up a majority of their business (Slim 1998). Some vendors have noted that the prohibition of credit cards under the portal prevents them from selling larger, more expensive items and therefore makes it difficult to produce such pieces. While this is probably true, and in spite of recommendations by some vendors to the contrary, the museum has continued to maintain that allowing credit card sales under the portal would be disruptive to the program. In discussions of the issue I have observed, a majority of vendors have sided with the museum. (Note to potential visitors and collectors: be sure to bring cash.)

The restriction on cameras is a bit more complicated. There is a standing joke that this regulation was implemented because vendors were sometimes taking photos of tourists, an act that some of the tourists found discomforting. This joke is a reflection of the fact that a number of the vendors do not like to have their photographs taken, and all expect the courtesy of being asked permission to be photographed by strangers. Many, if not most, of the tourists who visit the portal carry cameras[10] and often photograph the portal and the vendors, sometimes without permission and against vendors' wishes. Tourists often seek the most "traditional"-looking vendors, who are also usually the folks most opposed to being photographed. A main reason given for the prohibition of cameras among vendors, along with the restriction of other nonessential "modern appliances," is that the Portal is a place of business and the devices would be distracting and improper (Glenn Paquin, pers. com. 1999).

By the early 1980s the vendors and the museum staff had begun to work together to develop a more comprehensive set of rules and regulations for the program. Thomas Chávez had recently been named director of the Palace and new vendors were becoming involved in the program. Some, like Glenn Paquin, who had gained experience working with volunteer organizations at the University of New Mexico, had new ideas about how to improve the program.

Glenn Paquin, Laguna and Zuni

We'd sit in sessions, when we'd have our meetings. And Tom [Chávez] sat in on a lot of them and we'd go over the rationale of each rule, what kinds of rules [we should implement], and we would look at complaints. We'd ask people about things that they thought they would like to see, and we took a lot of that information from them. So my feeling was that if we take it from them it'll be easier to get it established as part of the rules because they can say, "I had something to do with it." So a lot of the rules are their ideas and we just put them into a formal, administrative type of wording that would make [them] sound like [they had their] own objectives in each category so [they had] to be done.

Formalizing the program entailed discovering ways to manage it physically. As more vendors competed for the limited space under the portal, the committee and museum staff had to find a way to distribute marketing space equitably. Before the 1970s demand for spaces was usually such that everyone who wanted to sell under the portal could find room to do so. As the program gained popularity as a result of the increasing demand for Indian art, the committee was given the authority to assign spaces. However, this proved problematic, as committee members were often accused of favoring vendors from their own village or tribe. The committee was left trying other ways to distribute spaces, eventually resorting to permitting mad dashes for spaces, such as "Dorothy's race" across the street. Finally, on Tom Chávez's recommendation it was decided that a daily lottery would be the most equitable means of assigning spaces. In July 1986 the portal was closed for two days so that the spaces could be delineated and numbered. From then on, on any day that more vendors came to sell than there were spaces available (now sixty-nine plus the duty officer's space), a drawing was held. Though there are still occasional complaints, especially when the committee miscounts the number of vendors or the number of chips needed, the draw has worked well for a number of years without requiring substantial modification.

One significant change that the draw has brought about is the mixing up of vendors from different cultural groups. Because the draw is random, vendors do not choose who they set up next to. This has promoted cross-cultural communication among Portal vendors. The random drawing for spaces also sometimes places individuals who do not get along next to each other. In extreme cases, the committee and the affected parties work out space trades to minimize problems.

Making the Program an Artists' Market

As the program became more well defined in the 1970s and 1980s, its emphasis changed. Before 1982 program regulations had required only that pieces sold be made by Native Americans and that they be bought directly from the craftsperson by the vendor if not made by the vendor himself or herself. While most vendors made at least some of the items they sold, many did, in fact, act as intermediate retailers. Through the traditional practice of trading among Native people, vendors thus made art from a greater variety of cultural groups available under the portal.

> ### Glenn Paquin, Laguna and Zuni
> I can remember when we first came in we were selling Acoma pottery. We were buying it and bringing it in and selling it. It was something that we had access to, and there was no one selling Acoma pottery [under the portal], no Acomas [were] coming out this far. So it added to the variety of things that were being sold and everybody really could sell anything they wanted and so it wasn't like it is today.

Though retailing was popular among the vendors, there began to be a movement toward restricting the practice as a way of controlling the quality of work sold under the portal. The program participants recognized that the Portal Program promised to support Native American artists using traditional production techniques and chose to steer the program in this direction. In 1982 the vendors voted to require resellers to obtain affidavits from the artists they bought pieces from that stated the artist's "name, address, tribal affiliation, census number, origin and quality of materials" in addition to a guarantee that the artist had personally handcrafted the items sold (Glenn Paquin to Jill Cooper, July 23, 1982, Portal Log).

In spite of these efforts, some vendors were becoming increasingly concerned about the quality of the goods being sold under the portal and informed the museum administration that the sale of inferior items by retailers was threatening the livelihoods of legitimate craftspeople (Phillips 1998). In 1987 David Phillips, acting director of the Palace, and the concerned vendors began to work together to effect changes in the program rules that would strengthen the program's support of Indian artists and craftspeople selling their work through the program. Working through the museum administration, Phillips and the vendors modified the rules to limit items sold by vendors to those made by themselves or members of their households and to require that the pieces sold be Indian handmade.[11] Though generally accepted by the vendors, a few program participants who had been particularly successful as retailers resisted the rule change. The most prominent of these was a Diné (Navajo) vendor named Francis Begay who refused to abide by the new rule and eventually brought a second lawsuit against the program.

The turmoil that the rule change caused gave Paul Livingston, now attorney at law, the opportunity he had been looking for to resume his challenge to the Portal Program (see Evans-Pritchard 1990:91). Livingston began to work with Francis Begay and her non-Indian husband, Russell Steinman, to oppose the new program rules. By all accounts, Begay had maintained a lucrative business under the portal reselling jewelry she had acquired from a number of sources, often at prices below those that other vendors could offer. Because she bought pieces at wholesale prices (which are generally no more than half of retail prices) instead of investing her own time in the manufacture of pieces, she could sell greater quantities of jewelry at a lower profit margin. Vendors who sold only pieces from their own households simply could not produce enough work to make a living selling at the lower prices set by Begay. When the rule revisions were made, Begay continued to conduct her business just as she had before, ignoring the new restrictions. After some minor disputes over Begay's jewelry, events came to a head at the end of June 1987. The committee found that among her jewelry were earrings that were not appropriately trademarked. David Phillips requested that she remove the pieces from her cloth. At the urging of her husband, Begay refused.

David Phillips, former acting director, Palace
They wanted a fight. And essentially what happened was I did my best to avoid it, but they finally got me in a position where I could

either enforce the rules established by the museum or I could walk in my office and tear them up, because I wasn't willing to take a stand.

Phillips composed a suspension order for Begay and asked her to leave the portal. She refused, and the police were summoned. When she refused the police order to vacate the portal, she was arrested.[12]

The next month Livingston filed suit on Begay's behalf against the museum, the Board of Regents, David Phillips, and each member of the Portal committee, charging that she was being denied the opportunity to pursue her livelihood. The case finally went to trial in July 1990. In August the judge dropped most of the counts of the lawsuit, and a few days later the jury found in favor of the defendants on all of the remaining charges. Begay, who had continued to sell under the portal during the lawsuit, resigned from the program after its conclusion and later moved away from Santa Fe.

This second round of legal challenges helped to further solidify the legitimacy of the program and ensured its survival. In finding for the program, the jury in *Begay v. Museum of New Mexico* affirmed the steps the vendors and the museum had taken to develop the program. It firmly established the program as a market for Native American artists to sell their own work directly to the tourist public and ended the use of the portal as a secondary retail outlet. By upholding the standards that the program participants had set for craftsmanship, the successful conclusion to the suit also set the stage for the vendors and the museum to develop additional standards for materials and techniques that would allow the program to be a haven for artists and craftspeople who handcraft their work and a place that valued the use of traditional methods, such as outside-fired pottery, that otherwise would be difficult to justify economically.[13]

While the museum had certainly accepted the Native American market before the 1970s, the legal challenges posed by the Livingston and Begay lawsuits forced it to accept responsibility for the program in a way it never had before.

David Phillips, former acting director, Palace
I think up to that point [when the program was legally challenged]
the museum had never really committed to the program in the
sense of putting its resources behind the program. It depended
very heavily on the volunteer committee to keep things going
out there, and it didn't realize, I think, just how important that
program was to the museum as well as to the vendors. It essentially is the most popular exhibit the museum has.... And it
has been very important in helping support Native American
arts and crafts. What's happened since then, I think, is that the
museum has finally put resources towards that program the
way it has to its other programs. And perhaps what it took was
this lawsuit in order to drive home to the museum it was not a
problem that would go away.

For the people who were involved in the lawsuits, Native and
non-Native alike, the experience was traumatic.

David Phillips, former acting director, Palace
While I was the acting director sometimes on a daily basis I
would have to be dealing with those three individuals [Livingston,
Begay, and Steinman], trying to make peace, trying to dodge their
little legal traps, and then after I was no longer director I still had
the threat of a lawsuit hanging over my head. I'd never been sued
before. It was a pretty scary experience.

Dorothy Chavez, Santo Domingo
Oh, that was something scary. It was something that I thought
I would never have to go through. It was a big mess, and what
we went through was something I'll never forget. You know for
me as an Indian I thought I would never end up going to court
and to me that was something big, something scary. And a big
experience I would say. I would have never seen a courtroom if
I hadn't been in that lawsuit. But it also worked out for the program too. Because of that lawsuit I think we have achieved a lot.
I would say we got something good out of the lawsuit.

One of the good things that came out of the lawsuits was that vendors from all of the cultural groups represented under the portal had to work together to support the program. This resulted in greater understanding, respect, and friendship among many of the vendors and reinforced vendors' commitment to the program.

Lori Hesuse, Diné (Navajo)

That's when I first came into the program. [The Livingston lawsuit] was going on and we all ended up going to Denver to the Tenth Circuit Court, so all of us were up there and we went in one of the Santo Domingo schoolbuses. (Laughter) It was very uncomfortable, we tried to get a shuttle bus but we were too late, we didn't get together in time. It was a very interesting trip. And nobody knew Denver, I was the only one; I had lived there in my earlier years, so I'm the only one that knew where the motels were so I had to guide the bus driver to go to an area where we could sleep.... That was really interesting, we had a real interesting trip. We ate a lot. (Laughter) ... It took us about ten hours in the bus, I mean it seemed like it was all day long. But, no, it was really something, because that was the first time I ever ate pueblo bread with salt. You know, everybody had fresh bread, they had their own little lunches, and I had always eaten pueblo bread with stew and all that, but they were passing it around they had a little salt shaker, so they told me, "Try it," and I did and it was good. // It was neat. We were just there, but we had a good time. Just the trip and all that. That's when I got to know some of the ladies, and Tony Tortalita and his wife, Dorothy, and just a few others. It was really nice, we had a good time.

The Portal vendors made great contributions in terms of time, energy, and money in combating the legal challenges to the program. Those who were involved recognize the importance of that period in the development of the program.

Lori Hesuse, Diné (Navajo)

We had to raise a lot of money. It's the vendors that raised it for our attorney. In fact I think that each one of us, at one time, had to give

a hundred and twenty-five each, you know everybody. And then
not only that, but we donated jewelry, and you know where the
committee space is now, that's where the cloth was where all the
donated jewelry was and everything that was sold from that cloth
was put into the fund. And we always had an account at First
National Bank, and that's where all the money went. And Tony
Tortalita was always our banker. (Laughter) Our treasurer. And
it was really good because nobody said, "Well, I can't pay that."
Everybody just offered it, you know, "This is how much I'm
going to give." And they would bring jewelry that they made
just specifically for that reason. So we didn't have any problems.
I think, I can't remember, I think we had to raise about $11,000,
and we did it without any problem, because everybody was
together. And you know I always tell the Navajos, you know
when they're really bad-mouthing sometimes some of the Pueblos,
I tell them, "You don't realize that that's who won this place back
for us. You need to appreciate..." That's why I was telling you,
you need to give a little bit of the history, this is what I'm talking
about when I asked you that, it's because it was these little women,
these little Pueblo women, are the only ones that were there, and
like you say, a handful of Navajos. They're the ones that put their
time, their money, their jewelry, and the younger generation needs
to realize that that's who fought for this place, so that we can be
there, so that we can have livelihoods and be able to support ourselves and our children and our grandchildren. And they need to
appreciate each other for what happened.

Glenn Paquin, a second-generation vendor whose children are also
vendors and whose grandchildren have participated in the program's
children's shows, felt a commitment to the program because of the
earlier efforts of his parents in the lawsuits.

Glenn Paquin, Laguna and Zuni
My mother and [some other vendors] were the ones that were
primarily involved in fund-raising and getting lawyers and all that,
so they basically saved it for us. And so I felt some obligation at

that point, because I felt it was a good program and they had been in it, and that it should be developed more fully once we were assured that we could sell, [that] it would be primarily for the Indian people.

Today some of the elders who were involved in the lawsuits and in formalizing the program no longer come regularly to sell under the portal. They continue their commitment to the program by encouraging younger vendors, visiting the portal, and coming to the annual meetings to lend their support.

To ensure that participants are actually making the work they sell under the portal, starting in 1991 new vendors have been required to demonstrate their arts for committee members or museum staff. Done informally at first, by 1993 the committee and the museum administration began a drive to have all vendors redemonstrate their work. Largely to assist in the monumental undertaking, the museum hired a part-time employee to serve as program coordinator. Though the museum administration had recognized for many years the need for staff support for the program (*Journal North*, July 4, 1987), this was the first time the museum had supported a salaried staff member whose main responsibility was the Portal Program. An office was established for the program in the Palace complex, and the Portal began to have an active presence within the museum as well as outside. The addition of an office inside the museum was practical but also symbolically important. During the first few years after the establishment of the office, vendors often commented on how far the program had come, saying things like "Look, now we even have an *office*."

With the help of the first Portal coordinator, Sarah Laughlin, the 1994–95 program committee undertook redemonstrations and recertification for all program participants. Jurors attended more than seven hundred demonstrations, almost all held at the homes or workshops of the individual vendors. Attending demonstrations required the committee and staff to travel all over New Mexico, frequently driving three to four hours each way to observe demonstrations in outlying communities and on the Navajo reservation.

Marvin Slim, Diné (Navajo)
When I was on committee, that's when we first started doing the demonstrations, there was like seven hundred people, wasn't there?
{SL: 720.}
Yeah, it was a lot of people.
{KH: What was it like that year, you know, with all the demos?}
Time-consuming. Yeah, I wouldn't do it [again], you know. (Laughs)
{SL: That year, that was unbelievable.}
Yeah, going to all those different places and it was a lot of time spent out on the road watching demonstrations, and you learn a lot, like how to do the sandpaintings, and how they did the pottery and jewelry and cutting turquoise slabs and stuff. You get people saying, "Oh, don't copy me," you know, discouraging you. (Laughs) I don't do that kind of stuff. That's about it, though.

There was some resistance to the redemonstrations, especially among artists and villages concerned about divulging particular production techniques, but the demonstration drive was ultimately completed. At Santo Domingo Pueblo, where knowledge of the details regarding the manufacture of turquoise and shell heishi jewelry is closely guarded, vendors conceded to the demonstrations when it was agreed by the committee that they would be observed by committee members from Santo Domingo.

The purpose of the demonstrations was not to establish subjective aesthetic valuations of participants' work but to show that they possessed the knowledge necessary to produce the pieces they sold under the portal. This is also the reason demonstrations were held at vendors' workshops: seeing where artists worked allowed the committee members to confirm that participants had the equipment necessary to produce their pieces. At one new-vendor demonstration I attended as second observer, I was asked by the primary observer to videotape the artists' work bench and tools for the benefit of other committee members who might wish to verify the demonstration. Demonstrations are not always successful. Occasionally program applicants do not demonstrate the ability to produce the art forms they intend to sell. In such cases the applicants are encouraged to continue to work with the materials and to demonstrate again when they have mastered the technique. Demonstrations are one of the only tools the committee possesses to ensure that vendors and their families make all of the pieces they sell under the portal. On a day-to-day basis, the program relies on participants' honesty in the representation of the pieces they sell, and problems are rare.

On successfully demonstrating their knowledge, vendors were issued new program identification cards. They were also given copies of the program's rules and regulations. It has been suggested that program participants demonstrate their work every few years (Slim 1998), but the time commitment required of the program committee for such an effort has prohibited such action. Considerable time is already spent by the committee each year observing demonstrations of new vendors and for added crafts of current vendors.

Budgets for all Museum of New Mexico programs are limited, and during the second half of the 1990s the committee put their energies into various fund-raising campaigns to support operations for the program and to provide funding for advertisements in the Eight Northern Pueblos' visitors' guides and elsewhere. A successful fry-bread stand at Indian Market one year, frito pie sales, beverage sales, and appeals to area businesses have allowed for some discretionary spending. In 1997 the committee raised more than $4,000, which was used to pay for a full-page advertisement in the Eight Northern Pueblos 1999 *Visitors Guide.* Fund-raising by the program committee and other participants in addition to funding from the Museum of New Mexico Foundation allowed the program to produce a new informational brochure in 1997, the first in a number of years and a much more significant product than ever before. At the insistence of the vendors, the brochure text included a summary of the history of the program, information about the different classes of objects sold, and advice for visitors to the portal.

As the program continues to grow, it also continues to become more structured. The rules developed during the 1980s set the stage for the Portal to become a program that could maintain its integrity in the face of a growing number of participants, but no set of rules is ever complete.

Glenn Paquin, Laguna and Zuni

You can develop things up to maybe 95 percent of your goal. You can reach 95 percent. It's the last 5 percent that is the most difficult and you may never get there, and that's what happened to us. We had developed, I think it was fifty-eight rules when I left. We had developed a number of rules and it covered just about everything. And after that I felt we had established just about everything that needed to be established, that anything that went on from now on was just fine tuning an engine, just really to keep it running smooth with the rules that we had.

The program rules have grown out of practices that had become customary over the decades. For example, every morning before 8:00 vendors come to the portal and place markers (such as blankets, cloths, and knee pads) outside of the spaces they would like to occupy for the day. Markers are not put on the spaces until the duty officer determines whether a drawing for spaces is necessary. Though not added to the program rules until 1997, this practice was used for a number of years to keep spaces from being claimed until the committee member in charge for the day said they could be taken, thus helping to minimize disputes.

Even today much of the smooth daily operation of the program relies on participants' following practices that are not explicitly laid out in the rules. An important example occurs during the drawing for spaces. After the committee members have counted the number of participants present and collected a corresponding number of chips to be drawn, a noncommittee vendor is asked to verify the number of chips and to put the chips in the bag from which they are drawn. This practice is not specified in the rules but serves as a check on the committee to help ensure accuracy and honesty in the draw. On one occasion the duty officer asked me if I would verify the chips but was immediately corrected by other committee members before I could decline the responsibility.

FIGURE 5: *Early morning under the portal, 1997.*
Photo by the author.

Rule changes generally come from two sources. The first is when new materials or techniques are introduced by participant artists. Starting in about 1996, a number of jewelers began to use gold and gold fill in their work. After consultation with those participants and other metalworkers in the program, the museum administration and committee proposed a rule regulating the marking of gold materials. The body of vendors voted in favor of the rule change at the 1997 annual meeting, and on approval by the MNMBOR the rule was adopted. Not all newly introduced materials or techniques are accepted by the program membership. As noted above, program rules allow only outside-fired pottery to be sold under the portal. At the 1994 annual meeting a representative from Jemez Pueblo made a presentation in favor of allowing kiln-fired pottery. The program's potters were invited to a later meeting to discuss the issue. At that meeting in May 1994, the majority of potters in attendance rejected the proposal. As a compromise, the museum administration offered the acceptance of kiln-fired pottery if it was labeled as kiln-fired. At the 1995 annual meeting the body of vendors voted against the compromise and the rule prohibiting kiln-firing remained unchanged (1998 Annual Meeting minutes, Portal Log).

Rules are also codified when customary practices of the program come into question. When the program was first established under the aegis of the museum in the 1970s and 1980s, rules were regularly added to address issues of procedure and protocol. In recent years, these additions to the rules have been minor. However, almost every year issues arise that are resolved through codification of practice into rules. When such situations occur, the committee, the vendors, and the museum work together to reach a satisfactory resolution. For example, in 1998 two additions were made to the existing rules regarding the distribution of spaces. The first came about in response to vendors trading the spaces they had been assigned with other vendors. A number of participants were bothered by the switching, and so the rule regarding the assignment of spaces was amended to prohibit space trading.[14] The other addition addressed the sharing of spaces. Sixty of the portal's seventy spaces may be shared. On some occasions vendors with little stock allowed others sharing their space to use more than half the space to display their pieces. This too caused frustration among some of the vendors, and the participants voted to add a provision to the rules requiring that spaces be shared equally (1998 Annual Meeting minutes, Portal Log).

The program rules provide a flexible framework for the maintenance of the Portal as a community. The continuing development of the program rules is a reflection of community building.

David Phillips, former acting director, Palace

Well, you have to understand that it's always the case that rules arise in response to a situation. People very rarely go about making rules except when there's a perceived need. And as long as no one actually tried to sit down and sell at the portal except Native Americans, there was no need to establish the legal precedent that you could have an all–Native American exhibit devoted to Native American jewelry. And then, until people started essentially worrying about the quality of what was being sold out there, then there was no reason to have those rules. So as long as the program exists there will always be further changes to the rules simply because someone will try something that no one ever imagined up to that point, and if it's something that's a threat to the program it'll have to be found out.

The Portal Program today is many things to many people. I now turn to some of the things that the Portal Program is at the beginning of the twenty-first century: a workplace, a community, a museum program, and a place where art happens.

FOUR

The Portal as Workplace

*I think you just simply cannot ignore the
importance of the program to the people who
make a livelihood from it.*

—David Phillips,
Former Acting Director, Palace

Though Native American people have been integrated into Euro-
American economic systems for centuries and many have been
engaged in wage labor and other employment outside of their home
communities, especially during the last century, studies of Native
American people in the workplace are fairly limited in scope. Considerable attention has been paid to the historical integration of
Native peoples into the dominant Euro-American society and economy by way of labor, particularly in the Pacific Northwest region of
the United States, in western Canada, and in Alaska (Barsh 1996;
Boxberger 1988; Burrows 1986; Wenzel 1983; Wyatt 1987). For the
American Southwest, Kurt Peters (1994, 1995) has described the
relationships between laborers from Laguna Pueblo, New Mexico,
and the Atchison, Topeka, and Santa Fe Railroad and the creation
of "colonies" of Laguna Pueblo along the rail line between Laguna
and Richmond, California, the line's terminus. Among the significant findings of these historical studies is that Indian people have

long been active in the workplaces of the dominant society and that they have often had a voice in dictating the terms of their employment. The employment of Laguna railroad workers, for example, grew from an 1880 agreement between the pueblo and the Atlantic and Pacific Railroad that was demanded by the Laguna people before they would allow the railroad right-of-way across Pueblo lands (Peters 1995:34–35). In southeastern Alaska at the end of the nineteenth century, Indian people refused to allow Anglo-owned salmon canneries to introduce Chinese laborers who would compete with them for jobs (Wyatt 1987:44).

Less research has been undertaken on more contemporary Indian experiences in the workplace. A few recent studies have been published by scholars in fields such as business administration (Gordon 1996), human resource development (Kawulich 1998), and organizational behavior and development (Keil 1997). These studies have sought to identify the motivations of Native Americans in the workplace and to chronicle their experiences. While valuable, they are limited by project size, by simplistic concepts of indigenous cultures, and by limited attention to the workplaces themselves. Most studies of Native Americans in the workplace have looked at their employment by non-Indians. Studies of Native people working in Indian-controlled workplaces are virtually nonexistent.

The Portal is, at its most basic level, an Indian-run workplace. To be sure, the Museum of New Mexico plays a role in managing the program. As is evident from the historical development of the Portal, however, the museum's role is negotiated with the vendors. The museum administration and the Board of Regents have final say in the program, but actions that affect the Portal (such as rule changes) are never taken without close consultation with the program committee and the vendors as a group.

The Portal is also different from other workplaces because each vendor is an independent businessperson. The program rules determine the basic structure of the marketplace, including how sales spaces are distributed and when the business day begins. The rules also regulate what materials can be used and what sorts of objects can be sold. Some vendors have argued that some of the program rules, such as limits on time allowed away from the portal during the day, restrict their independence, but the rules that structure the program provide for considerable freedom for participants nonetheless. Each vendor sets the prices for the pieces he or she sells, limited only by what the market will bear.[1] Vendors decide how often they will seek sales space under the portal. They purchase or collect the materials used by themselves and their households in the production of the pieces they sell; they maintain their own production sites away from the portal; and they decide how many or how few pieces they will produce. The most significant controls of vendors' business decisions come from the need for participants to support themselves and their families.

Making a Living Under the Portal

The economic importance of the Portal cannot be overestimated. As many as half of the more than nine hundred registered program participants regularly sell at the Portal or produce work that members of their household sell at the Portal. Of these, many make their entire household incomes from the sale of their art. Approximately 5 percent of the residents of Jemez Pueblo are registered as vendors in the program. At Santo Domingo, about 10 percent of the population participates in the Portal Program. Taking into consideration underage children and other household members, and other family members outside of participants' households who benefit from income derived from Portal sales, almost everyone in these villages is affected economically by the program either directly or through the sharing of resources in related households.[2]

Smaller numbers of vendors come from each of the other Pueblo villages in New Mexico,[3] with nearly thirty each from Santa Clara and Cochiti and nearly twenty each from San Felipe and Laguna. Though to a lesser degree than at Jemez and Santo Domingo, the economic impact of the Portal Program is significant at these villages too.

More than two hundred fifty Diné (Navajo) artists participate in the program. Many of them live away from reservation lands, but the economic impact of Portal sales on their immediate families and in terms of financial support to other family members is great. Some vendors describe the Portal as a piggybank or a pot of gold: it provides much-needed money for people from communities with some of the lowest per capita incomes in the United States.

Vendors are well aware of the economic motives that drive participation in the Portal Program.

Glenn Paquin, Laguna and Zuni

The one thing that drives them, is money. (Laughs) I don't care, you can come up with all kinds of freebies and benefits, but it all boils down to one thing: money. If they're not making money they're not going to come here.

When disputes arise, vendors remind each other of the economic needs that the Portal meets. After each interested party has had the opportunity to state an opinion, often one or more of the program participants will take a conciliatory stance in an effort to mend the social fabric. Frequently these mediators will refer to the economic purpose of the Portal. In a 1987 hearing on program rule changes, one of the vendors said, "I think we shouldn't be fighting, and we should get along as Indians. After all, we're just here for one purpose—to make a living for ourselves" (quoted in Evans-Pritchard 1990:110). This sentiment is reiterated at annual meetings, in program committee meetings, and under the portal. As noted in chapter 3, the program committee always considers the economic impact on a family when recommending the suspension of a vendor for rule violations.

A number of vendors have left other jobs because of the greater economic opportunities available through selling at the Portal.

Glenn Paquin, Laguna and Zuni

I wasn't very happy with the salaries [of various directorships I held], because my dad and my brothers were making more money than I was. (Laughs) ... So my dad said, "Why don't you go back to doing the things that we taught you?" So I came up here in November of 1979 with my mother and started out. [I was] very apprehensive about what to do, how to sell, and so it took me a little while. The first year we made, I don't know, maybe a few thousand dollars. But it was a good learning experience.

Sarah Martinez* tells how she quit a government job to become a full-time Portal artist, both because of the financial benefits and because of the freedom self-employment allowed her.

Sarah Martinez, Santo Domingo*

I went and I worked for the state for about five years, and then I was pregnant with my son, and that's when the new rule came in that you had to all be from the same household [to sell on one cloth]. So then I went on maternity leave, and I didn't want to go back to work. I wanted to stay home and take care of him, because I couldn't face the thought of sending him off to a baby-sitter. You know, you just hear [about] so many things going on. So a month before I was going to go back to work I said to myself, "I'm going to do some beadwork, and I'm going to start working on it every time that I can, and then before I go back to work I'm going to go selling." So I did, I went and I worked and I came selling, and I freaked out. In one weekend I made what I made at the state in one month! (Laughs) So I said, "Nope, this is it. This is what I'm going to do from now on and I can stay home and take care of my son." And I always say that he's my little blessing in disguise because with the jewelry work, with me being self-employed, I've gained a lot. If I was still working at the state I'd probably still be in ... you know!
   {SL: You got it!}
   I wouldn't have the things that I have today.

Scholars have noted the importance to Native American people, especially women, of being able to stay home with their children (Kawulich 1998:132, 202; Parezo 1983:146). While the desire to stay home with children is certainly not limited to Native American women (indeed, it is probably so culturally *nonspecific*, in the United States at least, that the argument that such a desire is culturally determined is invalid), participating in the Portal Program allows parents to spend more time working at home than is possible in most other formal employment.

Although the Portal is a flexible workplace, some vendors have encountered child care difficulties. Because of concerns about dangerous automobile traffic, program rules prohibit parents from keeping their children under the portal while they are selling. In summer 1999 there was a dispute within the program because some single parents brought their children to the portal in the mornings. The draw for spaces is held at 8:00 A.M., and the vendors' day care services would not accept the children before that hour. To get a sales space, the parents had to attend the draw and were thus caught in a bind. A suggestion was made that the museum or the program consider developing a child care program for the children of vendors and museum personnel, but this has not come to fruition. The proposition reflects the changing experiences of Native American parents: in the past many working parents could rely on nearby extended family to serve as child care providers. As Native Americans move away from their home communities, these family networks are stretched and such daily support can be unavailable.

Although child care is not solely a Native American concern, there are obligations related to participation in Native American communities that make it difficult to take employment in a typical workplace. Many of the program's participants are deeply traditional people with significant social and religious responsibilities in their home communities. Puebloan people, especially, have religious and social obligations that keep them away from the workplace for days at a time. In addition to the annual feast days (discussed below), members of the New Mexico pueblos frequently must stay home to participate in activities relating to the Catholic liturgical calendar and to indigenous ceremonial cycles. Preparation and participation in these periodic events frequently keeps vendors away from the Portal for days and even weeks at a time. During the most important events in each village, all village residents will be "home." When such activities are taking place at Santo Domingo or Jemez, it is readily apparent under the portal, where there are empty spaces, even during the middle of the summer tourist season.

Kawulich (1998:202) argues that employers should take into account Native Americans' need for flexible schedules, but few will or are able to do so. As a result, Native Americans living in urban settings have often had to settle for low-paying, irregular employment such as day labor, trading higher wages and job security for the freedom to return to their reservation homes to fulfill social and religious obligations (Mucha 1983:356). Since the Portal sets no limits on how often or how seldom a participant can attend, it provides vendors with the kind of flexibility in their employment that they require. As one participant explained to a newspaper reporter, "The Portal lets Indians be Indians" (Sarah Laughlin, pers. com. 1997).

It has been noted before (e.g., Parezo 1983:146–47) that one of the advantages for Native American artists of producing arts and crafts is that it allows them to stay within their home communities where they have the support of family and friends. Wage work often requires workers to move away from their homes in order to be nearer their place of employment. Participants in the Portal Program have greater freedom here, too. Because vendors are not required to commute to the workplace five or more days a week, it is easier for them to live in their home communities. Of course, success at the Portal demands fairly regular trips to Santa Fe, and so participants do not have the same freedom to stay at home as that enjoyed by artists producing piecework for wholesale or doing commission work. Some vendors do commute almost daily. However, participation in the program provides other benefits over wholesale production.

The most significant benefit of selling directly at the Portal is the price that artists can get for each piece. When asked about the differences between selling at the Portal and selling elsewhere, almost all participants interviewed commented that price was the major consideration. Typically, artists wholesaling to shops or to jobbers will receive no more than 50 percent of the retail price of each piece; and they frequently receive less. Even artists who are well known and who show at galleries receive only a portion of the retail price of each piece. Under the portal there are no middlemen, and vendors are able to charge retail prices for their pieces. The added expense of commuting, parking, and time spent selling under the portal is quickly balanced by the higher compensation received for each piece. In general, pricing under the portal is similar to that for equivalent work in the shops around the plaza. Visitors occasionally comment that they can get lower prices elsewhere, usually for pieces that are machine-made or of inferior materials (such as silver plate, reconstituted turquoise, or greenware pottery). Vendors generally respond by explaining the differences in production methods and materials and leave it to the visitors to decide what kind of work they want to buy. While there sometimes is friction between the Portal participants and non-Indian, city-permitted vendors who sell jewelry and other objects on the plaza across Palace Avenue, the desire for mutual success extends to other outlets for Indian art in Santa Fe.

Dorothy Chavez, Santo Domingo

The stores [don't really hurt our business] as long as the customers know when they come to the Portal here that this place has all the vendors who make all their own jewelry. If they know that, then they shop out here, but if they don't, then they go other places. But it's also nice if they go to the store and buy [pieces] from them that are made by some of the Indians. If the stores are honest about what they're selling, then that's okay.

In addition, the Portal allows Native American artists to maintain their personal and artistic integrity in a way that wholesaling from shop to shop does not.

Mary Eustace, Zuni and Cochiti

I think it's a privilege to sell here.... It's better than being degraded when you wholesale, go from shop to shop. And the majority of the time the buyers say no to you, or if you ask a certain price, they tell you, "No, we can get that from somebody else for three bucks." That's degrading, that's bad. Oh, I feel sorry for all the other Indian people that are out there doing that, having to be rejected on a continuous basis, because they're subjected to these owners that have the money.

Even more important, selling under the portal gives artists the opportunity to meet the consumers of their work. While visitors are drawn to the Portal by the opportunity to meet Native American artists, this interaction is no less important for the artists themselves.

Jennifer Juan, Diné (Navajo)

It's nice to be presented in a gallery, but being able to get the full satisfaction out of being connected to another person with your jewelry is very rewarding, especially if you've really worked hard on it.... I think a lot of people, the tourist people that don't understand, they're not aware of how much time is involved, and the money, and the materials. If you're committed to it, then you can work long hours and then that all comes to being able to meet somebody that appreciates it and that gives you your full price for it. That's very rewarding when you think of everything else that was involved in it. And there's quite a few people that come to the Portal that are like that, that appreciate the work of the different media that people work in on the Portal.

Many vendors take very seriously the opportunity to share their art that interaction with tourists gives them.

Mary Eustace, Zuni and Cochiti

It's an honor being on the portal and telling people who we are when we're out there. When I'm standing there I tell them we're under this program, through the Palace of the Governors. We're regulated, to legitimize who we are as authentic; we have our trademarks. This is us, you get to meet the real person.... So it's nice, it's the overall aspect of the thing, of being and seeing how tourists see us. And yeah, I give them a lot of information when I'm out there. // So when they ask us about pieces, and if you really did sit there and you really stamped out a certain piece and this is the kiva steps, this is the sun, the Zuni sun face and the Zuni sun face is for this reason, you talk about the Kachinas and ... the Zuni sun masks [and] all this, [and] they really appreciate it. It's really nice that you, yourself, as a person out there selling, that you're giving knowledge, you're feeding other people. Wisdom, stuff that they take back. Who knows, they might need it.

Not Just Another Job

For many workers, in particular those in nonprofessional and wage-labor positions, jobs frequently change and play only a limited role in their self-identities. In his research with Ecuadorian plantation laborers, Steve Striffler (1999) found that workers did not identify themselves as plantation workers but rather saw the work as something they would have to do until they could raise enough capital to do other work. In her work with Navajo sandpainters on and around the reservation in the late 1970s, Nancy Parezo (1983; pers. com. 1997) found that many painters saw the production of commercial sandpaintings as just another source of income: when other wage-labor opportunities arose, painters would take those jobs and return to sandpainting when necessary. Edwin L. Wade (1976:97–98) recognized similar attitudes among southwestern Native American arts and crafts producers during the 1950s; commercial craft production was seen as just another way to bring income into the household. It seems that most of these Native American art producers have not thought of themselves as artists but rather as craftspeople. They did not produce pieces for their own aesthetic fulfillment (see Parezo 1983:151, table 6.1) but rather to meet an economic need.

Some Portal vendors have expressed similar attitudes toward the piecework and wholesaling that they and especially their parents have done in the past. And for some vendors, the Portal is not a final or lifelong career. But for most, even those who do not intend to continue selling at the Portal over the long term, being a Portal participant is much more than "just a job." The artists interviewed unanimously expressed the feeling that they are privileged to have the opportunity to take part in the Portal Program. To be sure, there is an economic motive driving the creation of art for sale under the portal, but it is accompanied by attitudes toward the work and aesthetic desires on the part of the producers that make production for the Portal *artistic* production.

In the broader Native American arts and crafts market, producers rarely interact with consumers. While there is a long history of small numbers of white patrons seeking to procure art directly from Native artists (see, e.g., Lee 1999) and a number of artists in each Pueblo village in the Southwest and in many other communities throughout Native America sell their work from their homes or shops, these sales make up only a small part of the market. Most of the sales, and most of the representations of producers as artists, are made by middlemen, most of whom are not Native American. In the typical process of bringing Native American arts and crafts into the market, producers are removed from the representation of their work as art.[4] A silversmith, for example, might produce two dozen bracelets (or rings, or earrings, or pendants). When the producer sells those pieces to a jobber, a shop, or a gallery, the transaction is couched almost entirely in economic terms. The wholesale buyer often determines price based in part on a subjective aesthetic valuation of the pieces, but ultimately the transaction is about price. Pieces are often wholesaled by lot, with little or no discussion of individual items.

When the pieces are offered for retail sale, however, the emphasis of the transaction shifts from price—which in the retail environment is more or less set—to the subjective value of each piece as an example of Native American art. Shop clerks will often provide biographical sketches of a piece's maker, attempt to place the piece within the history of Native American art, or otherwise heighten its value in the eyes of potential consumers. Though presented as an "artist," through this process the maker is relegated to the status of remote and anonymous producer, not a real person but a figure fitting into the category "Indian artist." The artist reaps none of the personal, intellectual rewards of being perceived directly by others as an artist.

At the Portal, Native American artists gain the intellectual benefits of being recognized as artists by the consumer public. There is a shift from producer of objects with solely economic value to artist creating objects with aesthetic (as well as economic) value. This shift has many implications for how program participants perceive their work as art and how they participate in and interpret their interaction with consumers. These issues are addressed more fully in chapter 7. What is important here is that because vendors are perceived by consumers (and by themselves) as artists, selling at the Portal is not just another job. Being a Portal participant gives the producers of Native American art the opportunity to see their work as art and to see themselves as artists. Consumers express their appreciation directly and often treat the artists with the deference afforded to other artists in Western society. This leads to a stronger personal association with the occupation of producing for and selling at the Portal market. Native Americans who produce piecework or otherwise wholesale their work do not enjoy the regular interaction with appreciative consumers that reinforces their status as artists. Such producers are more likely to see the production of Native American art as just another economic opportunity, interchangeable with truck driving, mine labor, or any of a number of other sources of income. Participation in the Portal marketplace affords Native American artists a greater measure of support for the development of their personal identities as artists.

This distinction has implications for program participants' sales practices. Many tourists who come to Santa Fe have visited other ethnic tourist marketplaces where indigenous people sell indigenous arts and crafts items in a public place that is a tourist destination (see, e.g., Steiner 1995; van den Berghe 1994). At many of these marketplaces, tourists assume that prices are negotiable. They see bargaining as part of the experience and the only way to ensure that they get a "good" price. While indigenous salespeople might oppose and even be offended by such expectations (see O'Rourke 1987 for strongly worded objections by indigenous vendors to tourists' demands for "second prices" in Papua New Guinea), their ability to resist tourists' affronts is often limited by the need to sell—at any price. If only one tour boat or bus comes to the marketplace each day, a sale at a low profit margin versus no sale can literally mean the difference between buying food and going hungry. These marketing situations reflect the significantly asymmetrical power relations that frequently exist between tourists and indigenous "hosts."

Furthermore, in most tourist indigenous art markets, vendors are retailers who purchase the artwork at wholesale rates from the original producers (Steiner 1994; see also Graburn 1976). Retailers are able to closely control profit margins. They know exactly how much they paid for each piece and how much each piece must be sold for. Moreover, the relationship that retailers have with the pieces they sell is strictly economic: they have no personal investment in the production of the artistic works.

The Portal is a different kind of marketplace. Because of the vast numbers of potential customers who visit the Portal each day, vendors are more empowered to stick to their asking price. Some have pictured the Portal vendors as a poor, disempowered minority group relegated to sitting on a sidewalk selling whatever they can, using the market as an example of the subjugation of indigenous peoples.[5] The Native American artists who make up the Portal Program, however, are very much in control of the marketplace interactions that occur there. Portal vendors do not have to accept the ridiculously low prices that are sometimes offered by customers because there are generally numerous opportunities for other sales during the day. And because they are the artist-producers of the pieces being sold, vendors have personal ties to their work and are sometimes offended by customers' attempts to bargain. The vast majority of Portal program participants feel that they offer fair prices for their work and that the expectation of bargaining by tourists only leads to the artificial inflation of prices. Vendors know the price at which they must sell each piece in order to recoup material and labor costs. With this in mind, they would have to give an initial asking price significantly above their actual selling price in order to provide customers with the appearance (and experience) of bargaining. This artificial price inflation, along with resellers' ability to provide lower prices on larger quantities while maintaining a reasonable profit margin, is common practice in many tourist marketplaces.[6] Vendors note that this practice seems fundamentally dishonest, and they prefer to offer fair but firm prices.

Nonetheless, some tour operators and tourist guides continue to tell visitors that they should not accept offered prices, and many tourists continue to expect bargaining. Portal vendors have developed a number of responses to deal with bargainers. Some use humor to gently instruct visitors.

James Faks, Blackfoot, Onondaga-Oneida, Maya, Apache
I will allow them to haggle on [my big items], and I kind of
make a game [out of it], because you want them to be relaxed.
They say, "So what do you want for this belt?" and I'll say "Three
hundred," and they'll ask me, "Well, can you do better?" and
I say, "Yeah, four hundred." That just kind of throws them off
and breaks the ice and then I let them see how good they are at
haggling, which is fun.

Other vendors simply refuse to acknowledge attempts at bargaining. I have heard one illustrative story from two very different
sources. While working as a Jeep tour guide in Tucson, I found that
many of my passengers were familiar with Santa Fe and had been to
the Portal. When I told one client that I worked with the Portal
Program, he described how he had gone there thinking that haggling
over prices was expected. When he asked a vendor the price of a barrette, she told him it was $12. He then asked the price for two, and
she said it was $12 for each. I had heard the same story earlier from
a program participant.

Mary Eustace, Zuni and Cochiti
One tourist asked this lady, "How much is that barrette?" The
lady goes, "Eight dollars." "Well, how much for two?" and the
vendor says, "Sixteen." (Laughter) Like that. "You don't give me
a discount?" "No."

The Portal visitor who told me his version of the story acknowledged
that he had gained a considerable education that day.

Not all vendors object to bargaining but rather are opposed to
the expectation by visitors that they will bargain. When developing
the text for the program's 1997 brochure, there was considerable
debate over what to say about pricing under the portal. Some vendors opposed any reference to bargaining; others wanted to continue
to have the freedom to adjust their prices (Sarah Laughlin, pers. com.
1997). The compromise text reads: "Some program participants
negotiate prices, many do not. Please remember that authentic

The Portal as Workplace

Native American arts and crafts are labor-intensive and that hand-crafted objects cost more than those that are machine-made."

Some vendors are willing to bargain with visitors, and all recognize the realities of the free market. When tourism dips during the winter, some vendors adjust their prices in response to the decreased demand.

Mary Eustace, Zuni and Cochiti

I was born to negotiate. I'm the type of person, if I go buy something...out there at a flea market or the arts and crafts store I try to get [a good price]. But you don't go too low, where you disrespect that piece, disrespect the person. I mean we all try [to] save a buck here and there. I don't mind [if] people do that with me. In fact, I do a winter price, just a set, flat, low price, because I believe the more you can move out at a good cost where it doesn't stiff you, that's good business rather than to price it high and sell one piece and take home the rest.

Because the Portal is such a good marketplace, vendors do not have to accept potential customers' offers. Also, because vendors are not usually struggling just to make ends meet, they can sometimes afford to show great generosity to visitors. Program participants are some of the most generous people I know and not uncommonly will share their art with visitors who could not otherwise afford it. Many vendors will sometimes give pieces or provide significant discounts to visitors who appreciate their work.

Glenn Paquin, Laguna and Zuni

A guy came up to me this morning and I asked a hundred and fifty for a bracelet.... He took out a hundred dollar bill and said, "I'll give you a hundred dollars," and I said "No." It's like he felt that he could buy me off, or that my work wasn't worth a hundred and fifty dollars, you know, and I'm not going to do that. I might do it if it was [someone who really appreciated the work]. And we do that—Opal and I do that during the year—we see somebody that comes by and they really like something but they can't afford it, and ... I'll just take it and I'll give it to them, and they say, "Really, are you sure?" and I say, "Yeah." Because it's my gift, it's my life. If I want to give something to somebody, that's my option. And it makes me feel good that I'm giving something to somebody that really appreciates it but couldn't afford it. But I give it to them, and so now [they] can enjoy it and [not] worry about the money, because I can go back and make another one.

The Portal is an ideal location for Native American artists to gain exposure for themselves and their work. Most participants make their living by selling smaller pieces to large numbers of casual consumers, but there is always the opportunity for the sale of larger pieces or large quantities of pieces to single customers. Some participants occasionally sell their pieces to serious collectors under the portal. James Faks (Blackfoot, Onondaga-Oneida, Maya, Apache), who also sells his silverwork in galleries in a number of states, sees the Portal as his own personal gallery:

The Portal for me is my gallery, this is where I come to show my art. I guess a lot of us think that way also. The Portal is the most unique place in the world to come and to find Native-made jewelries. I say "jewelries" because that's how my people say it, just put some humor [in it].

Others develop sales relationships with gallery and shop owners and buyers from all over the world by way of the Portal. These relationships sometimes require the production of significant numbers of pieces at one time, but the rewards of the increased exposure in addition to the economic gain of a big sale can be worth the effort.

Mary Eustace, Zuni and Cochiti

{SL: Do you sell anywhere other than the portal?}
    Well, I was running [my earrings] through J.C. Penney's and Foley's department stores, Nordstrom's, [and the] Smithsonian.
    {SL: What kind of volume do you have to do for that?}
    Their minimum's like a hundred. But I make it all. But the

thing with that is that where do I meet them? I meet them out
here. That's [also] why I like selling here because I look for the
bigger fish. (Laughs)

Other artists have made contacts under the portal that have led to
acting jobs and other creative work. The Santa Fe area has become
a popular place to film movies, and Native American actors are often
in demand.

Kenneth T. White II, Dineh (Navajo)

Everything that I've received through the Palace—you know what
it is? It's being at the right place at the right time and that's basically how it all started. [New Mexico is] a nonunion state, so a lot
of film industry comes to film here. There's a couple of western
towns built here so the local casting director here in town is always
looking for Native people, and she came by one day and was desperate for a Native to make a film and . . . she set up this audition
for me to go to. She described what I needed to do, and I said,
"All right." So she gave me three days in advance to meet this
director, and I didn't do anything. She would call me every
evening and she would say, "Kenneth, have you rehearsed that
little skit that I've given you?" And I said, "No.". . . So she said,
"You really have to be serious about this." I said, "You know what,
it'll just naturally happen when it's time to do it." She said, "Oh,
so you're that good?" I didn't know anything about this thing, I
was just being introduced to it. So I did, I went to the audition,
and the audition was to come with this fear, you open this door
and see this ghost or imagery and you come with this fear. That
is basically what it was, so naturally I was scared to meet this
producer, director, [these] businesspeople.

{SL: Fear was easy to do!}

Yeah, my heart was pumping, I was nervous, I was a wreck.
There were all these Native guys there, that had longer hair and
stronger features, and you know what, I was scared. So anyway, I did
it, I did the audition and the director just told me right then and
there, he said, "You know what, I'm just going to tell you straight

out that you got the part. There's all these other guys I haven't seen, I don't know who they are. That's okay, because you're perfect for it. And I'd rather have you do it than those guys." So I did, and that's how it all started. So from there on the Palace of the Governors has given me that, so I just want to give something back. I appreciate it.

Working at Home

The workday at the Portal is only part of a participant's job. Many hours are spent making the pieces that will be sold. In some households, the person who usually sells at the Portal makes only a small percentage of the pieces displayed and sold, while other family members stay home to produce the bulk of the work. Other vendors do all of their own work in the evenings and on days when they do not sell.

A few vendors maintain studio spaces or workshops away from their homes, but the vast majority do their production work in areas or workshops set up inside or adjacent to their residences. As noted earlier, the ability to work at home can have significant benefits for program participants. Being at home allows parents to spend more time with their children and also saves the expenses of paid child care. Because children are exposed to their parents' (and often grandparents' and aunts' and uncles') work as artists, they often begin to learn the various art forms from an early age.

There seems to have been a significant shift in production work by children over the last generation. Many vendors tell of having had to help support their families by assisting in the production of pieces for sale when they were children. Producing piecework for wholesale at low rates of return required that all members of the family contribute. When a parent or other supporting adult died or was otherwise unable to continue to work, children would often have to take on added responsibilities.

Marvin Slim, Diné (Navajo)
{KH: How did you learn silverwork?}
  All my family does jewelry. My uncles, my mother, my brothers, my sister. Everybody does jewelry in my family.

{KH: So did you start when you were very young doing [jewelry]?}

Yeah, with my mom. She used to do piecework, back in the seventies. Squash blossoms were very popular. Before the squash part is soldered onto the piece, everything has to be filed, so that's all we used to do is file the pieces, file everything down. [It was] kind of an assembly line, because there's four kids. And so one filed, the other one [would] texture it off, and my mom would solder it and throw it in acid. She used to work all night.

Dennis Ramone, Diné (Navajo)

[My relatives] forced me, they really forced me [to learn silversmithing]. I didn't like it in the first place. They forced me, and they spanked me, and they made me learn. That's the way I learned.

{SL: Are you glad they did, now?}

Yeah. I was glad they did it to me, now it's what I live on. I didn't have that much education myself. As far as I went [was] about seventh grade, and my grandpa passed away so they took me back to my hometown. They told me, "We need your help." The two of us we got raised from that family, two boys. The rest were nothing but girls. So that's how far I went.

Children would often help with the tasks that required the least amount of skill. Many silverworkers tell of spending time in front of the buffer polishing finished pieces, a task that no one enjoys. Children also helped in the marketing of pieces, at the portal and elsewhere.

Today vendors have different attitudes about children working. Higher family incomes allow parents to provide more alternatives for their children. Like their own parents, most vendors want their children to understand the art and encourage them to experiment with the different media. Children play a central role in southwestern Native American families and communities, and parents want their children to have every opportunity possible. Parents recognize that formal education is critically important, but they also recognize the value—economic but especially cultural—of Native American art.

Sarah Martinez,* Santo Domingo

I want them to go and get an education. First of all, I want them to excel in school. And then after that, I'm teaching them the jewelry, the art on the side, so that they can supplement their income.

Jennifer Juan, Diné (Navajo)

{KH: I was reading in the Indian Market magazine (Salodof 1998:71) about you wanting your kids to know about the stuff that you do. Do your kids, are they involved in making silver or weaving or anything like that?}

Yeah, I didn't really force them to learn anything, but I know they're very committed to presenting their culture. I'm very lucky, I think, because my kids are more interested in learning about the things that I do, rather than—they go to malls—but rather than just hanging out and driving around. That's where I'm very lucky and yes, my daughter, she's sixteen years old, she's learning how to weave. She has her own loom stands, and we did a rug weaving demo at the Wheelwright Museum, her and I. So, yeah, and now they're working on jewelry. . . . [S]he does her own stuff. She does some weird stuff, but she's expressing herself too. I think it's important, it's like a piece of the past that you have to pass on to your kids, otherwise it'll just die.

James Faks, Blackfoot, Onondaga-Oneida, Maya, Apache

{KH: Are your children interested in the arts?}

Yeah. My eight-year-old is going to be a killer painter if she decides to go into it. She's already putting out some pretty cool pastel stuff. But I think that comes from the connection of parent and child. There's a connection and they see that I like what I do, and they want to do that. And they're starting to see my art all over, and they like that too. I think they want to be a part of that.

{KH: So would you like to see them selling on the portal in twenty years or so?}

Yeah (laughs) if we don't have our own gallery by then. But yeah, I think I would like to see that. . . . I want my kids to be part of whatever they want to be. // I want them to know that this is still alive so they can choose, not really choose, but know that there's another way. I think they're catching on, they're some smart kids.

Some program participants feel that the production of Native American art can be too limiting.

Marvin Slim, Diné (Navajo)
{SL: I want to ask you about your kids, are you teaching your kids this?}

No. I want my kids to go to school. With me, I was brought up different, I didn't have a father.... [M]y mom was there, but she was always busy too.

{SL: She worked real hard.}

Yeah, she worked to put food on the table, so we were left alone most of the time, or back home on the reservation. With me, I lost my father when I was like what, two years old, probably. I would like my kids to have a totally different life.... They're pretty bright, you know, my son is in third grade, but he's at a fifth-grade level, so he's very bright, and so I want him to go to college or go to [the] air force, see the world first before he settles down.... So I want their lives to be totally different. Jewelry's nice to know, to learn, but I want them to do something else.

The Portal Program allows parents to actively encourage their children to experiment with art. Although children cannot become program participants until they reach the age of eighteen and demonstrate their art for the program committee, parents are allowed to sell their children's work on the family's cloth. Frequently, parents will sell their children's work so that the children can earn extra spending money or save for purchases or school expenses. Portal visitors enjoy the children's art as they try new forms and designs in a manner less constrained by convention than most adult work.

Robert Naranjo (Nambe and Santa Clara), is very proud of his son Makowa Ko's work. Makowa is living with his mother on the East Coast. So that his son can earn extra spending money, Robert sends him clay that he forms into pots and sends back. Robert finishes and fires the pieces and sells them for Makowa. During the year in which this was written, eight-year-old Makowa had bought himself stereo equipment, a computer, and a vacuum cleaner and was working toward the purchase of a sofa so that he could relax after a hard day's work.

The program also sponsors an annual children's show before Christmas. Dozens of children and grandchildren of vendors produce pieces for the exhibition, and the kids sell their own work. Parents appreciate how the event gives their children the opportunity to learn firsthand about the Native American arts and crafts market.

Sarah Martinez, * *Santo Domingo*
The annual children's show [is] a really good thing for the kids because it really builds up their self-esteem, and it makes them understand what their parents have to go through.

Household-based Production

Native American arts and crafts production, like that in many other small-scale societies, has generally been household based. The labor involved in collecting materials, producing pieces, and marketing the finished goods can best be accomplished by a group of people working together. Though in some cases gender roles have shifted or become less defined—for example, the proliferation of male potters in the Tewa pueblos is a fairly recent phenomenon (see also Mills 1995 for examples at Zuni)—the household continues to be an important production unit in the making of Native American arts.

Since the late 1980s the Portal Program has required that all items sold under the portal be made within the household of the vendor. The household production rule has certainly had its intended effect: the Portal provides a sales outlet for Native American artists where they do not have to compete with retailers who might undercut pricing in order to sell a higher volume of pieces. At the same time, by articulating a strict definition of household, the rule places limits on the socioeconomic behaviors of program participants.

Among many Native American families, individuals not actually living under the same roof cooperate closely in supporting their families economically. Parents, adult children, and grandchildren, siblings, aunts and uncles, and nieces and nephews all help each other in agricultural work, in providing child care and supporting other domestic needs, and in the production and marketing of arts and crafts. The Portal Program's household rule does not, by and large, recognize this cooperation.

Ultimately, however, this program rule, along with many others, is the best attempt to deal with a complex reality. The protection of artists is a high priority of the program. But to meet the needs of participants, the program has to remain flexible. To keep the program accessible to as many participants as possible, the museum provides exceptions to the household rule for ill and elderly vendors and others who need help from family members outside the household. This flexibility is what makes the Portal such a unique and successful workplace for Native American people.

The Portal as Community

Feast Days

Feast days are important religious and social events at each of the New Mexico pueblos. They are occasions for celebrating religious ceremonies such as dances for patron saints and for families and friends to come together. The women of each family prepare huge quantities of food—bread baked outside in adobe ovens, green and red chile stews, bone stew, enchiladas, beans, posole, sandwiches, salads, fruit, cakes, cookies, and pies—to be shared with family, friends, and other visitors to each home. Throughout the day of the feast, dining tables are laden with serving dishes as waves of guests help to celebrate the abundance of the feast.

August 4 is the date of Santo Domingo Pueblo's annual feast day. Nineteen ninety-eight was the first year that my wife, Nancy, was able to join me for that occasion. At the first home we visited, I entered first. I was greeted cordially: "Come in, sit down and rest, we're glad you're here." But when our hosts saw Nancy, the response was different: "NANCY!!!" was followed by big hugs and other celebrations of her attendance. When we visited the next family's home, the same events occurred, only this time after the initial greetings one of our friends rushed to the back of the house to get a heishi necklace that she had made for Nancy, having inquired of me earlier in the summer as to Nancy's favorite colors.

Later in the afternoon we rested under a ramada in front of the home of another Portal artist. The home is on the main plaza, so we had an unobstructed view of the hundreds of dancers of all ages, the women and girls wearing manta dresses and the men and boys wearing traditional embroidered kilts. Toward the east end of the plaza a ramada for Saint Dominic had been erected in front of one of Santo Domingo's two large kivas. Off in the distance on a rise at the edge of the village a carnival was set up: we could see the top of the "Zipper" ride rising beyond the kiva ladder.

The feast day is a time of celebration, when everyone is welcomed to come to the village to enjoy the day: in addition to friends and family members who come to enjoy the feast at peoples' homes, tourists come to watch the corn dances, and, in the case of Santo Domingo at least, a number of people from surrounding communities come mostly for the carnival. One year at a friend's family home I met a late-middle-aged Hispano couple from the village of Peña Blanca—just north of Santo Domingo—who told me that the feast and the attendant festivities had been a significant annual event for them for many years. After the conclusion of the dances, many of the children who have danced throughout the day rush home, eager to change clothes and head to the carnival.

Sitting at the edge of the plaza watching the events of the feast, from the dances to the carnival, I began to think about the day and about Nancy's and my experiences. While all family, friends, neighbors, and acquaintances are welcomed, Nancy was a special guest. Over the last few years everyone has gotten used to seeing me around, yet Nancy is able to visit with the people from the Portal just once or twice a year. But more important, Nancy's reception is a reflection of the importance of family: she is important to me as part of my family and so is important to the people from the Portal as part of an extended family. I am humbled by the caring and the generosity of the people I work with under the portal. We have been given gifts of care and friendship that we can never repay.

Defining Communities

The Portal Program is much more than just a market, a workplace, or a program. It is a realm of interaction with great social, cultural, and political significance for its participants. In talking about the program, participants refer to it as a big family,[1] or as a "second home." It is a social place more than just a geographic one, where friends get together, where long-term relationships are formed and maintained, where people meet life partners. The Portal is a place where rivals come together and learn to coexist. It is a place where people find and develop social networks and a place where those social networks can be used for cultural learning and to reinforce identity. It is a place where people take leadership positions and serve their fellow participants. In short, the Portal community is an important part of a great many lives.

"Community" is a concept, like "culture," that is much used both in quotidian speech and in academic writing but that is also generally poorly defined. This ambiguity is not always problematic, for it provides a label for social groupings that are in fact often difficult to define. The concept and experience of community can take many different forms, and most people experience different forms of community during their lives.

Scholars have emphasized communities as being made up by groups of people that are in some way socially threatened (Hazan 1990:6). Groups whose membership is based on race, ethnicity, or sexual orientation are often identified as communities. These groups come together to provide mutual support, to reinforce group identity, or in response to social stigmas placed on group members by others. Studies of urban Native American communities have reflected this tendency. In discussions of Native American and First Nations communities in urban centers such as San Francisco (Ablon 1964), Vancouver, British Columbia (Morinis 1982), Chicago (Mucha 1983), and Los Angeles (Weibel-Orlando 1991), the status of Native Americans as a subjugated ethnic minority has been identified as a central feature of community development.[2]

More recently, the concept of community has been viewed more broadly. Putting aside such cultural elite–created manifestations as workplace communities designed to promote production or corporate image (see Naylor, Willimon, and Österberg 1996) or the bastion of modern upper-middle-class suburbia, the "gated community," which despite being so named by human resources officers and real estate developers are not necessarily true communities, community is beginning to be seen as a kind of social grouping that is not limited to minority groups. "Community" has always had a positive connotation (see Williams 1983:76) and periodically has been characterized as a cultural ideal in opposition to alienated industrial society at least since Ferdinand Tönnies's (1988) conception of gemeinschaft and gesellschaft in the late nineteenth century. It has begun to be seen as something that is lost or missing in contemporary society (Oldenquist 1991:93), that must be replaced (Edell 1998), or that can be "virtual" (Wellman et al. 1996). In other words, communities are now seen as social organizations that all members of complex societies do or should participate in.

Communities are not necessarily mutually exclusive, and most people are members of several communities. Communities can develop around geographic settlement patterns, around involvement in schools or churches, through common association based on ethnicity, or, as at the Portal, through interaction in the workplace. Different individuals can be more or less involved in various communities, and each community can have different meanings for different participants. Communities may be ecologically or economically grounded; that is, they are made up of individuals who come together out of material necessity. Communities can be formed around shared beliefs, as is found among religious communities. These social groupings may also be communities of sentiment, with the community taking form around its members' common concern and care for the interpersonal relationships that make up the institution of community and for the institution itself. As is the case with the Portal, communities usually have both material and social components.

Unlike earlier anthropologists who have used the term to refer to a geographic setting, boundary, or grouping within which social interaction occurs (e.g., Murdock 1949; Turner 1974:201), more recent scholars have recognized that in complex society the notion of community is more difficult to grasp and indeed can become so complex as to be unmanageable (Hannerz 1980:172). As Joan Weibel-Orlando (1991:51) notes in her discussion of the Los Angeles, California, Native American community, such traditionally identified characteristics as "territorial boundedness; geopolitical definition; differences in core and peripheral population and service densities; early and sustained enculturation within a small, age-graded group of peers with whom the individual has continuous, face-to-face interaction; and a constellation of established social institutions and public events as foci of assemblage to which every community member hypothetically has equal rights of participation" are inadequate to define an indigenous community in an urban setting. Communities in contemporary complex society often have vague, if any, physical territoriality. Members of a community can live and work significant distances from other community members and in the case of cyber-communities may never interact physically (see Smith and Kollock 1999; Wellman et al. 1996).[3] Lifelong involvement, enculturation, and continuous (or even regular) face-to-face interaction are not necessary attributes of community in complex society. There must be some continuity among core membership for a community to remain intact, but membership may be much more fluid than posited by earlier theories.

Though contemporary communities in complex society may not exhibit all of the classically defined characteristics of community, they share a number of defining features, and I borrow from a long tradition of theoretical development in defining the Portal. The first and most important characteristic of community is that its members have a common purpose, interest, or identity (Edell 1998). Unlike other urban Native American communities (see Ablon 1964; Mucha 1983; Weibel-Orlando 1991), the Portal is not based strictly on ethnic identity, an issue that I discuss more fully below. Rather, the common purpose that brings the Portal community together as a community is the maintenance of the program and the economic opportunities that it provides.

Hazan (1990:4–10) identifies four further frames of reference for the recognition of community: boundaries, cultural idioms, functional structure, and temporal experience. Boundaries of community do not have to be territorial, and in complex society geography is often a less important determinant of community than such factors as common interest and social inclusion. Communities share cultural idioms, ranging from ethnic identity to traditional social and religious practices to shared behavioral expectations to mutual agreement concerning word meanings that are specific to the community group. Communities have functional structure: human behavior is patterned, and participants in a community behave in a manner that conforms with and re-creates the structure of the community. Communities may also be structured by formal rules that regulate behavior. Finally, a community must have a temporal dimension. As communities are made up of people interacting with each other, the actors, interactions, and makeup of community change over time. Communities both form and dissipate as they meet new needs or fail to serve their members. In the remainder of this chapter, I explore the ways in which the Portal is an urban Native American community exhibiting these four characteristics in particular ways and how it is different from other such communities.

The Portal Community

The Portal community is different from other urban Native American communities in a number of ways. First, for many participants the Portal is a secondary community. A majority of Portal vendors live in and are intimately involved in the social life of their home communities (this is true for a much greater percentage of Puebloan vendors than Navajo because Navajo reservation lands are farther from Santa Fe, and this is more common among older than younger vendors).[4] While members of urban Indian communities such as those studied by Ablon (1964), Hoikkala (1995), Mucha (1983), and Weibel-Orlando (1991; see also Weibel 1978) have been more or less isolated from the support networks available in their home reservation communities, a majority of Portal participants are as (or more) involved in their home social groups as they are in the Portal.

Closely related to the strength of connections to home communities for Portal participants is ethnic identity. Contemporary Native American people must identify themselves, and identify with others, on several levels, ranging from family and (for some) clan and moiety to village, tribe, or nation membership to association with other Indian people through pan-Indian identity. As Native people move away from their families and tribal groups, association with Indian people from other tribal groups can become more important. Weibel-Orlando (1991:61) notes that the underlying principle of social organization of the Los Angeles Indian community is supratribal Indian ethnic identity. Under the portal, pan-Indian ethnic identity is less important. The Portal Program exists legally because of the unique relationship of Indian people to the U.S. government. However, supratribal Indian identity is not what brings the Portal community together on the most basic level socially. Rather ethnic identity is used as a discursive tool to unify the program participants in times of stress on the program. In the day-to-day reality of the Portal community, pan-Indianism is less important than tribal identity and interpersonal relationships.

Official participation in the Portal Program requires a person to identify ethnically (and be legally recognized) as Indian, but participation in the Portal community is not limited in the same way. A small number of non-Indian people who are employed on or around the plaza are also actively involved in the community of the Portal. Though these members are marginal—they do not sell under the portal or take part in the drawing for spaces or other "business" of the program (except for the Portal coordinator and the Palace director who have administrative roles) and thus have a different place in the social makeup of the group—they are no less members of the Portal community. Thus ethnicity is an important but not a determinant feature of the social organization of the Portal community. Acceptance and involvement in the group transcends ethnicity in the Portal community.

A third important difference between the Portal community and other urban Indian communities is that participants in the Portal are not a marginalized underclass. As I argue throughout this book, the Native American people who participate in the Portal Program are fully in control of their destiny. Indian cultures, particularly those elements of Indian cultures that lead to the production of the kinds of Native American arts that are sold under the portal, are given special value in Santa Fe and in the Southwest generally. Furthermore, many elements of traditional life remain very strong in the Native American communities of New Mexico. This is another reason why supratribal Indian ethnicity is not the most basic organizing principle of the Portal. When Native people are secure in their identities, ethnicity is less of an issue.

While many workplaces might serve as communities, few are as socially complex as the Portal. Portal participants have many social connections, ranging from family ties to decades-old friendships (and rivalries) that have developed from years of working together under the portal. A majority of the Portal participants have kin who also participate in the program; many are second-generation vendors, and a few are third-generation. A great many participants have been coming regularly to the portal for more than ten or even twenty years, a few for even longer. The shared connections and social histories among vendors, both under and away from the portal, create deeper relationships than those that exist among people in most other workplaces.

Because of the great diversity among Portal participants, the program as a community has different meanings for different members. The Portal is a secondary community for many participants, but for others, especially those who reside away from their home communities, the Portal is the location of primary contact with other Native American people. For some, it provides the only opportunity to interact with other Native people. For these vendors, the program plays a very important role in the development and maintenance of identity as Native American people.

Yet other vendors do not participate regularly in the program. Some of these are elderly people who have health or mobility problems; others have family obligations that keep them at home. Though not usually physically present under the portal, many of these vendors continue to play an active role in the Portal community by maintaining an interest in daily events and interacting with active program participants back in their home communities.

Some participants come to the Portal occasionally and are not actively involved in the social relations that make the Portal a community. For these occasional vendors, most of whom have other jobs or responsibilities, the Portal serves mostly as a source of supplementary income or as an occasional venue to display their art. A few vendors come to the Portal regularly but are not actively involved with the community because they do not have family or friends there and do not interact extensively with other vendors.

The Portal is a workplace that encourages social interaction: vendors do not sit in isolated offices or cubicles or booths, nor do they direct their attention toward detailed tasks such as jewelry manufacture, which is prohibited in the sales spaces. The job of Portal vendors is to interact with others and to sell their work. First and foremost, they are salespeople: vendors have to be able to sell enough of their work to support themselves and their families. If the Portal did not provide the opportunity for Native American artists to make a living, none would come. Portal participants are acutely aware that communicating with visitors is an important part of what they do and that success under the portal is dependent on this communication.

Glenn Paquin, Laguna and Zuni

{SL: What do you think [tourists] are looking for?}

I think that they're trying to get a feel [for us]—you know, they can read about Indians in books and all that—but they want to get a feel for the humanity: "Who are these people?" And they want to talk to you, they want to get into your mind and see how they are different from us.

Most of the visitors who come to the Portal are at best transitory participants in the Portal community, briefly interacting with vendors, perhaps buying a piece of Native American art, then moving on. Some, though, get to know one or more of the vendors and become friends. Through this process, the Portal community spans the globe.

Dorothy Chavez, Santo Domingo

I've met, through the Portal Program, a lot of friends which are very dear to me now. . . . They write to me, they call me, even if they're not buying anything they want to know how I am, what I'm doing. . . . I even have a friend from Switzerland that writes to me often and tells me how she is, about her family. She sends me pictures of her children because I met her over here and she went to my home, she visited my home. She sang a song for one of my grandchildren; my first grandchild was a newborn then when she came to my home. That was something interesting because she sang her song in her own language. So things like that happen, like meeting a lot of people here which are very good friends now is something very great that I have experienced in the Portal Program.

While vendors and visitors sometimes develop personal connections, the community of the Portal is centered on the people who interact on an almost daily basis throughout the year: the vendors, some members of the museum staff, and a few others such as the newspaper vendors who spend significant periods of time around the portal. A photograph I took on the portal one morning illustrates the relationships between program participants and visitors and the role of each in the Portal community. In the photo, the edges of the vendors' cloths marked a crisp line down the middle of the portal. One vendor knelt behind his cloth and reached out to give a piece to a customer, who in turn reached across the line, marked by the edges of the cloths, separating the vendors from the visitors. On either side of the vendor who was reaching out to his customer, program participants sat or stood in their spaces, visiting with their neighbors and reading the morning newspaper. Outside the cloths, dozens of tourists made their way down the sidewalk, as they do every day. The community of the Portal, by and large, is made up of the people behind the cloths. Because of their transient nature visitors to the program only penetrate the surface of the community for a brief moment, symbolized by the customer reaching across the vendor's cloth during the market exchange. The social, educational,

FIGURE 6: *Vendors under the portal, ca. 1998. Photo by the author.*

and personal exchange that accompanies the trade of money for artis-tic product—that brief insight into the Portal community—is what makes the interaction particularly meaningful for the visitor.

I took the photograph after I had been involved with the Portal Program for several years. When I first came to the program, I had thought that I would study the interaction between tourists and Native American artists under the portal. The vendors steered me away from this idea and showed me that the program is about much more than the interactions between Native people and ethnic tourists. It is a place where Native American people work together to support themselves and their families. Through working together, they make a new kind of Native American community that further strengthens the participants, the program, and in turn the partici-pants' home communities.

Building a Community

The Portal's growth as a Native American community cannot be taken for granted. Though popular conceptions of Indian people suggest that all Native American cultures are fundamentally the same, this is far from true. Promoters of Santa Fe tourism celebrate the tricultural city and state, where Native American, Spanish, and Anglo worlds come together to create the ideal destination for the cultural tourist. The visitors' bureau's mantra of triculturalism is accurate only on the surface. To speak of a single Native American culture (or a single Hispanic or Anglo culture) is far too simplistic. Visitors to the Portal are sometimes surprised to learn that all of the program participants don't speak the same "Indian language" and are even more surprised to learn that Diné and Keresan, the two most commonly spoken languages under the portal, are as different from each other as each is from English. Not only are the languages different, but other cultural expectations and practices and a history of tension, cooperation, and accommodation between different Native American cultural groups make the Portal a truly multicultural Native American community.

Before the 1970s most of the vendors under the portal were from the Pueblo villages near Santa Fe. In terms of historical subsistence strategies, social and political structure, religious beliefs and practices, and experiences of interaction with and subjugation to non-Native invading cultures, the Pueblo villages of the northern Rio Grande drainage are very similar. In spite of these similarities, the various pueblos have always been autonomous and consider themselves distinctive. Relations between villages have varied from close cooperation to occasional open conflict. Identity is strongest at the village level, and historically there has been tension between vendors from different villages. This has been especially the case when new villages have begun to be represented under the portal; this was the case for Santo Domingo in the 1950s (see chap. 3).

If the cultures of the Pueblo villages are similar to each other, the culture of the Navajo (Diné) people is not like that of the Pueblos. Since their arrival in the American Southwest some seven hundred or more years ago, the Navajo and Pueblo people have had a complicated relationship. There is a long history of trade and cooperation, beginning with the sharing between the Pueblos and the Navajos of technological knowledge of agriculture and crafts such as weaving shortly after the ancestors of today's Navajo people arrived in the Southwest. During the Pueblo Revolt of 1680, Navajo people helped to drive the Spanish from New Mexico and sheltered Pueblo refugees from the Revolt and the subsequent Spanish reconquest. However, the Navajos' use of raiding as a subsistence strategy and the Pueblo villages' status as targets for that raiding fostered an antagonistic relationship between the groups that has been perpetuated through centuries of interaction. I think it is important not to overstate the conflict between Navajo and Pueblo people. There is significant cooperation between the groups and between individuals from each group and there are large numbers of very strong bicultural Navajo-Pueblo families. Yet a measure of tension does continue to exist between them.

When more Navajo people began to sell under the portal in the 1970s, tensions were great and tempers sometimes flared. The first Navajo vendors came to the portal in about 1970. During the first part of the decade, their numbers were few and they were not perceived as a threat by the longer-tenured Pueblo vendors (Hesuse 1997). By the mid-1970s there were about twenty Navajo families selling regularly under the portal (Grace Ann Herrera, pers. com. 1999). Some Pueblo vendors were alarmed by the growing numbers of Navajo vendors and felt that the Portal market should be limited to Pueblo Indians. They sought to discourage the newly arrived Navajo people from selling under the portal. Navajo vendors' cloths would sometimes be thrown into the street before they set up their pieces, a great deal of grumbling took place on both sides, and verbal confrontations were not uncommon. Informal leaders of the Navajo vendors, particularly Lucille Joe, would gather the Navajo vendors on the plaza in the mornings to give them pep talks, urging them to stand their ground (Grace Ann Herrera, pers. com. 1999).

The tension was broken in 1976 when Paul and Sara Livingston and other non-Indian vendors attempted to sell their work under the portal. Though some of the Pueblo vendors still did not want to accept Navajo people into the Portal Program, the governors and other leaders of the villages instructed the vendors to work with the Navajos so that they could save the Portal for all Indian people (Tony Tortalita, pers. com. 1999). Indian people have a remarkable capacity to put aside intertribal conflicts when they encounter a mutual threat from non-Natives.

Cheryl Arviso, Diné (Navajo)

A lot of times when you have groups of people, when there's a cause, we may not get along and there might be some tension, but when there's something more important than that the groups tend to pull together and stand as one, because there's something important that they're aiming for, they're trying to resolve. It's a goal that they have. And even now if you look really at the porch and the Portal, that still happens. When there's something really important, that's more important than the petty little problems that we deal with, they have a tendency of coming together and supporting each other and going that route, putting their problems aside and coming together as one.

Since uniting against the challenges to the program, the Navajo and Pueblo vendors have generally worked in close cooperation. Every year, Navajo vendors and vendors from various pueblos are elected to the program committee.[5] A number of Navajo vendors have served as program committee chairs, though this is one place differences between the cultural groups is notable: several Navajo women have served as committee chairs, including Lillian Garcia, who led the program through much of the *Begay v. Phillips* lawsuit, and Cheryl Arviso, who at twenty-six was the youngest vendor elected committee chair; Pueblo women have not accepted nominations to this highest post on the committee.[6] Though they have never served as committee chairs, every year a number of Pueblo women serve on the program committee, sometimes for several terms. Positions of official responsibility such as this are generally unavailable to women in the Pueblo governmental systems, but the women show their capacity for leadership through managing the

Portal Program. These long-serving committee members also serve an important role in maintaining organizational memory.

Though Navajo and Pueblo vendors generally put aside cultural frictions in the daily operation of the Portal Program, they are never far from the surface. Navajo and Pueblo people have differing, culturally influenced views about such important issues as personal freedom in artistic expression (see chap. 7) and in earning and spending money. In times of conflict on the Portal, allegations of misconduct or unfairness are often made across cultural lines. Committee members and museum staff have to tread carefully in such situations to avoid accusations of favoritism. Every committee member that I have had the pleasure of working with has taken great pains to not show preference to his or her own people at the expense of others; however, dealing with this criticism is an ongoing challenge.

In spite of the underlying caution that exists between vendors from different cultural groups, Portal participants have come together to form a strong Native American community. The Portal community is significant to vendors with greatly varying life experiences. I have described how some vendors' lives are deeply rooted in their home communities while others live largely away from their home villages or reservations. Though it is impossible to fully understand the meaning of the Portal community to all participants, the sentiments of vendors near each end of this one spectrum illustrate the Portal community's importance.

For many of the vendors in the Portal Program, "home" has a meaning beyond the immediate understanding of most non-Indian people. For these vendors, most of whom are from the Pueblo villages near Santa Fe (Santo Domingo is the quintessential example because of its conservatism and its social cohesion), "home" means not just family and friends but also inclusion in a group with strong social, religious, and ritual bonds. The individual recognition and the relationships and mutual cooperation that exist can be found only in small communities that rely on kinship and face-to-face relations. Being a member of a Pueblo community has a significance that cannot be overstated.

Juanita Atencio, Santo Domingo

I'm from Santo Domingo Pueblo, and I've lived there all my life. I was born there, I live there, and I want to be there. I don't intend to move anywhere else; maybe for a visit, if I do a show, maybe a couple of weeks would be the longest I'll be away from [Santo Domingo], but I've lived right there all my life.

Vendors who are so tightly bound to their home communities do not need to be involved in another Native American community. For them, identity as Native people and association with other Native people is never in question. Nonetheless, the Portal is deeply meaningful to them in a way that transcends its economic benefits. They care about the program and their fellow participants and have chosen to make the program an important part of their lives.

The Portal has been described as a "second home." Spending time on the Portal is second only to being at home with family.

Dorothy Chavez, Santo Domingo

I just have this heart for the Portal. For some reason I just have this feeling for the Portal that it feels like I said at the committee meeting we had last week, this is my second home away from my own home. My brother calls it [that] too. If my family doesn't find me at home, my brother tells them, "You don't find her at home, go to Santa Fe. She's in her second home." So I consider it my second home because I'm always over here. And I like being over here. I miss it a lot when I'm not here. I really do.

Vendors also come to the Portal because it gives them the opportunity to spend time with their friends, even when they can sell their work just as successfully from home or in other venues.

Robert Naranjo, Nambe and Santa Clara

I sit here, I can sit here and sell here [at my house in Santa Clara] .... But then you miss your friends out there, and you go back out there and you sell out there and you have a good time with them and you enjoy yourself and you just have fun.

I really got depressed last year. So I just took off, down south, southern New Mexico. And it cost me some money to do that, but after about a week or two weeks of that I went down to Santa Fe. That's what I should have done. You get down there with your friends and talk to the people, that's good therapy. You're not spending money—well, you spend money eating, parking, stuff like that—but you enjoy your friends, talk with your friends there, and just have a good time. Like my friend P. . . . We sat there one day, the first thing she offers me, "Here, Robert, have an apple." I ate an apple. After that she opens up some chips, you know those canned ones. We had some of them. She reaches in the cooler and gets out a soda, gives me a soda. And about lunch-time, I didn't know where she went. She went to Kaune's, that little grocery store, and she bought some bologna or ham, I can't remember, she made sandwiches. I mean all day we were just eating. Three o'clock, I said, "P., I'm going to go about four o'clock, I'm going to go home." She said, "Why?" I said, "You're out of groceries."

Vendors who are no longer able to come to the Portal because of age, infirmity, or other obligations often miss it deeply. At the Portal Program's annual meeting in April 1999, a respected elder who was deeply involved in the development of the program in the 1970s and 1980s rose to admonish the vendors:

I don't even come here to sell anymore, but because I have interest and I want this porch to continue on the way it is supposed to be used I'm here to help you. Even sometimes I drive my husband up here, he's not able to come here anymore, we're both disabled, but because of the interest that we have we're here today. And what I want to say to you folks is, you take care of that porch. You make a living, I see a lot of you with nice cars, I see you with things that we never had, and it's because of this little porch here that we have. You'd better take care of it. You'd better do what the rules say, because we have rules here to protect us. And what are rules for anyway? They are supposed to be used to protect what you have here. I'm glad I'm here today, I'm thankful that I can still get around a little bit. But I do promise that I'll be back just to even ride up in front to see your faces. It's very important to me. Tony Tortalita and I, and some other older ones that have gone on, we were the ones that were sitting out here, and we got along. We were brothers and sisters, and that's what you should all be now: brothers and sisters. If you are really Indian, Indians always treat each other as brothers and sisters. And I hope that you'll continue to carry on this without any problems. It is hard when you get old, it is not very easy. But I miss this porch, that is why I'm here today.[7]

While the Portal is an important community for many of its participants, it has special meaning for vendors who otherwise would have limited contact with other Native people. These vendors, some of whom identify themselves as "urban Indians," live away from their reservations and villages in mixed-ethnicity communities in Santa Fe, Albuquerque, or other towns near Santa Fe. These vendors see the Portal Program as an opportunity to interact with other Native people on a daily basis. Some maintain family ties at one or more of the Pueblo villages and participate to some degree in village social and ceremonial life. Others, especially those whose tribe of origin is not in northern New Mexico, consider the Portal an alternative home community.

James Faks, Blackfoot, Onondaga-Oneida, Maya, Apache
{SL: What is it like to be from outside this region and be at the Portal with all the Pueblo people and Navajo people? Is that easy, hard?}

It's pretty easy for me. Everywhere I've been I've been fortunate enough to have been adopted into many different tribes and peoples' ways and so I guess I'm fortunate to say I have lots of grandpas and grandmas, and that's the oldest way, as far as we know from being Native, that's how it is.... But on the whole wide scale I'm pretty well accepted, so that makes me feel pretty good.

Some vendors have come to know other Native people for the first time on the Portal.

Mary Eustace, Cochiti and Zuni

{SL: Have you met or made friends with people, vendors, staff, or visitors to the porch that you wouldn't have otherwise probably met if you weren't at the porch?}

Yes. I've met Indian people. That's a big thing. Because being raised in the city [Albuquerque], nothing but Hispanics abounded where I lived, and prejudice also. So coming up here and meeting all these Pueblos and Plains Indians, it's interesting, it's exciting. I really appreciate their friendship....

{SL: So it was really when you came to the portal that you met more Indian people.}

Indian people, yes. And even I was stereotyped into thinking how they were.

{SL: What were your ideas? When you came here, what were you expecting?}

They were mean to me, growing up. When I was in junior high, they would ship them in from these boarding schools and it was a lot of Navajos that I ran across, and they didn't like me, because I wasn't like them. So I didn't like them, because they didn't accept me so I was caught between—because the Hispanics didn't like me because I was Indian, and yet the Indians didn't like me because I was urban. So coming up here, and thinking, Wow, they're not as mean as they look! (Laughter) They really are sweet people, they're just quiet. They're, like I talk about suppression, shyness, the withdrawal that whatever or whoever put them there, if you break that barrier they're really the sweetest people. They're the nicest, kindest people.

The Portal community accepts participants with different life experiences and gives them the opportunity to share their experiences with other participants and with the tourist public.

Sarah Martinez,* Santo Domingo

Even if somebody doesn't buy anything from me, I just feel good that I was able to give them part of the knowledge that I have, because actually I wasn't raised on a reservation, I was raised in a city [Española]. I'm what you call an "urban Indian" but I knew what it was like.... When we were growing up our mom was married to a Spanish man, so we were like half Spanish and half Indian, so when we went back to the reservation, it was like, you know, "They're Spanish," and they would make fun of us, and then we went back to the city and then we were Indians and they made fun of us, so I didn't learn very much about my culture until I was older, and what I did learn about the Pueblos and stuff I learned in books because I took Indian education in high school.... What I know I try to educate the tourists when they do come in. And if they don't buy anything from me I feel good that I helped them to understand a little about Pueblo or Indian culture.

In the Portal community, knowledgeable and experienced elders often give support and advice to younger participants who are just finding their way, acting as mentors in the same way grandparents or aunts and uncles might.

Sarah Martinez,* Santo Domingo

Trying to learn how to do the stamping, I didn't have any tools, all I did was use screwdrivers, awls, and, you know, just what I could find around the house and I remember Glenn Paquin was like my mentor. He would always encourage me, because he would see how my work was. And then I would tell him, "I don't have any tools! And I'm just doing it any way," I would tell him, and he would just smile and he'd tell me that's the best way to learn. He said, "See what you can find around your house and your yard and learn from that," he said, "because eventually when you get into the bigger stuff you'll know where you came from, and then it'll be a lot easier, your technique will get easier." So I did, and he's always encouraged me and whenever he sees my new pieces he'll tell me, "You're getting good, and better at your designing and your work."

The Portal community supports Native American artists in their artistic development, but it also offers participants opportunities to learn about their histories, cultural traditions, and indigenous languages. The Portal offers Native Americans who are not fully integrated into a village or tribal community social networks that allow them to maintain and develop their identities as Native people and as members of their own cultures.

The Portal community is accepting and inclusive. The museum guard staff, other museum personnel, and other members of the plaza-area community are included in the Portal community. The guard staff, made up almost exclusively of Hispanos, interacts closely with the Portal Program participants. While there is sometimes friction between the vendors and guards, there are also many friendships. During the time that I have been at the Portal, for example, there has been a running joke between a vendor and a young guard who resembles the vendor's grandson. In addition to the Portal coordinator, other museum staff not linked to the program through employment are members of the Portal's social world. Newspaper vendors and employees at area restaurants and shops also participate in the Portal community to varying degrees. Though not official participants in the program, these community members contribute to the social fabric of the Portal, and it is in part through these connections that the Portal community is integrated into the social fabric of Santa Fe.

Probably the most fully integrated nonparticipant is the world-famous, self-proclaimed "paperman dancer" James Douglas.[8] James has sold the *Santa Fe New Mexican* on Palace Avenue in front of the west end of the portal for more than a decade.

James Douglas, newspaper vendor

Three years after I came out here my mom and dad finally [came] out, and the people under the portal noticed right off the bat, they said, looking at the features of my mom, and my mom's mom was a full-blooded Creek Indian. And so right off the bat they click, you know, and so I really get along great with these people because my mom died two years ago, and the people under the portal just started handing me money because they knew I had long way to go back east back to the Cambridge area,

and you know we're towards [the] New Hampshire area where
my parents had the pig farm. These people just, I couldn't believe
all the money they gave me for the plane fare and spending money
and so forth. And I really consider them friends, true friends,
because if they know you're a good person they will bend over
backwards for you. // And, like I say, every time there's an event
they definitely make sure they notify me, and Christmas,
Thanksgiving they always invite me into the museum for turkey
and all the fixings and the whole bit, and like I say, I really consider them true friends. // And that was the first thing I told the
New Mexican. They said, "Hey James, we're having a Christmas
party." I said, "Hey, you guys can have your Christmas party,
I'm going with my friends."

Though the Portal community is inclusive, it is also bounded.
Not everyone who regularly spends time in the area around the portal
is included in the Portal community, nor do all want to be included.
On the plaza south of Palace Avenue about ten vendors hold city-
issued permits to set up booths. These non-Indian vendors are not
held to the Portal's standards regarding production or materials used
in the articles they sell, and a number of them sell machine-produced
"Indian"-style jewelry. Because they are in direct competition with
the Portal participants and because they sell items not up to Portal
standards, sometimes at lower prices, a measure of suspicion and mis-
trust exists between them and Portal participants. There is also tension between Hispano food vendors in the vicinity of the portal and
program participants, with the food vendors claiming the right (and
the city permit) to sell around the corner from the portal. The Portal
vendors regularly express concerns about the smoke, smell, and mess
of the foodstuffs.[9]

These community boundaries are largely constructed along
ethnic lines but are also reflected in the boundaries of the physical
environment. A number of people from Santo Domingo Pueblo sell
jewelry at various locations around the plaza area, but because they
are not part of the Portal Program, their interaction with Native
people from the program is limited. The space under the portal is

Museum of New Mexico property, and as a result of the Livingston lawsuits the physical space of the portal is legally bounded and restricted to Native American vendors. In contrast, the vendors who set up their booths around the corner on Washington Avenue and on the plaza are on city property and are subject to city regulations and permitting procedures. The physical bounding of the portal is reinforced by the architecture, which visually sets the portal apart from the surrounding environment.

Maintaining the Portal Community

The Portal community is maintained through many types of interactions. Potluck lunches held at Thanksgiving and Christmas give participants the opportunity to enjoy each other's company outside of the work environment of the portal proper. Visits to participants' homes on Pueblo feast days reaffirm and cement the bonds of friendship. Many of the younger vendors go out, play basketball, and otherwise socialize away from the Portal. The program's annual meeting provides the opportunity for participants to air concerns and for elders to reinforce their conceptions of the Portal and to give advice about appropriate behavior. The foundation of the Portal community, though, is the daily, face-to-face interaction between program participants that takes place under the portal. Daily interactions under the portal are full of discussion, consultation, agreement, disagreement, and negotiation. Maintaining the Portal is work for all involved.

Humor plays an important role under the portal. Vine Deloria, Jr. (1969), has commented on humor among Native Americans as a means of coping with cultural domination, and this verbal strategy has been documented by others (e.g., Basso 1979). On the portal, though, this role of Native American humor is less important. Because the Native American participants in the Portal Program are usually very much in control of the program, the marketplace, and their interaction with members of the dominant society, there is less need for humor to counteract or combat discrimination. On the portal, humor reflects people enjoying each other's company and helps to cement social relationships.

The Portal can be disconcerting for some visitors, perhaps because it is their first face-to-face encounter with Native people and they are unsure how to act. Some vendors use humor to help put these visitors at ease. As noted in chapter 4, humor is also used with visitors to gently illustrate proper behavior, such as the discouragement of attempts at bargaining. Some vendors take cues from T-shirts or conference name tags to address unsuspecting visitors by name or by hometown or state. This serves to draw visitors' attention to the pieces for sale on the vendor's cloth, but it is also a lighthearted way to instruct visitors on how to interact with the vendors. The use of humor to initiate interaction is both a vehicle for and a reflection of the vendors' control of the market interaction.

As is the case with so many elements of the Portal community, the use of humor is much more developed among the program participants than between participants and tourists. Laughter is a staple of Portal society.

Pamela Smith, former director, Palace Printshop
{KH: So what's the best thing about the Portal?}

What's the best thing.... You know what I think is one of the nicest things? I like hearing the language. I like hearing that kind of mix still going on because you can hear Spanish, you can hear all the different Pueblo languages going on out there, and I like that. Also, I love hearing the Native American ladies laughing in the bathroom.

Robert Naranjo, Nambe and Santa Clara
Do you know C.B.?... I shared a space with him. I got a space and he asked me to share. I said, "Sure." So we sat right there. The reason I did is I had that big space right there where you get to that doorway. We started talking and talking and laughing and laughing. This lady came up and looked at a bracelet. He says, "I've got my initials in there, 'C.B.'" I knew his name was C.B. "That's my initials," he goes. "Could stand for 'cute butt.'" And then he started laughing. Anyhow, that day after he got home his wife was talking, "You look tired, what's the matter?" He said,

"I am so tired." She says, "Why?" "Robert shared his space with me and we just laughed all day long." His wife was telling me that he never had so much fun selling. But I tell them, I enjoy having a good time. If I don't sell anything, but if this person here is selling, this person here is selling, I enjoy that, because I know they're buying something, not just sitting there looking at each other.

One day under the portal a vendor began to talk about her idea for a book about the funny things that have happened there. The stories told reflect some of the ways in which humor is used. Several are about scantily clad tourists and vendors' reactions. As in other world tourism destinations, Santa Fe tourists sometimes dress in a manner deemed inappropriate by local indigenous people (see, e.g., Lavie 1990). On one occasion, as a tourist crossed Palace Avenue her dress was blown over her head by a wind gust, exposing her revealing undergarments. Another time, a tourist's low-cut blouse left male vendors embarrassed and women vendors amused at the men's embarrassment. Other stories told of visits to the Portal by celebrities and vendors' reactions, ranging from the failure by some to recognize the celebrities—to the astonishment of their neighbors—to vendors having photos taken with them.

Practical jokes are not uncommon. On one occasion Sarah Laughlin and I had been invited to a family's feast at Santo Domingo to celebrate one of their sons' saint's day on a day when, for ceremonial reasons, the pueblo was closed to outsiders. During the morning, several people under the portal told us that we would not be allowed to enter the village. Our host met us at the roadblock, and after she had received permission from the Pueblo governor's office we were allowed to follow her to her home. When we returned to Santa Fe later that afternoon we told a committee member from Santo Domingo that my car had been impounded by the tribal police and asked for a ride back to the village to reclaim it. As neither Sarah nor I are particularly good practical jokers, we gave ourselves away by failing to contain our laughter. The recipient of our practical joke retaliated by setting the clock in the Portal office back an hour, leaving Sarah confused for a couple of days.

Humor is an important tool for incorporating peripheral figures into the Portal community. When I first became involved with the Portal, vendors often shared jokes with me in a way that helped me to feel more comfortable. When Nancy is able to join me, I often hear her laughing with the vendors, I suspect at my expense.

Occasionally jokes will be made that are found offensive by other vendors. When I have known this to occur, the offended parties have expressed their concerns in open discourse, either at committee meetings or at the program's annual meetings. As in other situations in which vendors have concerns, speakers use Pueblo-style verbal techniques that include great care not to identify offenders, even though the majority of people present may know who is being spoken about. Instead of publicly shaming another person, offended members of the Portal community express their concerns and suggest appropriate behavior.

When program participants become concerned about an issue, resolution is sought through dialogue and conciliation. Everyone is given the opportunity to speak. Museum administrators occasionally lament what they perceive as the protracted duration of such meetings, but they are uniformly unsuccessful in attempts to limit speakers. Though all concerned parties may not agree at the end of a discussion, they almost always seem to find an acceptable middle ground. Compromise and insistence on resolution are methods of effecting change, or maintaining norms, that also help to maintain interpersonal civility and cooperation in the tightly knit community of the Portal.

The alternative to cooperating in the Portal community is nonparticipation. While occasionally vendors stop coming to the Portal because of interpersonal conflicts or an inability or unwillingness to abide by the program rules or social norms, most find ways to remain within the Portal community so that they can continue to sell through the program. The Portal community is an enduring institution.

SIX

The Portal as Museum Program

*Today's Portal Committee meeting was
canceled by an undetermined person for
no apparent reason.*
                    —Santa Fe New Mexican,
                        February 8, 1983

As I sat in the Saint Francis Auditorium in the Fine Arts Museum
during the 1999 Portal Program annual meeting, I was struck by
how much of what makes the Portal an institution—its history, the
sentiments of participants, and the relations among participants,
between the tribal governments and the program, and between the
program and the museum—was represented and re-created through
the meeting.

The annual meeting is one of only a few occasions each year
when a large number of vendors come together with members of the
museum administration in a setting removed from the portal proper.
As the other occasions are social events such as holiday potluck
lunches, the annual meeting is the principal time when the body of
vendors and the museum staff assemble to discuss the business and
administration of the program. It is also the principal occasion
for Pueblo governors and other tribal leaders to express support for
the program or to publicly address issues of concern to their villages.

In 1999, for example, a representative was sent by the governor of Jemez Pueblo in response to an argument between two (non-Jemez) program participants who were selling at the village during the feast day. The incident had occurred months earlier and was outside the program's jurisdiction, but the village's leaders used the meeting as a forum to communicate their disapproval of the vendors' actions to a multitribal audience.

In a style characteristic of meetings among Puebloan people, at this meeting several participants spoke about the history of the program, emphasizing the struggles that they and earlier vendors had undergone to preserve it. The elders and others talked of the need for mutual respect and appropriate behavior under the portal. The annual meeting serves as a venue for the affirmation of the Portal by its participants. The annual meeting is sponsored by the museum, however, and thus also reflects the relations between the museum and the participants and illuminates the complexity of the program, particularly the interaction between the museum as a state bureaucratic institution and the vendors as individual businesspeople, artists, and representatives of indigenous communities.

During the first part of each annual meeting, general business and proposed changes or additions to program rules are discussed. When the museum administration or members of the program committee or other vendors suggest modification of the rules, the proposed revision is formalized and brought to the program participants for further discussion and vote. Changes that are approved by the vendors are then taken to the museum Board of Regents, which has the final authority to adopt or reject rule changes in a public hearing. The Board of Regents and the museum administration also have the authority to modify the rules without consultation with the program membership, but this authority has rarely been exercised.

The second part of the annual meeting is committed to the election of the program committee. Each year a total of thirteen committee members are selected: a committee chair, vice-chair, and secretary, seven committee members, and three alternates. Candidates are nominated by other participants, then given the opportunity to accept or decline the nomination. Generally two or more vendors will be nominated for each position, starting with the committee chairpersonship. After nominations for the position are closed, the vendors vote by raising their hands. Sometimes there is general agreement that the first nominee should have the position, and no other vendors are nominated (or any nominated persons decline). Sometimes a vendor is nominated but not selected in one round and then is renominated and wins overwhelmingly in another round. Voting frequently splits down tribal lines, but each year a fairly balanced group of vendors is selected for the committee. Every year at least some of the alternates are promoted to full committee membership as members leave because of other commitments that arise.

The meeting is set up in the manner of most institutional meetings in Western parliamentary tradition. An agenda is discussed with the committee and then completed by the museum staff, and copies are made available to everyone as they enter the auditorium. The agenda outlines the plan of the meeting, names scheduled speakers, and includes business items to be discussed and voted on. In 1999 there were four items to be voted on by the program membership. According to program rules, the meeting is chaired by the director of the Palace of the Governors. On this occasion Charles Bennett, associate director, served as chair because the director, Thomas Chávez, was at a meeting out of state. Bennett attempted to follow parliamentary procedure, at least roughly, and to work through the agenda in what he considered a timely manner.

Because this was the participants' meeting as much as the museum's, considerable negotiation was necessary on each side. As I have discussed previously, the Portal is in many ways a democratic institution: nearly everyone who wants the opportunity to speak on an issue will be heard. Included on the agenda for this meeting was an "information sheet" developed by the museum staff in consultation with the committee that contained ten items intended to clarify the rules for the vendors. One of these items stated, "All vendors are to be set up, ready to sell, and at their cloth by 10:00 A.M." The purpose of this point was to encourage vendors to be at their spaces and selling by 10:00 A.M. so that they might make enough sales that they could go home, leaving spaces open for vendors on the waiting list that day. However, this rule (2-E, see Appendix) does not require vendors to be *at* their spaces at 10:00 A.M., but only that they be completely set up. Vendors regularly add the allowed one-hour break to their time in the morning, returning to their spaces to sell by 11:00 A.M. Charles Bennett's reading of this item led to a discussion that lasted almost half an hour, during which time fifteen participants held the floor. Several did so more than once, and numerous others made comments without acknowledgment from the meeting chair. Many different views were expressed, ranging from those opposed to being required to be at their spaces at 10:00 on the grounds of their status as independent businesspeople to others who supported the item. Recommendations were made that the rule be changed to reflect the item as presented. At the end several elder vendors admonished the participants to respect one another.

What was most interesting about this exchange, in terms of interaction between the participants and the museum, was the collision of the two parties' ways of conducting business. The museum, personified by the meeting chair, was interested in working through the agenda and finishing the meeting as quickly as possible. The program participants, on the other hand, demanded that controversial issues be discussed to the satisfaction of the people present. The first few minutes of discussion were spent determining what the standard practice was and that the rule and the "informational item" were not entirely consistent. Then several vendors presented their thoughts on the issue, both for and against the stricter regulation being proposed.

About fourteen minutes after the discussion was initiated, the meeting chair attempted to conclude the debate:

> OK, I'm not sure we need to discuss this very much more. How about two more comments. How about from people we haven't heard yet? R., we haven't heard from you yet.[1]

Two more participants spoke, then the chair tried unsuccessfully to stop a third speaker. He next turned to humor to attempt to move the meeting along.

OK. You guys, we want to get on with the meeting. We have
to do the election, and we're going to draw for a Ford Explorer
here too, so....

At this point, the chair began to realize that the discussion would
end when the program participants were satisfied that enough had
been said.

> **C.B.:** All we're doing right now is kind of reiterating what
> the rules are, you guys, let's go on. OK? Everybody's had a
> chance to say....
>> **Unidentified vendor:** Not everybody.
>> **C.B.:** OK, number 8. What?
>> **Unidentified vendor:** Not everybody.
>> **C.B.:** OK. All right you guys.

An elder vendor rose and spoke to the participants in the audience, followed by two other longtime vendors. Each acknowledged the changes that had occurred in the program over the
years and encouraged appropriate behavior and mutual concern
among the vendors. A fourth longtime vendor rose to express her
concerns about inappropriate humor under the portal and
likewise urged unity and respect among the vendors. As the four
vendors spoke, the auditorium fell silent for the first time since the
issue of 10:00 A.M. attendance had first been raised. After the last
vendor spoke, the meeting chair simply said, "Thank you," and
went on to the next item with the apparent approval of everyone
at the meeting.

In this case the process was more important than the product.
Ultimately, no agreement was reached and no action was actually
taken on the issue. It was recognized by the museum staff and
participants that the rules do not require vendors to be at their
spaces at 10:00 A.M. and that adding that requirement would
require a rule change. However, the extended discussion gave
vendors the opportunity to express their concerns and, perhaps
more important, for senior vendors to reassert the importance of

working together and showing respect for one another. Both are vitally important to the continuing operation of the program. The museum staff had to compromise their ideas of how a meeting should be conducted to meet the needs of the attendees.

The Portal operates as a museum program in this way: museum administrators and program participants work together to meet the needs of the vendors while fulfilling the expectations of the institution. To fit the category "museum program" into a Euro-American conceptual and legal framework, the program must have (and follow) rules that govern its operation and administration, including a formal annual meeting. To function as an institution within the conceptual frameworks brought to it by Native American participants, the program's operation and administration must be flexible. With vendors and administrators coming to the Portal with different, sometimes contradictory perspectives that are influenced by cultural expectations and individual experiences, the daily operation of the Portal as a program is a dynamic process.

This is at least in part because the Portal Program is the product of many intertwined histories. The program is possible because over the past century Santa Fe has developed as a tourist center that now hosts more than two million visitors each year. The presence of Indian people selling ethnic art in Santa Fe has played an important role in that development. The history of the Palace of the Governors as a public building on the city's main plaza and the availability of space under the Palace's front portal where Indian people could sell the things they make have also been important. As discussed in chapter 2, the local and regional businesspeople and politicians interested in promoting Santa Fe as a tourist destination and the social advocates interested in improving the economic opportunities available to Indian people have encouraged the development of the portal market. Most important, however, the Portal is the product of a historical interest (and economic need) by Native people to market their arts and crafts production combined with the desire of museum professionals and their staffs to support and promote that production and marketing of Native American art.

Displaying People

The Portal Program is officially considered an educational program of the museum, supporting traditional Native American culture and serving to educate the public through the opportunity to interact with Native American artists. As such, the program stems from a long history of the display of the cultural products, traditional activities, and bodies (both living and dead) of indigenous peoples by individuals and institutions of colonizing, dominant societies. Native American people have been subject to collection and display at least since Columbus captured Taino people from several Caribbean islands and took them to Europe where they were exhibited as part of his booty:

> Christopher Columbus, now Admiral, left Seville with as much finery as he could gather, taking with him the seven Indians who had survived the voyage. I saw them in Seville, where they stayed near the Arch of St. Nicholas, called the Arch of the Images. He had brought beautiful green parrots, guaycas, or masks, made of precious stones and fishbone, strips of the same composition admirably contrived, sizable samples of very fine gold, and many other things never before seen in Spain.... [In Barcelona] the streets were crammed with people come to see this eminent person who had found another world, as well as to see the Indians, the parrots, the gold and other novelties (Las Casas 1971:37–38 [bk. 1, chap. 78]).

The display of colonized peoples by imperial powers continued into the nineteenth and twentieth centuries, forming a basis for many of the world's great museums. Living displays found their widest expression in the world's fairs, starting with the Paris Exposition of 1867 and continuing well into the twentieth century. Burton Benedict (1994:34, 59–61) has documented more than two hundred displays of living people at fifty-seven international and colonial expositions between 1867 and 1986. Twenty of these exhibits featured Native North American and Inuit people. World's fairs were staged as tributes to industrial progress and celebrations of imperialist power.

The display of colonized peoples, much like the display of raw materials and manufactures from those colonies, represented the glory of the imperial nation. Implicit (and sometimes explicit) in these displays were ideologies of social evolutionism and racism that placed people of Western European origin at the supposed pinnacle of human development, ideologies that were celebrated at the fairs. The placement of indigenous peoples in displays located them at various points down the (supposed) evolutionary ladder of social and racial progress.

The display of people at world's fairs also amused and educated fairgoers. In exhibiting Native American people, U.S. government exhibits sought to demonstrate how Indian people were becoming "civilized." At the 1904 Louisiana Purchase Exposition in St. Louis, for example, a model Indian school was exhibited, complete with Indian children being educated (Benedict 1983:50). Social evolutionism held sway at this fair, as at others, with "living exhibits" placed in a supposed hierarchical order from "the more advanced tribes" located around the Indian school to the "less advanced" peoples placed farther away (Hanson 1904:266, quoted in Benedict 1983:50).[2] Among the least "advanced" were Igorot people from the United States' newly acquired colony, the Philippines, whose consumption of dog meat was scandalous but also apparently a major attraction (Benedict 1983:44)

As Benedict (1983:43) points out, the display of people has much to do with power relations between the displayers and the displayed. The ability of an imperialist government to exhibit tribal people who have been transported from their homes to a metropolitan center, sometimes literally half a world away, is a compelling demonstration of the power of the government and the subjugation of the tribal people. That the government can determine, in large measure, what cultural elements are displayed, what sort of clothing is worn, and how the public should perceive the colonized people who are on display is further testament to the inequalities of power of such displays. At the same time, the displays reflect popular opinion even as they reinforce it, helping to perpetuate the perceptions of members of dominant ethnic groups. The juxtaposition of uniformed Native American schoolchildren in a model school with scantily clad Igorot people squatting around a fire (Benedict 1983:44) at St. Louis in 1904 is a prime example of these inequalities of power on several levels. Not only did the caricaturization of Igorot ways of life firmly label them as savages, but the uniforming of Native American children helped to demonstrate the control of the dominant culture over the minds and bodies of Indian children while at the same time decivilizing traditional Native American cultures.

Though we in the academic community like to think that we have gained considerable enlightenment over the last century, in many ways the treatment of indigenous peoples in the context of heritage festivals (as events displaying non-Western people are now sometimes called) has not changed significantly. Richard Price and Sally Price (1994) provide a valuable critique of the Smithsonian Institution's 1992 Folk Arts Festival where they served as facilitators for Maroon "Tradition-Bearers." From the failure of event organizers to provide appropriate food to extremely demanding performance schedules to differential payment for Florida Seminole presenters over South American Maroon presenters, Price and Price clearly illustrate that indigenous peoples continue to be dealt with poorly as participants in fairs.

Though Price and Price provide some insights into the perspectives of the Maroon "tradition-bearers," what is missing from most critiques is the attitudes and motivations of the indigenous people who are on display. While undoubtedly some indigenous individuals who have been part of "living exhibits" have had little more freedom to choose their roles than did the Taino people captured and displayed by Columbus, the interaction between dominant powers and subjugated people is not a one-way street. Indigenous people *chose* to participate in world's fairs and other expositions, with motivations that were not necessarily tied to those of the colonial powers.

An example is the participation of twenty-eight families from San Ildefonso in the San Diego Panama-California Exposition of 1915 (Wilson 1997:129). There are a number of links between the San Diego exposition and the later development of the Portal market. Edgar Lee Hewett served as the director of exhibits for the fair, and several of the exhibits were designed and constructed by Museum of New Mexico and School of American Archaeology (subsequently renamed the School of American Research) staff. Included among those exhibits was the Santa Fe Railway's *Painted Desert* exhibit, a five-acre commercial attraction featuring Native American–style architecture designed by Kenneth Chapman and built by Jesse Nusbaum (Walter 1915:9; Wilson 1997:129).

Hewett helped to arrange for the families from San Ildefonso to exhibit at San Diego (Chauvenet 1983:191), and the popularity of the *Painted Desert* exhibit demonstrated to Hewett and other museum staff members that tourists were very interested in Pueblo Indians (Wilson 1997:129). Hewett and Chapman were key figures in the organization of the Santa Fe Indian fairs beginning in 1922, and they certainly recalled their experiences in San Diego in 1915 in developing both the Santa Fe Fiesta and the Indian fairs (see chap. 3). The importance Hewett and others placed on Native American dances, demonstrations, and other cultural exhibits at these events is at least in part a result of the successes at San Diego.

The San Ildefonso contingent to San Diego also included some of the same people who participated in and played important roles in the Santa Fe fairs during the next decade. Among the San Diego exhibitors were Maria and Julian Martinez, the stars of the Rio Grande Pueblo pottery market. The Pueblo people who exhibited at San Diego were not forced to participate; they attended by choice. Though information is not available about specific motivations, the Martinezes and other families had a sophisticated understanding of the Native American arts and crafts market, and there is little doubt that their decision to participate in the San Diego fair was informed by their expectation of selling pottery. In fact, this was not the Martinezes' first fair; they had honeymooned as exhibitors for the Fred Harvey Company at the 1904 St. Louis fair (Berlo and Phillips 1998:59). Their success at this exposition is reflected in the fact that they participated in subsequent fairs as well, including the San Francisco Golden Gate International Exposition in 1939.

Native peoples' economic motivations for participation in the display of (frequently idealized) culture has been recognized in

Indian involvement in the Wild West shows of Bill Cody and others (Moses 1996; Muccigrosso 1993:149). While reformers railed against Native people performing in the Wild West shows because the shows were perceived to be antithetical to "civilizing" the Indians (Moses 1996:26–27; Muccigrosso 1993:149–50; Reddin 1999:114–15), cultural performances that exhibited civilization or industry such as the demonstration of handicrafts were viewed with approval. For Native American performers in either context, the motivations were likely very similar: participation allowed Native people the opportunity to use elements of their cultural traditions to provide economically for their families and also to share parts of their history, experiences, and cultures with others. Though there are aspects of Native American cultures that cannot be shared with outsiders (see chap. 7; see also Norcini 1995), many Native American people want to share aspects of their lives with interested outsiders.

Something Different

The Portal Program has its origins in the long history of living displays but is at the same time a unique and remarkable institution. When the museum officially sanctioned the program in the 1970s, the administration sought to define the program's role within the mission of the museum. The Regents and staff felt a commitment to support the continuing production of Native American art and recognized the importance of sales under the portal. At the same time, because of the legal challenges the program faced, it could not be considered merely a market. The museum had to affirm that the program had an educational content and was not simply a commercial venture. During the early years, the program was sometimes designated a "living exhibit," using the language of the colonial displays of the world's fairs (see, e.g., *Santa Fe New Mexican,* June 14, 1979). As the relationship between the program and the museum has become better defined, it has come to be called an "educational program" in an effort to move away from the blatant objectification of indigenous people inherent in the language of living exhibits.

Though the idea of a living exhibit sometimes conjures images of people in cages, program participants have transformed the terminology into something of great value, even while members of the museum staff (and I) flounder through feelings of dominant-culture guilt about the use of such terminology.

Mary Eustace, Zuni and Cochiti

You know we're actually listed as living exhibits? I tell people that. I say "See? But I'm not on a wall. You know, I'm not hung on a wall, but we are living exhibits."

{SL: What do you think about those words, being called a living exhibit?}

I feel like a monkey in a zoo. (Laughs) Because they take pictures of you, and they want to take pictures of the most authentic, traditional-looking one.

{SL: Oh really?}

Yeah, and then they get mad, the vendors [do]. And I can understand that because it's like, "Wow, there's a real live Indian, let me take a picture." One person even said that he sat there and he pulled out a camera and took a picture of the tourist. (Laughs)

Glenn Paquin, Laguna and Zuni

In terms of what we give to the museum, I guess [what we give is] the idea that you have a living museum out there. A modern, changing, dynamic museum that is there every day. Good weather or bad weather, you've got us out there.

James Faks, Blackfoot, Onondaga-Oneida, Maya, Apache

We're the living museum, as far as I'm concerned. We are the indigenous ones, so this is a living museum, living art, visual art. I think that's basically what we contribute.

{KH: Does it bother you at all, the language that indicates that the portal is a living exhibit?}

Naw. You know, because I feel the same way about it. I mean it's not a zoo.

{SL: It's always a very weird thing. I just call it the Portal,
I never call it a living exhibit, I call it a market, or a...}
    Yeah, it's a market, for sure. But I also want them to know
that we do still exist and yeah, we are museum pieces. I mean
I see some of my grandmas out there, you know like S. and a lot
of the old ladies, they look like they need to be in a museum,
as far as I'm concerned, just the way they dress and carry themselves, it's the old way.

The goals of the Portal as an educational program aim to serve
both visitors and the Native American communities of New Mexico.
The communities of the vendors are served through the support of
the arts and crafts market that encourages the survival of traditional
artistic production.[3] Visitors learn through their interaction with
Native people.
    Not all Portal participants put a lot of effort into providing an
educational service to visitors, and some are only vaguely aware of
the educational directive of the program. But many vendors have
devoted considerable thought to the program's potential as an educational resource and their roles as educators.

Sarah Martinez,* Santo Domingo
I think the vendors benefit the museum a lot because, well when
I first started selling here we were referred to as a living exhibit.
(Laughs) And I thought, well, we're a living exhibit, shouldn't we
be dressing in our traditional clothes, or what's our role, you know?
But I think that what they were thinking was that when a tourist
comes to us, that they want to know more about our personal lives,
well not real personal, but how we live, and [that] we go to school,
or how we learn how to do what we're doing, and I think that's
probably what they thought a living exhibit was. We were able
to talk to people, and a lot of people aren't educated about the
Pueblos, and they all believe that we all speak one language and
we all follow the same culture, but it's not like that. // I try to
educate the tourists when they do come in. And if they don't buy
anything from me I feel good that I helped them to understand

a little about Pueblo or Indian culture. And the museum, the museum helps us out by allowing us to sit under the portal and [be] able to meet with other people and know where other people come from and know that, I think that we're all in the same boat, we all have the same problems, it's that we deal with them differently, and we educate each other.

Glenn Paquin, Laguna and Zuni

People that come out there, they're looking, you can just see it in their eyes they want so much to talk to you. This guy came up to me this morning, he was interested [in learning] about the language. He said, "I heard a language down there and it sounded different from the one down here." He didn't know anything about languages. So I started telling him a little about the people out here, that each tribe has their own language, and their own dialect. And he said, "Man, that's interesting. The only thing we have are Senecas up where I live, but we never hear them talking." But the people that come out here somehow it's like they're coming to the porch and they're thinking, "I'm here, what do I do now?" And a lot of times the Indian people out there don't say anything to the visitors, they don't get engaged in any conversation with them. But if the visitors had the time, some of these people would probably sit there and listen to you for hours talking about you and your family. It's so interesting to them to see another culture. We're like ambassadors for our people.

James Faks, Blackfoot, Onondaga-Oneida, Maya, Apache

{KH: The Portal is deemed an educational exhibit of the Museum of New Mexico. What do you think the tourists who come to visit the portal get out of their experience?}

Well, I know what I'd like for them to get. I'd like for them to go home and to know a little more about their piece. And when they talk to me and they buy a piece from me they're generally interested because of the difference in appearance and everything, so I like to give them the story on it. I think a lot of people, like I have, this is really funny: I had this man ask me the other day, he asked me, "Why did the Native people build the ruins next to the highway?" (Laughter) And I had to stop for a minute and think. But then I don't think I really answered him directly, I kind of went around it and we talked about the jewelry. But a lot of them are just not informed, and it's good for them to come here and interact with the artists because then they do get informed and they go away with more knowledge. And they're always very respectful and that's the good part of interacting with the people.

{KH: So you think that they gain a greater appreciation of Indian peoples through . . . }

I think so, yeah. I know that in some cases a lot of the Native people because of their native tongue they're reluctant to speak out and to extensively talk to them. They're reluctant to do that. But I think generally people come away with a better knowledge and understanding.

{SL: Well, I always think just the fact that there's guys with Dallas Cowboy jackets, I mean that we're all in the same world. I think a lot of visitors don't even know that.}

That's true, and just to recognize each other and that's a good feeling. And it's coming more and more. What I remember, as far as my elders talked about, it began in this continent with the Native people and now it's coming full circle because now the knowledge is coming back to the Native people and people are now wanting to find out more, which is a good thing. The knowledge is still the same, it's still because of this earth, why we're here, so it's coming in full circle. It's a good time.

{KH: What do you think that the people who come to Santa Fe and who come to the Portal as visitors, as tourists, what are they looking for? What are they trying to find here?}

Well, mostly what I see on the portal is just the interaction, inter-reaction, with Natives. Just to be able to spend some time and to find out how they made the piece or what certain dances [mean] or what means what. I think that's mostly what they want to know, but they do also want to know the artist. When people are buying art it always seemed that to interact with the actual artist is always the best way. And people like what they're getting, they're satisfied. And to me that's the best way to do it also. This is why the Portal Program is the most unique [program], because you deal directly with us, and that's cool, I think.

Organizational Structure or Paternalism?

On her next-to-last day as Portal coordinator in 1998, Sarah Laughlin met with an official from a European institution. He asked about the daily drawing for spaces and was surprised to learn that Sarah did not attend the draw every day, nor did she *ever* manage it. He seemed to assume that the vendors were "like children" and thus not fully capable of managing their own affairs, an attitude that seems better placed at the end of the nineteenth century than at the end of the twentieth but that nonetheless continues to be widely held (Sarah Laughlin, pers. com. 1998). Even among socially conscious museum administrators there exists occasional cultural misunderstandings that can perpetuate such ethnocentric perspectives. The differing ideas of how the annual meeting should be conducted serve as evidence.

In many ways, the Museum of New Mexico is a very progressive institution. Other proximate reasons such as staff shortages notwithstanding, from the first official recognition of the Portal as a museum program in the 1970s, the museum administration has recognized the vendors' ability to operate the program and has largely let them do so. At the same time, the museum maintains authority over the program. Like other cultural institutions with multiple levels of administration (such as universities), final responsibility and authority lies with the Board of Regents. Decisions regarding the program's rules and even its continued existence are dependent on the Museum of New Mexico Board of Regents' approval. However, this organizational structure does not have its origins in the desire of the museum to control the program. Rather, the responsibility was forced on the museum as it reacted to the legal challenges of the 1970s and 1980s and sought to protect the program.

In the end, even this authority is negotiated in a manner generally unseen in other institutions. The museum administration and the Board of Regents recognize the importance of the program to the tourism industry in Santa Fe and to the museum and have followed the recommendations of the program committee and the museum staff. On one occasion, a situation arose in which the then director of the Museum of New Mexico, Tom Livesay, moved to reduce the suspension of a vendor from the program. In response to this failure to support their recommendations, the committee threatened to resign. Aware of the turmoil this would cause, Livesay reversed his decision (Sarah Laughlin, pers. com. 1999).

In terms of day-to-day operation, the director of the Palace of the Governors has the authority to settle disputes. Suspensions levied against vendors for rules violations are handed down by the Palace director by way of a formal letter to the vendor spelling out the nature of the violation and the term of the suspension. As the director of the Palace and the program committee have negotiated their roles, the penalties that are imposed are almost always those recommended by the committee.

Having an authority figure outside the Portal play the "heavy" (or as former director Chávez alternatively identified himself, "benevolent despot") serves the important purpose of maintaining decorum within the program. The program committee is made up of vendors; as such the committee members are peers with a vested interest in maintaining relationships with the other vendors in the program and in selling under the portal themselves. By placing disciplinary authority in the museum administration instead of in the program, accusations of bias or unfairness against the committee can be minimized.

In fact, some vendors feel that the Palace director does not take a strong enough stand as overseer of the program. On numerous occasions during Chávez's tenure as director I heard vendors tell the program coordinator to "have Tom send down a memo" in response to problems that occurred under the portal. Though voiced by Pueblo and non-Pueblo vendors alike, this conception of the role of the director is tied closely to Puebloan notions of authority, whereby governors and religious leaders play a central role in directing and advising the people of their villages.

"This Is the Only Place This Can Happen, Really"[4]

The Portal is a unique venue in a unique location. Few museums have the luxury of so many annual visitors or accessible space for so many artists to display and sell their work each day. Furthermore, few museums are willing or able to provide sales space at no charge to indigenous artists. With limited budgets and constant concern for bottom lines, museums frequently have to consider the viability of exhibits based on the salability of souvenirs and other objects relating to them. If museum shops cannot foresee profitability in certain exhibits, they may not be funded. More directly relevant to the Portal, the staffs of some museums see indigenous artists and vendors as direct competition with shop sales and oppose any sales events at which a percentage of the proceeds does not go to the museum.[5]

The Museum of New Mexico Foundation operates a museum store in the Palace of the Governors complex, just around the corner of the building from the portal. Though the shop sells items similar to those sold by Portal vendors, and in fact carries the work of a few vendors, I know of no concerns regarding competition. Downtown store owners recognize the importance of the Portal Program for bringing visitors to the plaza area, and some are active advocates of the program. Just as the annual SWAIA Indian Market brings twenty to thirty times the revenue earned by participating artists to Santa Fe's shops, restaurants, and hotels,[6] the Portal Program brings significant revenue to all of the plaza-area businesses.

Alfonso Tenorio, Santo Domingo

I meet a lot of people from everywhere. Japan, Germany, and I meet a lot of people from Canada, Switzerland, England. They all come to the Portal [to see us.] Because I think if the plaza is cut off, [if there's] no more vendors under there, I think Santa Fe would die like Taos.

{SL: I always try, you know sometimes when I'm here downtown at night and the vendors aren't here, and I just try to think, What would this place be like if the vendors weren't here? It would be so lonely and quiet.}

I think Santa Fe would shut down. I think that's where all the revenue's coming [from][,] . . . having that Portal Program.

IGURE 7: *Portal committee meeting in the program office, 1997. Photo by the author.*

As an example of the cooperation that is possible between Native people and state-sponsored cultural institutions, the program is instructive as well as unique. Museums and other cultural institutions play an important role in the commercial development, promotion, and marketing of Native American art. They set standards for authenticity and value in contemporary Native art through exhibitions, juried shows, and the objects that are selected for sale at museum shops. In spite of the importance of these institutions to Native artists, in very few places are Native people given the decision-making authority or leadership roles found under the portal.[7]

Two elements are key to the program's success. The first is the participants' proprietary interest. From the very beginning of the market it has belonged to the Native American vendors. Following the Saturday Markets of the 1930s, neither the museum, the city, the New Mexico Association on Indian Affairs, nor any other non-Indian organization played any real role in maintaining the market.

Rather, Native American artists themselves came together from the communities around Santa Fe to make the Portal an institution of value for them and for the tourist public. Participants' concern for and direction of the program is evident in their efforts in court to protect the program and in their efforts to make the program a marketplace for artists. If not for the considerable investment of time and interest on the part of its Native American participants, the program would not survive.

The second key element to the program's success is the support it has received from the Museum of New Mexico. The museum has fought to maintain the program as a Native American marketplace, and the court decisions resulting from those fights have allowed the program to continue in this form. Adding to this support is the recognition by museum administrators that the program can best be defined and managed through cooperation with the program participants. This provides the program with a firm institutional foundation but also has allowed it to continue to evolve to meet the needs of its participants.

SEVEN

Being an Artist

A Pottery Firing

At 5:00 A.M. I stop by Dunkin Donuts on St. Francis Drive to pick up a dozen donuts—my contribution to the morning. A few minutes later I pick up Sarah and we head for Merton and Linda Sisneros's house at Santa Clara. After we've passed through Española Sarah recognizes the turnoff from the main highway but not the road to Merton's family's place. We drive up and down the road a couple of times, then I see smoke rising from a cluster of buildings a few hundred yards off the road. I figure it must be Merton's fire, as there is no evidence of anyone else stirring this early in the morning.

We're a little late getting to Merton's; he has already put the pots he and Linda have made in the fire, and they are well on their way to firing temperature. His fire is neatly formed: thinly split pieces of pine and white fir stacked around a metal milk crate that holds the pots. The crate is supported by three iron supports, old generator housings that his late mother used for the same purpose. The supports are laid out in the form of a triangle, which Merton says is his family's symbol. The triangle sign of his grandmother and mother is included on all of the pottery his family makes, as a sort of family signature to go along with the signature on the bottom of each piece that is required by the Portal Program. Merton says that the three supports also represent the three elements: fire, water, and air. The firewood he is using is salvaged from an old corral. Many people will only use cedar, because pine tends to have a lot of sap that can get on the pots as they are being fired. Merton avoids this by covering the crate holding the pottery with a metal sheet.

He watches the pottery in the fire as it heats and changes colors. When the pieces reach the appropriate temperature (according to Merton, between 1300°F and 1400°F), he puts ashes around the base of the fire and then piles horse manure all over and around the fire, smothering it. He uses a metal-handled shovel and rake that were his mother's firing tools. The key to producing the black ware that his family makes is eliminating oxygen from the firing environment. Merton explains that it is not the burning of the manure that makes the pots black (in fact, most of the manure doesn't burn) but rather the carbon being released from the wood in the reducing environment of the smothered fire. The manure has to totally seal out oxygen from the fire in which the pots are placed. He watches the color of the smoke; if blue smoke comes out, then air is getting into the fire. He moves the manure around to seal all remaining gaps and the smoke turns to a yellow color that indicates the oxygen has been removed.

Once the fire is covered, it is left for the time it takes to really enjoy a cup of coffee. Merton says that he used to go over to his mother's house, just to the west of the firing spot, for a cup of coffee and something to eat while he waited on the firing. His mother used to cook three hot meals a day. While we wait for the pottery, Merton tells us about this place where he fires. It is the same place his mother and grandmother used, a central spot at the family home. His mother's house is to the west, his house to the north. On the east there is an old corral and pastureland, and to the south there is a field he has been clearing. The firing spot is beautiful in the morning, with trees all around and the sun coming up over the mountains to the east. Though the trees were small when Merton was a child, he says that one of the reasons that his family picked this spot is because of the wild roses growing all around. In Tewa, Santa Clara is called Kha P'o, which means "Valley of the Wild Roses." An irrigation ditch runs along the edge of the site, and Merton indicates the connection between the ditch and the water serpent that is important to the Pueblo people and that is sometimes represented on Merton's family's pottery. Merton puts the ash from the fires in the irrigation ditch, where it can be washed down to fertilize the fields.

When the appropriate time has passed, Merton says a prayer and then begins to carefully remove the manure and wood from around the firing crate. He spreads out the charred wood pieces and the manure so that they can be separated and used again. Merton has his own horses and so does not have to buy manure, but many potters must purchase manure to fire their pottery. He lifts the cover from the crate and removes the pottery pieces from the basket using a cotton towel. He wipes any ash from the pieces as he pulls them out and sets them on a cookie sheet to cool. Merton had been a bit concerned about the outcome: he was firing larger and smaller pieces together, and it is sometimes difficult to get different-sized pieces to the proper firing temperature at the same time. Today the firing has been successful: two bowls, the larger about six inches in diameter, and eight or so of Merton and Linda's summer and winter owls. The owls are a specialty, and at about three inches high the figurines are small enough and inexpensive enough to be very quick sellers under the portal.

The beautiful, shining black pots and pottery owls will still be warm from the firing when the first visitors arrive at the portal this morning. They will pick them up and inspect them; the warmth of the pieces is reminiscent of fresh-baked bread. Merton and Linda, who is of Navajo and Papago (Tohono O'Odham) ancestry, have been making pottery together since their marriage in 1978 and are strong advocates of traditional pottery making. After hearing Merton's presentation (which is as polished as his pottery), many visitors will take a piece home.

After the piece leaves the porch, what will it become? A memento? A gift? A curio? A tie between the purchasers and the artist, between the purchasers and their conception of Native America, made stronger by their visit to Santa Fe? An investment? An object of Native American art? An object of art?

Native American Art

The discourse on Native American art as Art is of long duration and largely unsatisfying. Orbiting around the issue are a number of sometimes competing, sometimes complementary, frequently vehemently argued forces. On the most basic level, there is the long-standing but often vague set of categories developed by artists, art critics, gallery owners, and others involved in various art worlds (see Becker 1982) that distinguish between such phenomena as Art (or fine art) and craft, between pure art (Art) and marked forms of art such as commercial art, academic art, folk art, ethnic art, and tourist art. The creative work of autochthonous people may be considered by marketers and consumers to be ethnic art, tourist art, craft, or, more rarely, Art.

Since the aesthetic production of indigenous people is almost always categorized as a marked art form, it is also given economic and aesthetic values by consumers as something less than Art. This labeling and valuation tends to discount the creative efforts that go into the production of that art.[1] Cross-culturally differing conceptions of art serve to magnify this tendency. As a result, consumers are more likely to look at the work of indigenous artists as souvenirs or curios than as meaningful aesthetic objects.

Simply defining Art can be a daunting task. Rather than exhaustively review various definitions, here I would like to outline some conceptions of Art and how those conceptions might be applied to the aesthetic work of Portal participants. First, as Daniel Miller (1991:50) points out, the concept "art" is not based on any "absolute quality of the world" or universal human construct but is the product of certain historical and cultural conditions. In the case of Western European and Euro-American traditions, the conception of art has evolved over the course of the last three centuries from the sense of a human skill to an "institution," in which art as an "imaginative truth" is produced by "a special kind of person," an "artist" (Williams 1958:xiii–xiv).

Howard Becker (1982:276) provides as a starting point a "folk definition" of art in contemporary Western society. The definition includes "an emphasis on beauty as typified in the tradition of some particular art, on the traditions and concerns of the art world itself as the source of value, on expression of someone's thoughts and feelings, and on the relative freedom of the artist from outside interference with the work." "High" Art should also "give the knowledgeable viewer a 'transcendental' aesthetic experience that can change the way the viewer looks at reality" (Plattner 1996:7). To be pure Art (as opposed to "commercial art"), the artist should not care about the economic value or salability of his or her work (Mitchell 1993:1–2). Furthermore, as Parezo (1990:563) writes, within Western art worlds there exists a fiction that art should have "no other function than to exist, be pleasurable to look at, carry an aesthetic message, and convey the emotions and insights of the artist" (see also Becker 1982:278).

As I discuss below, much of the work sold by Portal participants meets Becker's criteria of art. Beauty, as mutually conceived by the Native American artists and their (usually) non-Indian customers, is a primary criterion by which pieces are measured. Value also comes from the placement of pieces within the art world of Native American art. The work sold under the portal can be identified as Native American by way of form, materials, or design elements that are accepted as being "traditional." Those rare pieces that do not exhibit one or more of these markers can be located within the realm of Native American art by the fact that the pieces must be made by Native artists to be sold in this venue. The artists who produce pieces for the Portal often put considerable thought and feeling into their work, and many seek to provide different perspectives—the "transcendental" experiences noted by Plattner—to the viewers and consumers of their art.

Portal artists also do their work with the expectation that it will be sold. Decisions about the types of pieces to make and in some cases size and design are made with consideration for the marketability of the work. By one of the accepted definitions of art, the work sold under the portal is thus "commercial" (Becker 1982:291–96) or "business" art (Plattner 1996:78). Under this hierarchical model, the recognition of market forces in production relegates the work to a status somewhere below that of pure Art. Besides the obvious elitism that exists in this assertion—and certainly the fine art world is built on the elevation of a very limited number of exceptional individuals to the status of artist—the idea that pure Art is produced by artists removed from the economics of art is largely fantasy.

In recent decades the inflationary markets of the fine art worlds have made the close association between art and money very clear (Marcus and Myers 1995:21). Artists make their living producing and distributing the special commodity identified as art (Parezo 1990:563). Reputations are made, groceries are bought, and houses and cars are financed through participation in the fine art world. Removal of the production of art from its marketing is relative. With very few exceptions, "fine artists" are not different from "commercial artists" in absolute terms but by degrees of apparent separation from economic considerations and marketing forces. Even among artists who produce "Art" there is a paradoxical relationship to the art market. While "fine artists" are not supposed to be economizing individuals, most would like to be able to fully support themselves through their work (Plattner 1996:12). In reality, however, few are able to do so. As I argue, the thought and sentiment that goes into artistic production is not profaned by the fact that the work is produced for a consumer public. The Portal artists are acutely aware of the economics of art, and many use that necessity to strengthen their artistic production.

James Faks, Blackfoot, Onondaga-Oneida, Maya, Apache

I'm a contemporary artist, but I also am a warrior and I see that in this time and day and age the way that we can be warriors is with our art and our music and everything we say. And that's a good thing, it's got to be mounted in a more positive direction in order for people to actually listen to us . . .

{SL: And how is your art a political statement?}

Well, mostly in the way that I do it and the way that I feel comfortable doing it. And the fact that I can remain self-employed in this society of high dollars—high-dollar rent and whatnot—I can remain self-employed and still do the things I want, and that to me is a statement. I mean this is what I want to do and so I'm going to do it. But do it well.

Even so, it is often not easy to support oneself in Santa Fe. Art is a luxury market that is subject to significant fluctuations in response to trends in the wider world economy. Selling art in Santa Fe is further affected by fluctuations in tourism. Thus there are significant seasonal variations in the market; summer is high season in Santa Fe, while winter brings far fewer visitors. The popularity of Santa Fe as a tourist destination fluctuates from year to year as well. The tourist revenue coming into Santa Fe has dropped considerably from the 1980s and early 1990s when it was one of *the* places to be among wealthy travelers. Portal vendors maintain an upbeat, sometimes tongue-in-cheek outlook on the realities of life as an artist.

Kenneth T. White II, Dineh (Navajo)

My goal was to be a full-time artist. I started out as a weekend artist, I could only do it on weekends, and slowly progressed to become a part-time artist. And by having a goal to be a full-time artist, I didn't want to label myself as a starving artist, so I did a lot of kitchen work. I did mainly prep-work for Spanish cuisine or Mexican food. Everything was prep so it wasn't all that hard, so I had access to food. I didn't want to be a starving artist, so I had access to food. That was my part-time job.

Much like the artificial separation of art and economics, the idea that aesthetic production cannot be fine art if it is "functional" is seated in artistic elitism. While some of the work marketed under the portal fits the criterion of "true art," as it is "nonfunctional"—that is, with no practical use beyond aesthetic appreciation (in particular, sculpture, two-dimensional graphic arts,[2] and most pottery)—the majority of work sold under the portal is jewelry that is meant to be worn. Though some collectors may not value this sort of work as highly as paintings (see Plattner 1996:207–8), I do not think that the functionality of a piece changes the aesthetic efforts involved in the production of that piece. In other words, jewelry can be Art.

A second major factor to address in a consideration of Native American art is the figuration of aesthetic production as Art as opposed to ethnographic specimen, souvenir, or "tourist art." In the southwestern United States, since the early twentieth century a body of white patron-activists has worked steadfastly to promote Native American aesthetic production to the category "Art." As discussed in chapter 2, a major goal of the Museum of New Mexico and the School of American Research in sponsoring the Indian Fairs of the 1920s was to encourage Native artists to produce "good" art as opposed to inferior curios and to encourage consumers to favor the former over the latter.

These efforts were continued by the New Mexico Association on Indian Affairs and related organizations. Perhaps the best example of the early efforts is the Exposition of Indian Tribal Arts, which opened in Manhattan in 1931 with the goal of presenting "Indian art as art, not ethnology" (exposition brochure, quoted in Mullin 1995:166). The show was organized by John Sloan and Amelia Elizabeth White and others who were also actively involved in the efforts of the NMAIA. The Southwestern Association for Indian Arts has continued these efforts to promote Native American art as Art. This is especially clear in the recent addition of a "Masters of Indian Market" show, separate from the larger Indian Market and meant to highlight the work of a small number of "master" artists.[3]

Still, Native American art continues to be categorized separately from other fine art traditions; it continues to be identified as an ethnic art. The vast majority of Native American artists are not afforded the same treatment as are other artists. Promotional material provided over the Internet for the second Indian Art Northwest show in Portland, Oregon, in 1999 advertised a preview for the show to give "the public its first opportunity to meet the artists and see the best of the best works of art."[4] Such previews are commonplace in Native American art shows, and while they might bear a superficial resemblance to gallery openings in the fine art world, there is a difference in the treatment of both the artists and the works. This is most evident in the promotional language used: one would never advertise displaying "the best of the best" of an Artist's work at an opening, as this would suggest that lesser work would be available later. Likewise, though demonstrations of artistic production are commonplace at Native American art shows, Artists are rarely asked to demonstrate their techniques to the public in an effort to draw visitors to a show.

Many Native American artists work in media that are generally accepted as "traditional." In the Southwest this includes such forms as pottery, stone and silver jewelry, and sandpainting. These media, because of their affinity with "craft" traditions, are often categorized by critics and collectors in an inferior position to Art, labeled as "decorative" or "minor arts" (Becker 1982:277). Even when elevated to the status of Art through showings in galleries and fine art museums, such work has not commanded the same prices as painting, sculpture, or other "nonfunctional" art (Plattner 1996:208). This explains in part the differential treatment of Indian artists in galleries and the nature of Native American art shows; demonstrations are popular because cultural tourists and other consumers are interested in seeing Native American artists working with "traditional" materials. Part of the value attributed to ethnic and indigenous arts comes from the association of the pieces with the "authentic" producers. The emphasis on public demonstration of techniques that is so widespread in the Native American art market is a product of this valuation: ethnic tourists want to see how objects of indigenous art are made by indigenous people because the experience adds to the consumers' stories about the pieces they buy, making the pieces that much more meaningful for them.[5] In the Portal Program, such demonstrations are limited. The space of the portal itself is set aside for sales, with rules allowing "only simple adjustments or repairs to items already made" (Rule 2-G; see Appendix). During the summer months, admission to the museum is free on Friday evenings, and occasionally vendors demonstrate their work in the Palace patio at this time. Few participants have shown an interest in demonstrating their work; the time and effort involved in dismantling and transporting equipment to the museum, setting it up to demonstrate for a few hours, then repeating the process to get everything back home tends to restrict vendors' enthusiasm. When vendors do demonstrate their work, interest among tourists is often very strong, and it can prove a valuable marketing strategy. One Friday I observed a tourist couple spend the entire afternoon watching a potter work. At the end of the evening they purchased several of his pieces.

However, this typification of Indian art hinders artists in their attempts to enter the realm of Art. Those who work within the canon of historically developed traditional Indian art find themselves marginalized in the fine art world or labeled as folk or primitive artists (Wade 1985:188). At the same time, Native American artists who attempt to work outside of traditional genres have been excluded from juried shows of Native American art because their work "didn't look Indian" (Ben Nighthorse Campbell, quoted in U.S. House 1992:54). The Yankton Sioux painter Oscar Howe experienced this sort of discrimination as early as 1958 when one of his abstract works was rejected by the Philbrook Annual Exhibition (Berlo and Phillips 1998:221). Howe's forceful protest caused officials at the Philbrook Museum to reconsider their policies and provide more support for innovative work, but discrimination against "nontraditional" art continues. Artists are also constrained from using new materials or techniques such as the pottery wheel because the resulting pieces might be considered inauthentic (Evans-Pritchard 1987:294).

There is considerable discussion among Native people about what Art is and whether Native peoples' aesthetic production can be understood in terms of Western conceptions of art at all. There is a truism that in most Indian languages "there is no word for art." Advocates of this position suggest that aesthetic production is such a central aspect of indigenous cultural traditions that the Western category of Art as something separate from and privileged over categories of everyday action and production is meaningless to Indian people. It is true that among many Native American cultural groups, art is an integrative cultural category. Rather than create the hierarchies of aesthetic production that are central to valuation in Western artistic traditions, all aesthetic production is seen as valuable and equally valid. Rina Swentzell, writing about her experiences growing up in Santa Clara Pueblo, articulates this point of view:

The Tewa Pueblo way accepts the intertwining of life activities. Humans, plants, and all things flow in the Po-wa-ha or, literally, the breath of life. That way is inclusive. Every person is recognized as partaking in the creative force and therefore has creative potential. Every child, every person, can make pottery—can coil, can polish, can fire. That is the way. The creative force, and therefore the world, is nondiscriminating—it does not choose only a few people to be geniuses. It embraces all who desire to participate.... Therefore, that special activity of being an artist in the outside world is seen as not special but as a necessary part of traditional Pueblo life. (Swentzell 1987:4)

Of course, different cultural perspectives complicate the picture. Illustrative of this complexity are the results of a session at the 1999 Native American Art Studies Association meeting entitled "Yes, There Is a Word for It: Educating the Educators about American Indian Art and Culture."[6] George H. J. Abrams, the session organizer, started the discussion by pointing out that the idea of there being just one word for art is Eurocentric and extremely problematic in cross-cultural analysis of aesthetic production. Later, Beatrice Medicine (1999) presented a paper in which she indicated that she was troubled by the idea that there is no concept of art in Indian languages. She pointed to a lack of evaluation of the complexity of Indian languages and to the singular model of the American Indian imposed by the dominant society as sources for the truism about the word "art" in Native languages.

A paper by JoAllyn Archambault (1999) addressed the issue among modern Plains Indian people. When considering traditional aesthetic forms, Plains people rarely call the work "ART" but never call it craft. In competitions, "fine art" is distinguished from "traditional arts," but the two categories are awarded equal prizes and both are called "ART." Archambault's paper also pointed out that modern Native peoples are aware of the economic benefits that come with the production of "ART" and that Native people, like other artists, are adept at socially positioning themselves as artists.

Gloria Cranmer Webster, discussant for the session, addressed the situation in her home community, Alert Bay, British Columbia. In Kwakiutl, there are no words for the Western concept of art or artist. Rather, a person who might be called an artist in English is identified as someone who does something very well. While there are some woodcarvers, printmakers, and workers in other media from Alert Bay who call themselves artists, most of these are people who produce work to sell outside the community. Her eldest brother, who is a carver, says that he is not an artist, he is a woodcarver.

Making Art Under the Portal

Many of these same issues are played out under the portal. Throughout this work I have referred to the people who produce pieces to be sold under the portal as "artists" because I feel that this is the appropriate term to identify what most of the participants do. Among the vendors, a variety of terms are used, though many participants rarely address the issue of categorizing the work they do or categorizing themselves as specialized producers. Some participants call themselves artists and the work that they produce art. Most have thought deeply and critically about the work of aesthetic production that they do. Others call themselves and other vendors "artist-craftsmen," "artisans," or "craftspeople" when pressed to categorize themselves, but this identification does not necessarily mean that these participants think of themselves as producing something less than art.

The vast majority of Portal Program participants put a great deal of thought and care into the work they produce. Technical abilities vary greatly among Portal vendors, as would be expected in a program whose membership is not limited based on evaluations of skill or creativity. The program's inclusiveness is one of its strengths. The Tewa (and more generally Native American) belief that everyone can produce art is at work here, as is the historical and economic reality that Native people can earn income through the production of art. In chapter 4 I discussed how the interaction with consumers under the portal helps to support Portal artists as artists. Because they are able to interact with consumers who appreciate their work, Portal artists are not alienated from their aesthetic production in the way that wholesale producers are.

Though not all Portal participants identify themselves as artists, for most the production of pieces for the market is an exercise that is personally and culturally more significant than any other employment would be. The production of art is a vocation, not just a job. This is evident in the relationship that artists have with the materials they use. Potters, for example, are required by program rules to use earth clays gathered from deposits on their reservations.[7] Most families of potters gather the clay themselves and process it by crushing, sifting, and soaking the raw clay, then mixing it with a tempering agent before it is worked. For many, the preparation of clay has social, cultural, and ritual elements in addition to the physical labor of the work.

Jewelers purchase the metals and stones they use in their work, but this does not diminish the importance of the materials to them. For many Native American artists, turquoise is a sacred stone. Many Santo Domingo people produce turquoise jewelry to be sold outside the village. Even though the stone becomes a commodity, there are culturally prescribed ways in which the stone should be handled and spiritual and physical consequences for those who act improperly.

The respect for the work of making art extends to the acts of production as well. The production of pieces is something that you should only do when you are in the right frame of mind.

Dorothy Chavez, Santo Domingo

I have this good feeling when I'm working, and I only work when I'm feeling good, when I'm happy. In our ways they tell us when you're working, enjoy what you're doing and make sure you have all your feelings in your work, because that's the only way that tourists will come and . . . they have feelings too. The feelings come out between your type of work and the customer. They know that the work was made in a happy way, in a happy mood. So we were taught to always make our work in a happy mood. So when my husband's working he's always singing away. He's always singing away his Indian songs and all that so I know that he's always happy when he's making, and I do try to do the same. And I always teach my children, talk about nice things when you're working. Also, when you're stringing or making earrings and stuff we sit around the table and do it together. We talk about nicer things so that all your feelings go towards what you're working at. So they always have to be good feelings otherwise [pause] who knows, you might keep your necklace for forever and ever.

{SL: That's what I was going to say, have you ever made one in a bad mood and it didn't sell?}

I won't. I teach my children, if you're in a bad mood but if I need something real bad and if I'm trying to make you do something that you don't want to do, please don't do what I tell. And I tell myself that too. I tell myself I'm not going to work because I don't feel good. So I always do something else in between that time until I'm feeling better.

Alfonso Tenorio, Santo Domingo

Oh, you have to enjoy what you do. I learned if you don't enjoy it, you're putting negative stuff towards your pieces. You've got to put positive stuff towards your pieces in order to feel good about what you're selling. That's the way I look at it.

{SL: And so if you don't, a lot of the folks that we've talked to that's what they'll say, if they don't feel good they don't work.}

Yeah, same thing with me. You know, I'll do other stuff like clean the yard, feed my horse, feed my dogs, pay attention to my dogs, clean them, groom them. And then after that I'll feel better. But I always work when I have a positive attitude towards my pieces.

This respect for the act of creating and for the products of the act extends into the marketing of the pieces. As Mary Eustace noted (see chap. 4), in negotiating prices with customers you have to maintain respect not just for the artist but for the piece as well. One should not sell a piece for a price that compromises the object's value as a piece of art.

Robert Naranjo, Nambe and Santa Clara

[P.] and T. got upset at me one day. I had car insurance due that day, and I had completely forgot about it and went and bought

something and I was short so I went down there to the Portal
and said, "Do any of you guys want to buy some pottery?"
They said, "Why?" I said, "Because I'm going to put them at
half-price until I make just enough to pay that car insurance."
Boy, I tell you what, they went like crazy! "Wasn't this so and so
yesterday?" "Yes it was." "Well, I'm going to take it."

{KH: You're doing like those stores on the plaza that have
the 50 percent off sales.}

Yeah. T. goes, "Robert, don't you ever sell that like that.
Your pottery is too nice to be selling it at half price." I said,
"Well, are you going to give me the money to pay?" "No, but
don't do that again!"

Even setting up one's cloth in the morning is an act of respect
for the pieces. Though critics might argue that the status of the art-
works is diminished because they are displayed on a sidewalk, this
reflects a lack of understanding.[8] Many vendors take a considerable
amount of time—as much as half an hour or more—to set up their
cloths. Pieces are laid out with care and respect, to give potential customers the best opportunity to see the pieces but also because the
pieces are important in themselves and have meaning to the vendors.

Portal artists invest a considerable amount of themselves in the
work they do, not just in terms of time and physical effort but also
in terms of intellectual and creative energy. Putting the sort of concentrated effort into each piece that is necessary in the creation of
art can be difficult, particularly when one must continually work to
maintain an adequate inventory for sale. Some Portal artists liken
the process to putting a bit of themselves into each piece that is for
sale, something that they are willing to do so that they can provide
for their families (Rodger Montoya, pers. com. 1998).

Glenn Paquin, Laguna and Zuni

I think what they're buying out there [are] creations that are
created in the mind of the American Indian.... It gives you as
an artist the feeling that, well I worked hard and I did a nice
piece and I'm proud of it and somebody that's going to get it

should be proud to pay for it and cherish it. That's the way my dad used to tell us, when someone buys a bracelet from you they're not just buying silver and turquoise, they're buying part of your life because it took you maybe two hours of your life to make that item and how do you price something like that? How do you price your life, you know, two hours of your life? It's priceless. And so it's not something that we can just go out and take off the shelf and take it down to the porch and sell it.

Some Portal artists explicitly identify themselves as artists and the work that they do as art, though how they define those terms varies from person to person. For Mary Eustace (Zuni and Cochiti), a poet, painter, and jeweler, all the different things she produces are art because they have the potential to have an impact on others' lives:

I'm always looking for something that will benefit mankind, even in my poetry. My poetry is, when I speak it hits everybody, not just a certain point, person, where a person sits there and says, "What does she say?" (Laughs) They can relate and they know and they can feel, and I, that's what I think a true artist is. When you can hit home to everybody, not just a very few people.

{SL: So in all the work you do—in your drawing, your jewelry, your poetry—you do think about where it's going and the impact it'll have?}

Yeah, it's like me crying out and shouting out to everybody that it's OK, because there's a lot of victims from dysfunctional backgrounds, and they don't know the answer, and I'm here to say, you know, everything's OK. Because we all grow up and sometimes we just don't let go, and that's where I think I come in. And, even with the ear twirl, the whole objective was to invent something that we didn't lose, because women would always walk by and say, "I always lose my earring. The back falls off and the French hook slides out." So I thought, "Well . . ." And I tell people, the women, "I bet you I haven't found one woman that hasn't lost one side of their earring," and they all laugh and they say, "that's true." And then with the poetry the same thing: I'll read my poetry or they'll

read my poems in the books and they [say], "Wow,
I can understand."
{SL: And it's something that they won't lose too.}
Exactly.

An important part of doing art is sharing it with others.

Kenneth T. White II, Dineh (Navajo)

I just want to express what I have to give, I just want to share
that. I [don't] have a message to give [to] the world, through
my art, [I just want to share with people]. People see that,
they get emotional sometimes. They see the passion and love
that I put into my work. People feel that, so in turn, you
know what, it's really honoring. I'm really honored to be allowed
to give that to somebody. And I just want to be focused and
keep myself grounded.

Portal artists draw on their life experiences and share those experiences with their customers. Ranging from the use of traditional
materials, techniques, and design elements to the development of
abstract forms, art produced for the Portal has great significance to
the artists who make it.

Jennifer Juan, Diné (Navajo)

The root of my jewelry is mostly being connected to my culture,
the tradition. The overlay style which I want to tell people [about],
because that's how I was raised, just herding sheep, and ... I have
a lot of respect for my mom, I have a lot of respect for women.
Because I've been through a lot myself, as I was growing up. So
I depict a lot of women in my jewelry. And my rug designs are
connected to just growing up, you know, growing up and learning
how to do each loom, or how to do repairs, and then this one here
represents the way I grew up, in a hogan. And I represent women
because I think I've had a lot of bad experiences in my life, so
I think women are a big strength to me.... And then this one,
this one here I think it just means stuff to me, but mostly I think

I look at the town that I'm in, Santa Fe, so I call it my Southwest designs. But it still has meaning to me, like this one represents all living, green things, plants, flowers. And then the hummingbird represents all the people that have wings, you know the birds and the eagles; and this is another one of my rug designs right here; and then the bear, it represents strength, and the arrowhead represents direction. The Navajo, they use a lot of arrowheads for protection and it's like a vision or seeing that they use for the arrowheads. And the Kokopelli, Kokopelli doesn't really have any meaning to me.

{SL: It means Santa Fe. (Laughter)}

From what I know he was a philanderer. (Laughter) But the turtle, the turtle it represents my sons S. and T. because they're from the Lakota tribe, their mom beaded this turtle pouch for us where we keep their umbilical cord, so that's what that means to me and also represents so that it'll make them have long life, and so that's where they keep their umbilical cord. And this one here is the person that owns this bracelet and the people that they migrate with, you know people that they meet from all over, all races of people. And this one represents the four directions. And the lizard, the lizard I usually, some of the designs that I use I usually connect them with their personality, like the lizard is quick and they're shrewd. That's how I represent my designs is the way that the animal is, you know, their personality. And then this one represents the thunder and lightning and the snow and the clouds. This bracelet has a lot of meaning in it, and I think it's really neat.

Alfonso Tenorio, Santo Domingo

I've had this design for a while, ever since I was a little kid.... This one came out of when we used to go hummingbird hunting, and we used to take hangers, make them into a "U," hammer the ends out—sometimes you hammer them out too thin—and you pull 'em out, leaves this little design in here. I never thought of that, that this would make me a living, until I started getting older and started saying, "Hey, I should make a bracelet out of that." So that's where this design came from. // What we did long time ago is we used just a coat hanger, long time ago coat hangers were thicker, and we just made slingshots out of the coat hanger, tie little rubber bands end to end together and we used those little hangers that we shaped into "U"s and hammered the ends on and then just used it as a slingshot.

But the Portal is not a venue that allows artists total freedom to express themselves as artists. The world of fine arts is one that idealizes the artist's freedom from almost all forms of outside control or interference (Becker 1982:276). While I was writing this chapter, a minor scandal rippled through the art community when New York City mayor Rudolf Giuliani attempted to revoke funding to the Brooklyn Museum of Art in response to the museum's exhibition of a piece by artist Chris Ofili depicting an image of the Virgin Mary that included a shellacked piece of elephant dung as part of the composition. Giuliani was eventually ordered to restore funding to the museum (Barstow 1999). This was a victory for the First Amendment, the museum, and for "Art," but the turmoil that the issue caused illuminates the complex interaction that takes place among artists, cultural institutions, patrons, and other sources of funding. Under the portal, artists must constantly negotiate their art with their customers, with other vendors, with the expectations of their home communities, and with themselves.

Anthropologists studying Native American arts and crafts in the Southwest have long recognized the impact of market participation on Native American arts. The white activists who sponsored the first Indian Fairs (see chap. 2; see also Bernstein 1993a, 1993b; Dauber 1993; Mullin 1993, 1995) and other Indian arts and crafts competitions and shows in the 1920s and 1930s were appalled by what they saw as abysmal work being produced for the curio trade. One of the key purposes of these shows was to promote appreciation for "good" art among consumers and an interest in producing that "good" work among Native American artists. The aversion to tourist curios by academics continued through the twentieth century. In writing about "Tesuque-modelled hatchets decorated in poster paints," Clara Lee Tanner (1960:143) opined, "It is amazing what favor the Tesuque wares have found in the eyes of White men."

Though they wouldn't dream of producing such work today, some vendors look back fondly at the pieces their families used to make. They remember helping their parents collect discarded automobile battery housings to substitute for jet and cutting up colored plastic colanders to use as "stones" in thunderbird necklaces and other mid-twentieth-century tourist curios. They do not disparage the work but remember it with amusement. It was a way to make a living in difficult economic times when natural stones and other materials were unavailable.

The vast majority of Native American art is produced for sale, and thus market demands and fluctuations are taken into account by artists. Maria Martinez, one of the most celebrated Pueblo potters, told Edwin L. Wade that she and her husband, Julian, began to make wedding vases and pottery candlesticks when they realized "that's what the tourists wanted" (Wade 1976:89). Portal participants likewise produce work that they know will meet the demands of their customers.

Juanita Atencio, Santo Domingo

Most of the necklaces that we have now are all modern and contemporary. . . . Like I know how to make jaclas, but I don't. Even for my own use I only have a couple of them that I made at home and I work with turquoise all the time. But I don't know why I don't find the time to do the jaclas any more. So we've gotten to the point where we more or less make what the tourists like.

Because many of the Portal visitors are looking for less expensive pieces, artists are constrained in the work that they do. Many artists will produce a few bigger, more expensive pieces each year but also make larger numbers of smaller, "bread and butter" items that will move readily.[10]

Marvin Slim, Diné (Navajo)

I could do sculpturing, other stuff, too, but it's just time consuming, and you make more earrings in one day than you

can on a sculpture, [and] still make the same money. All those
earrings add up to the same price as that sculpture, you can
sell the earrings faster than you sell the sculpture. (Laughs)
So you'll do just about anything, you know. But jewelry's my
main thing because it puts bread on the table for me.

Because the artistic production of Portal participants is market
driven, issues of originality sometimes arise, and designs that are successful are sometimes adopted by other vendors. Unlike other shows
that occur only once a year over a weekend, the Portal is open every
day and artists are exposed to each other's work constantly. This fact
helps to make the Portal a bellwether of the Native American arts
and crafts market. The intensive nature of the Portal also leads to a
steady stream of innovation and stylistic change.

Glenn Paquin, Zuni and Laguna

Ideas will develop, and we've gone through various stages. I
remember when everybody had watch bands, now you don't see
them anymore. You've got a lot of bookmarks; you never saw
bookmarks before. So that's what I mean about the dynamics
of this whole program. You've got all these artisans out there,
and it's good that we have a lot because every one of them has
their own contribution. At one point it might not seem like
much, but, what's her name, G., has designed these rings. I
don't know if you've seen the rings, but you look at the design
and it's just a wire that is twisted, and everybody says, "Well,
anybody can do that." But the way she weaves the wire is what
makes her designs unique. And people come and they all stand
around and admire them. When you go down the porch you
don't see any designs like that. And that's the uniqueness about
having all these artists out there, is that they develop new designs,
then that design fades and somebody else comes up with a new
design, so you've got this dynamic organization out there continually creating new jewelry. //

  E.P. came up with this design. He went to the University
of New Mexico [where he took a jewelry class], and his teacher

told him right out, "I don't want anything Indian. I want you
to create something that's totally different from what would be
identified [as Indian]." So he designed a simple bracelet, wrapped
with gold around the center, and one offset, and turned his design
in for his class project . . . He started making his new design and
selling them on the portal, and now everybody's making them.
They are doing them with offset, full-wrap, and now they're
adding their own interpretations. So, this process adds to the
whole design pot. That's what's going on out there.

Artists on the Portal handle imitation in a number of ways. Some
are deeply concerned that their designs might be copied, and a few
have applied for and received design patents for unique forms they
have created. Others see imitation as flattery and use the pressure of
it to drive themselves toward further innovation.

Marvin Slim, Diné (Navajo)

{KH: As you've developed as an artist, have you branched out into
new styles and using new materials and things like that?}

Yeah, [I] try to get my own separate, unique style. I base my
styles around my family, just try to be different from them. And
on the porch, too, [there's] so much jewelry out there you've got
to keep something totally different. And then people start copying
you and so you've got to go with something else again, something
new all the time. You get your old customers, too, they always
come back. They want to see something new, all the time, [they are]
always asking, "What are you doing now, Marvin? What's new?"

Alfonso Tenorio, Santo Domingo

When I learned my work, one thing my grandfather taught is
you never copy anybody. You have your own ideas in your head.
Whatever comes to you, you just go with the flow. //

{SL: I know sometimes you'll come up with a really beautiful
design, and then people will see it selling, and they'll think, Oh,
I want to try that design, too. How do you think about that, how
do you cope with that?}

The way I think about it is I think it's a good feeling, because I think you must be doing good in order for somebody to copy your work. But they still come back to the people who really make [it]. A lot of the people out there, [who] are sitting out there, you can tell each cloth has their own special way of doing their stuff, so you can see the unique patterns where one person [is] doing that pattern. Like me, I've been doing just these four patterns that I have, and I've been sticking to this pattern, I don't go out and just steal other designs from everybody else.

Glenn Paquin, Zuni and Laguna

It's natural for creative people to be sort of self-centered anyway. Some have this sort of "the world revolves around us" thing. And that's why we're creative, because we think that everything we do is unique, and in a way it is, because we have that ability to create things. And so when you have this creativity, you're centered on what you do. When you go to do the sales it carries over, and you say, "God, I don't want anybody copying my design." And that's why you hear a lot of them complaining about their work being copied. I've done it in the past, when I've developed something, and I felt like I didn't want anybody to copy it, but they copy it anyway. // And it can be frustrating. However, I enjoy it now, because I'm at a point in my life where I don't get upset with anyone doing any of the designs I've created. I feel the more they copy, the more power to them. [Unknowingly, they are carrying on the legacy of the Portal.]

More problematic than the intentional or unintentional sharing of ideas and designs between artists under the portal is the appropriation by non-Natives of designs and even whole pieces for mass reproduction. Manufacturers sometimes buy pieces that are then copied overseas, often mechanically using synthetic materials, and imported to the United States where they can be sold at prices significantly lower than those of originals (see Mobley-Martinez 1997).

Glenn Paquin, Zuni and Laguna

The problem comes with wax casting. That's something that anybody can do.... With just a few lessons you can go in and replicate something in real detail. It's just like prints. You can do an original, but it's hard to do a lot of originals. So you can go in and get it printed and you can make some money off the prints.... It's primarily because of wax casting of Zuni inlay channel work that hurt the Zuni artisans. It doesn't look the same, when you get done with it, but it's still inlay work. It's sold off as being Zuni channel inlay at a fraction of the cost, but it's actually wax-cast silver. And manufacturers just send these castings overseas to where they have stones [set] in, in Hong Kong or wherever it is that they do that work. And the problem that my brother was talking about a long time ago, and my dad, was that these people can take my bracelet, take the stones out, and run a cast, a duplicate of it, cast it, and then start making bracelets like mine. That's what they've done, there's a lot of people that make the original designs that my dad and S. do.

Artists working in the environment of the Portal are able to use each other's ideas to further their own and each other's work. Borrowing among artists becomes an important part of the process of artistic innovation. To the contrary, the mass-production of copies only hurts artists' ability to market original work.

The dynamics of artistic creation and expression under the portal are also affected by the intercultural transmission of knowledge between vendors and consumers and by the intercultural interaction among vendors from different Native communities. A significant portion of the allure of the Southwest generally and Santa Fe specifically is built on a mystification of Native American cultures. Over the course of the past century, non-Indian people have come to the Southwest in droves, searching for the spirituality, the unity with the natural world, the exotic mysticism that visitors perceive in the lives of the Native people of the region. Around 1940 Ernest Thompson Seton (n.d.:14), artist-naturalist and Indian lore enthusiast, proclaimed the Southwest "the last stronghold of the Redman's faith," and "a chosen Promised

Land" where he could celebrate that faith. Some came before Seton, and many have come after, seeking the spirituality that they perceive is missing in contemporary Western society.

For the Indian people who are the subject of this interest, this romanticism can be problematic. As a direct response to Spanish religious oppression and persecution, for centuries the eastern Pueblo villages have maintained strict privacy of their traditional religious beliefs. Since the late nineteenth century increasing numbers of (mostly Anglo) tourists, many of whom have not respected Puebloan practices, have compelled the Pueblos to prohibit non-Indian visitors from observing many ceremonies. Outsiders play no part in, nor are they allowed to witness, the most important events, and most Pueblo people do not talk to outsiders about such matters or about traditional spirituality.

Yet Native Americans recognize that non-Indian people come to the Southwest in search of these things and that this is one of the forces that brings tourists to the Portal to meet Indian artists. Many Portal participants recognize real value in their opportunity to interact with and teach non-Indian people.

Sarah Martinez,* Santo Domingo

{SL: What do you think tourists are looking for when they come here?}

I know some come to look at the jewelry and to find something really, I mean kind of like a souvenir of New Mexico. And I think that they come here to look at the artists, to meet the artists and to know a little bit about their background and maybe even to make friends with somebody, because I've made a lot of friends out here . . . . I think they come here to learn about culture, to buy some souvenirs and learn about the people that make it, that's what I think.

Mary Eustace, Zuni and Cochiti

The good part is that they get to meet us, they get to see our work, and we talk. [We tell them] where we come from and we tell them of our traditions and, oh, I mean it's like another human race looking for that natural, nature, the people that are so close, closer they think in spirituality to God. Which everybody looks for.

{SL: You think that's one of the things the tourists are looking for?}

Oh yeah, because they pick up a piece, and if it's a fetish bear or a turtle or any type of symbolism we stamp on it they always say, "What does this mean?" And sometimes it's just the stamp, but in all reality that stamp is made for something. Let's say if it's a rain cloud, some of the Indian people here, too, are naive to what it actually means, and they'll just stamp it and just say it's a rain cloud or it's this. But each symbol is a symbolism to what we believe in, we carry within ourselves. So when they ask us about pieces, and if you really did sit there and you really stamped out a certain piece and this is the kiva steps, this is the sun, the Zuni sun face and the Zuni sun face is for this reason....

They really appreciate it, it's really nice that you, yourself as a person out there selling, that you're giving knowledge, you're feeding other people. Wisdom, stuff that they take back. Who knows, they might need it, you know.

While sharing knowledge can help those in need, there is a limit to what should be shared. Because of the very public nature of participants' lives on the Portal, they have to walk a thin line between sharing knowledge and giving away too much.

Mary Eustace, Zuni and Cochiti

You see the younger ones coming in and listen to them talk, and give away secrets that they shouldn't give away. In fact I hate to say this but there's a lot of people out there that—it's like you sell your soul, you sell your people, your culture. You're not supposed to put a price on stuff like that. And that is wrong. And they should respect not just the older vendors, they should respect the piece. Just like when you go to a pueblo they say no picture-taking when they're having certain dances, because it's not [allowed]. It's funny how we commercialize everything, we have to survive, you know, but you do it to a point. You don't just go out there and—and they say everything has a price—and some people sit there and try to sell their soul and that's wrong, it's real wrong for them to do that.

Jennifer Juan, Diné (Navajo)

That's a really hard issue, because I think we should hold on to something, at least, that we cannot totally expose ourselves [and] our tradition for other people. I think we should hold on to something, because there's a lot of things that are very traditional to me that I don't use in my work, otherwise I'd be exposing everything.

Marvin Slim, Diné (Navajo)

You know, when that point came out to where people were saying, back in the seventies, sixties, it was a disgrace to be Native. Nobody would say come out and say "I have Indian blood in me" or something like that. Now, everybody says, "Oh, I have Comanche in me." Nowadays everybody's like they want to be Native or something. People ask me, "Where can I go to see a medicine man?" or something. And you know, you don't tell them those things.

The situation becomes even more complicated when different cultural perspectives must be taken into account. Among the eastern Pueblos especially there are definite limits on the kinds of images that should be publicly displayed or sold. In particular, there is an extremely strong aversion to the display of images of spiritual beings and the masked dancers that represent those beings. Just seeing such images causes great distress to some vendors, particularly traditional Puebloan women. A prime example is Kachina dolls. Though Kachina dolls are widely produced by Hopi carvers and others[11] and are sold through many market outlets, including many shops in Santa Fe, they are not found under the portal because of the fierce resistance to their sale by vendors from the eastern Pueblos. On several occasions potential vendors have proposed selling Kachinas but have ultimately withdrawn the idea out of respect for the wishes of other vendors.

As a matter of policy, the museum places no limitations on the subject matter of art sold under the portal. Though some vendors would like to prohibit the depiction of religious images, as a state institution the museum is obligated to adhere to the legal mandates against state regulation of religious expression. This is difficult for some of the Pueblo people whose village officials and religious leaders have full authority to prohibit such displays. This is a matter in which both the museum and the vendors must tread lightly. The museum cannot, constitutionally, proscribe religious expression. At the same time, many of the Pueblo people cannot allow, for very important cultural and religious reasons, the exhibition of some images. Ultimately when such situations arise, the vendors and museum administration must work together to negotiate resolutions that adequately meet the needs of all concerned parties. In the end there is always some measure of restriction of artistic expression, but it is usually a restriction that is agreed upon by the artist and the offended vendors.

In 1997 Jennifer Juan created a silver belt composed of conchos made in the forms of masked dancers from a number of tribal groups, including both Navajo and Puebloan dancers. Aesthetically, the belt was remarkable. Each dancer was depicted in careful detail, with the movements of the dances captured in the forms of the dancers and their clothing. Because of the subject matter of the belt, however, when Jennifer placed the piece on her cloth a number of other vendors were immediately greatly upset by it.

Jennifer Juan, Diné (Navajo)
Well, [the belt] represented different tribes, my tribe and then the [others]; it was an overlay piece with different dancers. I think I stirred up some controversy with that belt, with the different dancers. Being able to do other tribes' dancers, you know. The reason why I did that was because I've been to a lot of art shows and all of the dancers that were represented there just stayed in my mind, just the way they were dancing, and I put a lot of

movement in it and I felt that it was OK with me, and as an
artist I really wanted to do it, and if they were able to dance in
front of a lot of people that I could do it, you know. So that was
my thinking when I did that belt.

The artist and the offended vendors discussed the issue, and as
is the norm, everyone was given the opportunity to express their concerns. Jennifer agreed to remove the belt from her cloth. Later that
summer she submitted the belt for judging at the SWAIA Indian
Market. She received a first place ribbon and the next year was
awarded the Smoyer Fellowship, a grant given to promising artists
by SWAIA.

Jennifer Juan, Diné (Navajo)

I do have a lot of respect for my elders, whatever tribe they are,
and yet at that time when I had my piece out there I was offended,
too, because I was an artist. And the fact [is] that it was really hard
for me, but in a way I do understand. It's a difficult question, it's
about religion. But I can say that just through what I've seen and
what I know is that things are changing, there's so many things
that are changing and it's hard to just continually grasp on to
what you know.

The production of art is a social process. To be an artist under
the portal is to be a member of a social group. As a result, artistic production involves negotiation between artists and consumers, among
artists with differing cultural expectations and needs, and within
artists themselves as they find ways to express themselves as artists
and Native people.

EIGHT

Conclusion

The Challenges of a Tourism Economy

Under the Portal Winter Enters
As she walks toward the portal
she shuffles the leaves that fall beneath her feet.
With hands in pockets
the chill of the wind is a reminder
that summer has passed.
As the geese flock toward the south
for the winter
and the robin nestles in its bed
so goes the tourist
her only bread and butter
she dreads.
She reaches the portal
where other venders are there.
Reluctantly, she lays her cloth down,
upon it, will sit her wares.
For sales will be slow or none at all.
There she will sit on these bricks
her back against the wall.
She recognizes the look on her fellow vendors'

faces of winters past.
That old familiar look of forlorn.
She questions, "How long will this last?"
She reminisces of one summer day,
for all were carefree and warm.
When the tourist was plenty
like corn ready for harvest,
satisfaction to her palate.
What really caught her eye then
was this ant that crossed her path.
this tiny work ant with food on its back.
Now as the cold wind nips at her nose,
and her fingers become numb.
The thought of not taking heed.
Thus now, she must succumb.

         —Mary Eustace, 1994[1]

To participate in a tourism economy can be to live like the frivolous grasshopper in the fable rather than the ant "with food on its back." The peak tourist season can be very good, but the off-season can also be very bad. Portal Program participants, and much of the population of Santa Fe, are subject to the whims of national and international tourism.

Program participants and downtown merchants agree that Santa Fe is not the lucrative place it once was. During the most recent peak in the 1980s, when Santa Fe was *the* place to be, program participants remember being able to sell as much on a good day as they are able sometimes to sell in a week now. Santa Fe continues to be a prime tourism locale and hotel occupancy rates have continued to climb, but visitors in the late 1990s came for shorter periods and spent less money than before. More recent visitors also seem to be more interested in cultural and historical experiences and less interested in the conspicuous consumption that marked the previous generation of wealthy Santa Fe tourists.

Santa Fe is also a seasonal tourist destination. On peak summer days, as many as five thousand visitors come to shop under the portal. During the winter, especially when an absence of snow in New Mexico sends skiers to Colorado or elsewhere, only a few hundred tourists may visit the portal, and at intervals throughout the day there will be more vendors than customers. During the winter, times can be hard. Vendors must save during the summer, or travel to shows held in Arizona, California, and elsewhere during Santa Fe's slow season to make ends meet.

When temperatures peak in the twenties and clouds block the solar heating that makes the portal bearable in the cold, it is easy to doubt that summer will ever come again. Some vendors stay home during the cold months; others occasionally take jobs "inside" at restaurants or stores. One cold day, two Navajo ladies told me that selling under the portal was not very much different from their experiences tending their families' sheep as children: wind, rain, or snow, you are always out in the weather. When asked how the program could be improved, vendors often ask for heating for the portal. Long-range plans include the installation of a radiant heating system under the bricks.

Though participating in the Portal Program proves to be more rewarding financially for many vendors than are other jobs, it is not without difficulties. In addition to exposure to the elements, the constant need to engage in production work takes its toll as well. Silverworkers are constantly exposed to the nitric acid used to clean pieces as they are finished. All artists must engage in many hours of detailed, precise work each week. Because they make a living from the work of their hands, an injured finger or sprained wrist is equivalent to being unemployed while recuperating. Being self-employed means that no unemployment benefits or workers' compensation insurance is available when a vendor is injured or unable to work.

As noted in chapter 7, it is sometimes difficult to maintain the levels of artistic production necessary to support a family. Native American basket weavers have reported to Catherine Fowler (1999) that they are sometimes unable to support themselves producing beaded baskets full time and that they burn out from the intensity of that effort. While Portal participants enjoy the benefit of being able to sell their work at retail prices, they still must produce a lot of art each year. Maintaining the regimen of work can be physically and intellectually exhausting.[2]

Finally, being a self-employed artist provides little long-term security. A friend and occasional Portal vendor who has taken a government job remarked to me that the new job is one she will be able to retire from some day. Participation in the Portal offers no retirement plan, nor does it provide health benefits or paid vacation. The greater immediate economic returns of the Portal over other jobs is not without cost.

Continued Growth

The Portal has served as an important institution for Native American artists and their families, for tourists, and for the city of Santa Fe for most of a century. During that time, a market has evolved into a museum program, and the program has continued to evolve to meet the changing needs of both participants and visitors. Its success may be measured by the continual flow of new applicants to the program. Before the recertification of vendors in 1994 and 1995, more than nine hundred vendors were enrolled in the program. About two hundred vendors did not participate in the recertification process. However, by 1999 the number of registered participants had topped nine hundred again. In 2000 it reached one thousand. This continuing interest in the program is a testament to its success but also creates new challenges.

The space under the Palace portal is finite, and so too is the number of available sales spaces. As a result, it is not uncommon during busy periods for there to be twice as many vendors as there are spaces. On such days many vendors never have the opportunity to sell. Various proposals have been put forward to handle this shortage of spaces, ranging from decreasing space sizes to requiring all vendors to share spaces. However, no new proposal so far has gained the support of the program participants. The distribution of spaces by lottery has met the needs of the program since 1986 and will likely continue. Participants prefer the opportunity to sell on any day they choose, with the real possibility of not being able to sell on any given day, to alternatives that provide greater certainty but less flexibility.

In 1998 the committee raised the possibility of placing a moratorium on new applicants, but the museum administration determined that the program must remain open to new vendors because of the museum's status as a public institution, and most of the vendors are opposed to the exclusion of other Native American artists from the program. Active participation will ultimately be limited by the ability of vendors to get sales spaces regularly enough to support themselves and to offset the cost of days on which they do not draw a space.

Staying "Home" Under the Portal

During the time I have been involved with the program, various alternative sites have been proposed to accommodate overflow vendors. In 1996 participants set up tables in front of the Museum of Indian Arts and Culture on Camino Lejo on the outskirts of the city. This location had the advantage of drawing visitors specifically interested in Native American art, but numbers proved too low to support sales there. In 1998 the program began to work with the State Monuments division of the museum to sponsor weekend markets at Coronado State Monument at Bernalillo and at Jemez State Monument north of the village of Jemez. These events have had some success, but limited numbers of visitors limit the viability of selling at these sites as well.

The Palace portal draws many times the numbers of visitors these other sites offer, but participants' attachment to the portal is based on more than just customer traffic. The Palace and the portal have a long history, one in which many of the program's vendors have actively participated. Program participants feel a strong attachment to the portal, in addition to holding a proprietary interest in it. When we asked interviewees where they would like to see the Portal in five or ten or fifteen years, almost all expressed some form of the same sentiment: Right here.

The Portal has changed over the past century, from the location of occasional sales and shows to a daily marketplace to a museum program. The participants have changed over the years; as artists grow older, they come to Santa Fe less often, eventually staying home while their children, or others, take their place. As village and tribal economies have changed and as transportation has improved, the cultural composition of the Portal has changed. As fashions and styles change, both within and external to Native American art, so does the work that is marketed under the portal.

However, though the people who participate in the Portal Program live fully twenty-first century lives, the image of the portal painted by Pablita Velarde in 1941 remains remarkably familiar. Clothing styles have changed, and the majority of vendors sell jewelry instead of the pottery and drums pictured by Velarde (though to be sure, pottery and occasionally drums may still be found under the portal). But still, the Portal of 1941 is immediately recognizable to those who know the Portal at the beginning of the twenty-first century. This, too, is a testament to the dynamic energy of the Portal. It has evolved, all the while maintaining its integrity and purpose. The future will hold new challenges, to which the Portal is sure to respond.

Just as the end of each day under the portal marks the continuity that leads to the beginning of the next, the conclusion of this book is not an end but a beginning. With that, I finish where I began:

> As the bells of Saint Francis Cathedral chime 7:00 a.m. each day on the Santa Fe plaza, the heart of New Mexico's capital begins to come to life. The shops, galleries, and museums that occupy most of the downtown area will not open for at least two hours, but already there is a bustle of activity along the north side of the plaza. Singly and in small groups, Native American artists walk along the *portal*, or porch, that fronts the Palace of the Governors, home of the Museum of New Mexico's history museum. Each artist drops a brightly colored cloth, a foam kneeling pad, or a carpet square at a spot along the sidewalk in front of one of the sixty-four numbered spaces that line the wall of the Palace. As the minutes pass cars, trucks, and vans slowly pull up to the curb and other artists emerge and place their cloths along the portal.

Each of the artists has come to the plaza from their homes in the Pueblo villages, on the Indian reservations, or in Albuquerque or Santa Fe for the opportunity to sell the artwork they and their family members have produced as participants in the Native American Vendors Program of the Palace of the Governors.

Appendix

Guidelines, Rules, and Regulations Governing the Portal Program at the Palace of the Governors

(MNM Rule 57, Adopted 5/30/1999).

WHEREAS, the presence of Indian artists and artisans at the Palace of the Governors is an integral part of the history, tradition, and function of the Museum of New Mexico; and

WHEREAS, the Museum of New Mexico has determined that reserving the Portal of the Palace of the Governors for the display and sale of New Mexico Indian crafts would not only help preserve traditional aspects of New Mexico Indian culture but would be of educational value to the visiting public by providing the opportunity for contact with New Mexico Indian artists and artisans in a historically relevant context;

NOW, THEREFORE, BE IT RESOLVED BY THE REGENTS OF THE MUSEUM OF NEW MEXICO, that the policy of the Museum of New Mexico (the "Museum") with respect to the display and sale of New Mexican arts and crafts at the Portal of the Palace of the Governors (the "Portal") shall be as follows:

1. Location of the Portal Program:

A. The Portal Program shall be conducted in an area along the south wall of the Palace of the Governors, extending four feet south from that wall and extending between the plane of the east wall and the plane of the west wall of the same building. One space shall be situated against the banco (bench) and curb on each side of the Portal at the corner structures.

B. The area extending west seven feet across from the Palace of the Governors main entrance shall be excluded from use by the Portal Program participants.

C. During times of repair to the Portal area, during times of peak sales, or because of similar needs, the Museum may designate supplemental or alternate selling locations.

D. During regularly scheduled events, such as the Spanish Market, Indian Market, and the Garden Club Sale, the Museum shall not conduct the Portal Program.

E. The program area shall be divided into a number of spaces, each six feet deep (measures out from the wall) and three feet, six inches wide (measures along the wall). One space only may be used by a household.

F. *A household is defined as*: those persons residing in the same house, who are related by blood or marriage, and who qualify as members of New Mexican Indian tribes or pueblos. However, recognizing the sometimes complex nature of kinship, the Director of the Palace may, after consulting the Portal committee, allow in writing for minor exceptions to this definition with regards to specific households. In doing so, however, the Palace Director may stipulate such conditions or restrictions as needed to ensure that the intent of the program is to preserve and exhibit New Mexican Indian arts and crafts. The exceptions and conditions made in each case shall be considered unique to that case and not applicable to any other case.

2. Operation of the Portal Program:

Within the area defined, the Museum will permit a program involving the daily sale of handmade New Mexican Indian arts and crafts by qualified participants, subject to the following conditions:

A. Participants in the Portal Program must keep the area clean.

B. The sales activities of the Portal Program participants shall be conducted upon the brick surface; no tables or elevated stands are permitted, and no materials or advertising may be hung or posted on walls or posts.

C. The use by Portal Program participants of televisions, radios, tape recorders and players, binoculars, cellular phones, cameras, credit card machines and other modern appliances or equipment not essential to participation in the Portal Program shall not be permitted.

D. On occasion when there are more participants who want to be vendors on a particular day than spaces, a drawing shall be held by the Portal Committee and/or the Director of the Palace or designee for the available spaces. On these occasions the participants shall be counted, and a chip for each participant present at the Portal shall be put into a hopper or other type of container. The hopper or other type of container shall contain numbered chips for the spaces under the Portal, except for the duty officer's space, as well as blank chips. The total number of chips shall equal the number of participants present. Each participant shall draw a chip. If, after draw has been completed, all the numbered chips have not been drawn, a second draw shall be held for those participants who are present and who initially drew blank chips, and subsequent draws shall be held as necessary, until all spaces under the Portal have been drawn. A waiting list for vending spaces vacated during the day shall be kept. The first person on the waiting list shall be assigned the first vacated space. If the first person is not present when a space has been vacated, the second person on the waiting list shall be assigned the vacated space, and so on until the waiting list has been exhausted. Vendors coming to the Portal after the draw for vending spaces shall have their names added to the waiting list in the order of their appearance. Spaces, once assigned, cannot be traded.

E. The Portal Program shall commence at 8:00 A.M. each day of operation, and shall terminate each day upon departure of the last participant vendor from the program area. Participants may place their cloths along the curb opposite the space they want at 7:00 A.M. No participant may claim a space (by placing their cloth against the wall of the Palace) prior to 8:00 A.M., and all participants must be completely set up by 10:00 A.M. even if there is no draw and no waiting list. The 10:00 A.M. set-up time applies to the west side of the Palace when, during peak sales times, the Museum makes spaces available there, and to vendors who are sharing spaces. With the exception of the first space west of the building entrance, which shall be held each day for the designated duty officer of the Portal Committee, no spaces shall be reserved.

F. After 10:00 A.M., any participant who has left his/her space for a period exceeding one hour shall be considered to have abandoned that space, and it shall be available for reassignment to another. Neither the Museum, nor the members of the Portal Committee, assumes any responsibility for merchandise left unattended.

G. The making of items for sale in the area designated is not permitted; only simple adjustments or repairs to items already made is allowed.

H. No participant in the Portal Program may engage another individual, not a member of his or her household, to sell, nor may any participant solicit sales for another within the designated area.

I. For reasons of safety, children shall not be allowed to accompany participants in the Portal Program while the participants sell under the Portal.

J. The Director of the Palace shall require identity badges for Portal Participants, to be worn or displayed on cloth when selling under the Portal or taking part in other Portal activities. Any such badges, if issued, shall remain the property of the Museum and shall be surrendered by the participant on the Museum's request. If the badge is lost or stolen, the Museum shall charge a $5.00 replacement fee.

3. Qualifications and Required Conduct of Participants in the Portal Program:

A. To qualify as a participant vendor in the Portal Program individuals shall be at least eighteen years of age, shall be American Indians, as defined in NMSA 1978, Section 30–38–4(B), and shall be from recognized tribes and pueblos of New Mexico.

B. Any person who desires to participate as a vendor in the Portal Program must apply to the Museum for the privilege of selling goods at the Portal. The application form, as submitted, shall include proof of enrollment in a New Mexican tribe or pueblo. In addition, as part of the application, the applicant shall submit to the Museum the marker's mark he/she will use to identify his/her arts and crafts.

C. As part of the review process, the applicant shall demonstrate his/her art or craft to the Director of the Palace of the Governors, the Director's designee, and/or one or more members of the Portal Committee, to establish whether the items for sale meet minimum legal and quality standards. No person may sell under the Portal until his/her application form has been approved by the Director of the Palace of the Governors.

D. The Museum may require a signed and notarized affidavit from an applicant or a participant in the Portal Program attesting to the facts presented in the affidavit. The Museum may use the affidavit to verify the qualifications of a participant in the program. Intentional misrepresentations on the affidavit will be grounds for denial in participation or expulsion from the Portal Program.

E. All participants in the Portal Program shall accept and abide by the rules and regulations of the Museum governing the program. Violations of provisions of Museum policy or failure to abide by the rules and regulations may result in suspension or expulsion from the program.

F. The Museum shall deny permission to sell to any participant in the Portal Program whose goods or presence are, in the judgment of the Museum, inconsistent with these rules and regulations.

G. Participants in the Portal Program accept that admittance into the Program does not make them employees or agents of the Museum, nor does it mean that they are acting on behalf of the Museum in any official capacity except to the extent that members of the Portal Committee are exercising duties described in Paragraph 5 of this Rule.

H. Participants in the Portal Program shall accept the Museum's absolute right to require persons to leave the Portal if, in the sole judgment of the Museum, they are not conducting themselves in a manner consistent with the Museum's program.

I. The Director of the Palace may, after consulting with the Portal Committee, allow in writing for a waiver of the requirement that participants be members of New Mexico pueblos or tribes. Such waivers shall be granted only to members of United States pueblos or tribes, and residents of the United States who can document their Museum approved participation in the Portal Program prior to May 1987.

4. Annual Meeting and Public Hearing to Adopt Rules and Regulations:

A. Annually, on a day in April, at a place to be provided by the Museum, a meeting shall be held of participants and all other interested public. Said meeting shall be held in accordance with provisions of the Open Meetings Act, NMSA 1978, Sections 10–15–1 through 10–15–4. The annual meeting shall be announced four weeks in advance of the date and shall be open to the public.

B. No action of any type shall be taken on applications (new applications and demonstrations) two months prior to the annual meeting. This rule does not apply to participant violation.

C. On matters requiring a vote, the vote shall be restricted to qualified participants in the Portal Program.

D. At such meetings, copies of the proposed revisions to the guidelines, rules and regulations governing the Portal Program of the Palace of the Governors, if any, and copies of existing guidelines, rules and regulations governing the Portal Program shall be available for explanation and discussion and the Portal Committee shall be elected by vote of the participants present at the meeting.

E. The Board of Regents, Museum of New Mexico, shall hold a public hearing in accordance with NMSA 9–6–11(e) of the Cultural Affairs Act, to adopt these rules and regulations.

5. The Responsibilities of the Portal Committee:

A. The Portal Committee shall be responsible for monitoring the program on a daily basis for compliance with the policy and the rules and regulations of the Museum.

B. The Portal Committee shall appoint daily one or more duty officers who shall be responsible for the assignment of spaces when necessary.

C. The Portal Committee shall inspect all goods for sale to determine whether they are Indian handmade goods and meet minimum standards of quality as established by the Museum.

D. The Portal Committee, as representative of the Portal Program participants, may from time to time propose changes in these rules and regulations for consideration and adoption by the Museum Director pursuant to Section 18–3–5(A), NMSA 1978.

E. Violations of policy, rules, or regulations shall be reported by the Portal Committee to the Museum. For simple minor violations the Portal Committee may issue oral warnings to the offender. For more serious, or repeated violations the Portal Committee may recommend to the Museum that the violator be warned in writing, suspended in writing from the program for a specified period of time, expelled in writing from the program, or that other appropriate action be taken.

F. The Portal Committee shall assist participants in the program in presenting the traditional and educational aspects of the Portal Program.

6. Administration of the Program by the Museum of New Mexico:

A. Administration of the program shall be the responsibility of the Director of the Palace of the Governors who shall chair the annual meeting of Portal Program participants and who shall work directly with the Portal Committee in the conduct of the Portal Program. The Director of the Palace may issue such rulings and judgments as are necessary to interpret and enforce the Museum's polities, rules, and regulations on the Portal Program.

B. The Museum reserves the absolute right to eject participants for conduct inconsistent with the Portal Program or for behavior that is disorderly or lacks due regard for the public or other Portal Program participants.

C. The Museum is authorized to utilize the services of law enforcement authorities to enforce and maintain its policies, rules, and regulations.

D. Any participant in the Portal Program who is aggrieved by actions taken under the rules and regulations shall first present his or her concern to the Portal Committee in a bona fide effort to effect resolution; if not resolved, the matter shall be presented in writing to the Director of the Palace of the Governors who shall hear all parties to the matter and render a decision on the matter; such decision may be appealed to the Director of the Museum of New Mexico, also in writing, and the decision of the Director shall be final. Copies of all paperwork relevant to the matter being appealed will be made available to the Director for his consideration.

E. The Museum shall provide interpretive materials on the history and culture of Indians in the Santa Fe region, and on the tradition of the Portal Program.

F. The Director of the Museum of New Mexico may request the assistance of the Office of Indian Affairs and other specialists in the operation of the Portal Program.

7. Portal Program Participants' General Vending Rules:

A. All items the Portal Program participant vendors offer for sale shall have been made by members of the same household. (See Paragraph 1-F for the definition of household.) All merchandise offered for sale shall be handmade by members of recognized tribes and pueblos of New Mexico, and shall conform to provisions of the New Mexico Indian Arts and Crafts Sales Act. Representations made to prospective buyers are solely the responsibility of the vendor.

B. Each participant in the Portal Program may have an assistant, who shall also be an approved participant in the Portal Program. The assistant must sit with the participant whom she/he assists within the assigned space.

C. While selling, participants in the Portal Program shall not engage in activities which disrupt the flow of pedestrian traffic at the Portal. Disruptive activities shall include, but not be limited to, verbal and/or physical assault on visitors or other participants.

D. Participants in the Portal Program shall not consume alcohol nor be intoxicated while vending. Consumption of alcohol or intoxication while vending is automatic grounds for suspension.

E. Participants in the Portal Program shall not fight while vending. Any participant who is involved in any fight or altercation while vending may be subject to suspension. Fighting is automatic grounds for suspension.

F. Any time a participant leaves his/her space, for any reason, he/she shall completely cover his/her goods with a cloth.

G. On any occasion when there are more participants in the Portal Program who want to vend on a particular day than spaces, and after the draw, any participant may volunteer to share his/her space with another participant. Shared spaces will be divided equally between vendors, six bricks each. Spaces 1, 6, 7, 59, 60, 65, 66, 67, 70, and 71 cannot be shared. Once the space has been awarded, if either of the pair leaves, his/her portion of the goods shall be completely covered with a cloth. Only participants in the draw may share spaces in addition to having their names on the waiting list. Vendors arriving at the Portal after the draw has taken place shall not be permitted to share spaces, but may have their names added to the waiting list in the order of their appearance to be eligible for assignment to vacated vending spaces. If a vendor draws a blank and shares with another vendor who, for whatever reason, is away from his/her space for more than a hour between 10:00 A.M. and noon or who leaves before noon, the vendor who drew the blank must pack up and the full space be given to the first person on the waiting list.

H. The waiting list procedure when the west side of the Palace is open to vendors is as follows: A vendor may choose not to draw for a space on the west side. If a vendor does not draw for the west side he/she can share a space with another vendor under the Portal, but his/her name will be placed at the bottom of the waiting list. The vendor will not get a full space under the Portal until: 1) vendors who drew blanks for both the front and west side and 2) vendors who drew spaces on the west side have been given an opportunity to move to the front. If you are going to share under the Portal, do not draw for the west side.

I. Waivers: The Director of the Palace may, after consulting with the Portal Committee, allow in writing for a waiver of the requirement that all items sold by a participant be from the same household (see paragraph 1-F for the definition of household). Such waivers shall be granted only to persons who have been a part of the Program prior to May 1987, especially those former artists and artisans who are no longer physically able to prepare handmade arts or crafts and whose economic livelihood would otherwise be destroyed. In doing so, however, the Palace Director may stipulate such conditions or restrictions as are needed to ensure that the intent of the program is to preserve and exhibit New Mexico Indian arts and crafts. The exceptions made in each case shall be considered unique to that case and not applicable to any other case.

J. Any vendor providing knee pads for customers must keep the knee pads within the boundaries of his/her space or offer them to customers as needed. No knee pads may be taped beyond the boundaries of vending spaces. Vendors who draw bench vending spaces must not put additional seats of any kind on the surface of the benches.

8. Authenticity of Maker of Goods (Maker's Mark):

A. All goods offered for sale under the Portal shall be marked with the maker's mark. Any exceptions to this can be issued a waiver by the Director of the Palace of the Governors, after consulting with the Portal Committee.

B. Metal jewelry shall have a stamped maker's mark, and pottery shall have a maker's mark added before firing. This maker's mark shall be recorded with the Museum as part of the application to qualify as a vendor. The same maker's mark shall appear on all goods being sold by a single vendor.

C. On metal jewelry with stones, the maker's mark shall be placed on the back of the piece opposite the center of the stone. The intention of this provision is to require the jeweler to stamp the piece before the stones are set, and to make it impossible to stamp such pieces after they are completed. Metal plates with the maker's mark which are soldered or attached by other means to a piece of metal jewelry shall not be permitted.

D. If the design of a reversible pendant (or other piece of jewelry) makes it impossible to stamp the maker's mark behind the stone, the pendant (or other piece of jewelry) shall be stamped on the bezel.

9. Jewelry Materials:

A. Silver and gold:
Silver jewelry must be made of sterling silver, and *not* silver plate or commercial liquid silver. Gold overlay on silver is allowable. All jewelry using gold should be stamped 10K, 14K, 18K etc. All jewelry using gold fill shall be stamped 12KGF or 14KGF. The use of coin silver is prohibited.

B. Prohibited Materials
In addition to the above prohibited materials, no artist or artisan shall use any reconstituted materials; color-shot, pre-drilled, semi-precious stones; imported heishi; or pre-carved pieces in any jewelry exhibited or offered for sale under the Portal.

10. Jewelry Findings:

All jewelry must be as traditional and handmade as possible. Jewelry "findings" (as defined by NMSA 1978, § 30–33–3(H), of the Indian Arts and Crafts Sales Act) means "an ingredient part of a product which adapts the product for wearing or display, including silver beads, leather backing, binding material, bolo tie clips, tie bar clips, tie tac pins, earring pins, earring clips, earring screw backs, cuff-link toggles, money clips, pin stems, combs and chains." All jewelry offered for sale under the Portal must be finished, i.e., complete with necessary findings. The only exceptions are pendants, which can be offered for sale without chains. Acceptable findings used on jewelry sold at the Portal shall be the following:

A. *Sterling Silver Findings*: all neck chains; all jump rings; all spring rings; all tie-on hooks and eyes; all crimp type hook and eye earring part; all screw-on, clip-on types; all ear wire types; all ear posts, ear nuts; omega clips; all cuff link and components; all necklace cones; all bolo tips; all bench made beads (2 mm to 9 mm seamless are acceptable); all size money clips; surgical wire for earrings; all size melon beads; bezel cups in all sizes and shapes from 2 mm to 5 mm.

B. *Nickel or Base Metal Findings*: all size buckles backs; all bolo backs; all foxtail and tigertail; all concho backs; all key rings including split rings; all barrel catches including eyeglass/chain attachments; all tie tacks, sets and clutches (backs); all scarf pins (stick pins) backs; all pin bars and pinsets (backs); all barrette backs; all tie bar slides; all alligator clips; all expansion centers; all size spring bars; keyholders (safety pins), large and medium sizes; all size money clips; wire used in "memory bracelets." Surgical steel is permitted in wire post earrings.

C. *14K Gold Findings*: All ear posts and nuts; joint catches; jump rings; spring rings; bolo backs; bolo tips; necklace cones; all size cones.

D. *Gold Filled Findings*: All posts and nut sets; all French wire styles; all hooks and eyes; all spring rings; all size jump rings; all neck chains, all beads; all tie tack backs; all bolo tips, all ear clips; stick pins and clutches; all size cones.

E. *Red Brass or Brass Findings*: All buckle backs; all key ring backs; all concho backs; all bolo backs; all bolo tips, all hooks and eyes; all brass beads; all size money clips.

F. *Leather Findings*: All size straps for concho belts; all size braided bolo cords. Vinyl bolo cords are permitted.

11. Beadwork:

A. Permitted Beadwork Materials:
   On beadwork offered for sale under the Portal, the bead-worker must have made the silver, brass, or any other

metal which has been incorporated with beadwork into the final product. The following materials shall be permitted: all size glass beads; brass and copper beads from 2 mm to 9 mm; all types of legal feathers; all types of leather; porcupine quills (natural color only); genuine natural bone hair pipes; genuine natural bone disc beads; dentallie shells, lead crystals and sweetwater pearls (also know as freshwater pearls). The use of sweetwater pearls is also approved for metal work.

B. Beadwork findings:

Because beadwork is a totally different craft from silversmithing, the following findings shall be permitted when incorporated into beadwork items: buckle backings (blanks); barrette backings; bolo backings; sterling silver bolo tips; sterling silver, aluminum and tin cones for fringe dangles only metal spots of nickel or brass; barrel screw clasps; hooks and eyes; spring rings, crimp beads; eye pins and head pins; jump rings; split key rings; tie tack mounts; tiger tail, all earring findings.

C. Prohibited Beadwork Materials:

The following materials shall not be permitted when incorporated into beadwork: plastic bone hair pipe; pre-cut, pre-shaped, and abalone disk.

12. Pottery:

A. All pottery shall be handmade of earth clay from sources on the participant's reservation or pueblo, and fired using traditional materials. Clay sources other than the participant's reservation or pueblo may be approved in writing from the Director of the Palace of the Governors.

B. All pottery shall be engraved before firing.

C. All pottery may be hand painted in natural mineral paints, poster paint colors, or bright acrylic color paints.

D. The use of commercial protective sealants on pottery is allowed.

13. Vending Traditional Food Stuffs:

A. Traditional food stuff may be offered for sale and shall be derived from the household of the participant vendor. The participant shall have prepared the food stuff within 24 hours of offering.

B. The following food may be sold: oven bread, Indian melons, tamales, pies, fried bread, piñon nuts, parched corn, piki bread (paper bread), and ristras (chili strings).

C. The participant who vends food shall obtain from the City of Santa Fe a valid food handler's card or certificate, which must be exhibited by the participant food vendor at all times.

D. All food must be packaged and labeled with the maker's name and ingredients.

E. Other additional kinds of foods shall be approved by the Portal Committee and/or the Director of the Palace of the Governors before the participant vendor offers it for sale to the public.

14. Sandpainting:

A. All sandpainting shall be handmade of natural materials. No commercial sand shall be permitted.

B. No dyed sand shall be permitted.

C. No sandpainting sold under the Portal of the Palace of the Governors shall have a frame.

D. Each sandpainting shall be signed on the face of the painting with the maker's mark impressed into the design of the painting while the sand is wet. This does not preclude *additional* marking or signatures, e.g., on the back of the painting.

E. The use of commercial protective sealants on sandpaintings is allowed.

15. Leatherwork:

A. All leatherwork shall be permanently marked. Marking in ink is not permitted.

B. Leatherwork without beadwork should have a branded or stamped maker's mark.

C. Leatherwork with beadwork can have a branded, stamped or beaded maker's mark. The maker's mark may also be incorporated into the beaded design.

16. Payment to Participants:

A. No participant shall accept any payment prior to delivery of the item. Cash-On-Delivery (C.O.D.) orders are permitted. Any violation of this section shall result in immediate suspension.

B. Participants may receive arts and craft items as payment for their own goods, so long as they do not re-sell the items at the Portal.

17. Statement:

This statement of rules and regulations supersedes all previous statements of policy, rules, and regulations concerning the Portal Program of the Palace of the Governors, Museum of New Mexico.

Notes

Prologue

1. For example, Patricia Fogelman Lange (1993:231) suggests that the portal market is less than a favorable place for Native people to work. And Margaret Dubin (2001:137) writes that Portal vendors "change out of jeans and flannel shirts into more 'traditional' (stereotypical) clothing and jewelry before their customers arrive," something that absolutely does not happen. The sources for these impressions are complex, as evidenced by Dubin's (2001:110) quoting of Navajo painter Tony Abeyta, who in turn quotes "critics" talking of Indians "still just evolving from selling trinkets and baubles under the portal."

2. Penny Gomez, interview, 1997; Pamela Smith, interview, 1997.

3. Of course, Feld was not the first to recognize subjects as readers. Américo Paredes (1978:2), for example, noted that Mexican Americans who were the subject of anthropological writing were "people who read what you write and are more than willing to talk back."

Chapter 1

1. Two million is the figure provided by the Santa Fe Convention and Visitors Bureau for annual visitation. Precise numbers are difficult to calculate. While many visitors stay at hotels in Santa Fe, many others stay with family or friends or are day visitors to the city and thus are invisible to statisticians. On average, there are 120,000 paid entrants to the Palace of the Governors Museum each year. Thomas Chávez, former director of the Palace, estimates that only one in every twenty visitors to the portal enters the museum. By this estimate, some 2.4 million people visit the portal each year.

2. Quoted from interview with George Ewing, 1998.

3. In fact, the only contact the consumers of ethnic arts often have with non-Western people and cultural traditions occurs in the purchase of ethnic arts (Jules-Rosette 1984:8). This exchange is frequently not directly between artists and consumers but rather is effected by art dealers or other middlemen (Steiner 1995).

4. See Appendix for Portal Program rules. Machine-made findings, including bench-made beads in sizes ranging from 2 mm to 9 mm, are allowed.

5. Though vendors of arts and crafts, food, T-shirts, and other goods can be found in many villages during feast days, they are never from the village holding the feast but are from other tribal groups or are non-Native. Vendors are generally asked to make a donation or pay a nominal fee to the host village, but this is not an economically significant activity for the villages.

6. Of course, defining "traditional" clothing is problematic. When the idea of vendors dressing traditionally for a special event came up in late 1999, some vendors noted that they do not have any clothing that would be considered traditional.

7. I use the term "costumes" here, because the use of traditional clothing in this setting would be costuming, that is, dressing for an act. By contrast, traditional clothing worn for traditional dances is not costuming but the appropriate clothing for that activity.

Chapter 2

1. In fact, the Casas Reales may well have entirely surrounded the area of the contemporary plaza (Snow 1993:5).

2. The collections of the Palace of the Governors contain a copy of a voucher signed by Governor Don Bernardo López de Mendizábal to Juan Chamiso, a carpenter from Pecos Pueblo, for money owed for carpentry work on the Palace in 1661.

3. Selenite, a variety of gypsum found in the form of transparent crystals, was sometimes used as a substitute for glass in windows. Gypsum was also commonly used for whitewash. In 1660 Governor López de Mendizábal wrote to his district officer for Galisteo, Diego González, asking him to send thirty Indian laborers to Santa Fe with ground gypsum for whitewashing the Casas Reales (quoted in Kessell 1987:177–78).

4. According to the testimony of a Tegua rebel named Antonio, who was captured by the retreating Spanish on August 23, 1680 (Hackett 1942:1:20).

5. Vargas apparently later freed at least some of these people, with the goal of resettling them at the abandoned pueblo of Cieneguilla, west of Santa Fe (Kessell, Hendricks, and Dodge 1998:582).

6. A monument erected at the center of the Santa Fe plaza in the 1860s bore as one of several inscriptions the following: "To the heroes who have fallen in various battles with savage Indians in the territory of New Mexico." In 1973 members of the American Indian Movement protested the monument and demanded its removal. The governor and then the city council concurred, and plans were made for it to be removed. As noted by Grimes (1976:46–50), that led to a heated controversy and protests from many who did not want the monument removed. As a compromise, it was proposed that an explanatory plaque be added to the monument. Before that could happen, however, someone took a chisel to the monument and removed the word "savage" from the inscription. After reading an early draft of this chapter, then Palace director Thomas Chávez explained the complexity of interactions among Hispano and Indian peoples throughout New Mexican history: after the word was removed, a Pueblo man asked him why they had taken out the word "savage," because the Indians they had been fighting (i.e., the non-Puebloans) *had* been savages.

7. John Greiner, who took over the duties of Superintendent of Indian Affairs from the ailing James S. Calhoun in 1852, kept a daily log of his activities. During the six months between April and September 1852, representatives of the various pueblos visited almost daily, and the office almost always provided the visitors with meals (Abel 1916).

8. It is possible that a portal existed on the south side of the Palace even though it was not drawn by Urrutia on his map. The Urrutia map seems to indicate no portales in Santa Fe, though they were common in both Spanish and Spanish colonial cities of the time. Furthermore, the early portales were generally shed-roofed attachments to buildings and may not have seemed worthy of indication on the map. Bunting and Conron (1966:41) suggest that the first portal in front of the Palace was built in 1705.

9. A reproduction of the plan is on exhibit at the Palace of the Governors.

10. Mexican filigree jewelry was popular enough to be advertised in an early (probably 1919) Santa Fe Fiesta program, though no Native American arts were advertised (Hewett Collection, Box 54).

11. Spanish Colonial-style arts and crafts have enjoyed something of a rebound in popularity. The annual Spanish Market, held in Santa Fe each summer under the sponsorship of the Spanish Colonial Arts Society, has grown continuously over the past few years and has added a winter market. The weekend of the summer Spanish Market makes up two of the four days each year the Portal Program does not operate. Rancho de las Golondrinas, an interpretive museum just south of Santa Fe dedicated to Spanish history in New Mexico, and the Hispanic Cultural Center in Albuquerque are active supporters of Hispanic arts in New Mexico.

12. Restrooms continued to be an issue at the end of the twentieth century, though now for tourists. In her interview, one vendor commented on the fact that there are no public restroom facilities for visitors to the plaza area. She expressed frustration that visitors had to pay the museum admission fee in order to use the restrooms in the Palace. Vendors have free access to the Palace restrooms, as long as they wear their program ID badges when they enter the museum.

13. There were many reasons for promoting Indian dances at the Fiesta. In addition to their entertainment value, there was a desire on the part of Fiesta organizers to promote Indian-style dancing in the schools to replace German folk dancing at a time when all things German were suspect. During a planning meeting for the Fiesta in 1918, Edgar Lee Hewett announced that the School of American Research was planning to give a scholarship for the study of Indian dancing being adopted for use in the schools (*Santa Fe New Mexican,* July 27, 1918).

14. The potter was most likely Maria Martinez. In October of that year, a New Jersey patron sent a letter acknowledging his receipt of two "bowls of Maria's which I purchased from you last August, and which you very kindly had boxed and sent on to me here" (Herbert W. Smith to Curator, The New Museum, Santa Fe, New Mexico, October 22, 1922, Hewett Collection, Box 29, History Library). It is not clear whether the pottery was offered at the Palace or at the Museum of Fine

Arts. The "American School of Research" building would presumably be the Palace, but the "New Museum" to which Mr. Smith's letter was addressed would presumably be Fine Arts.

15. Rose Dougan also provided funding for housing construction at San Ildefonso Pueblo around this same time, encouraging the residents to sleep fewer to a room, to use beds, and to locate houses so that exterior areas could be kept clean (Edgar L. Hewett to Rose Dougan, September 15, 1922; Rose Dougan to Edgar L. Hewett, September 19, 1922; both in Hewett Collection, Box 29, History Library).

16. Or at least, in the case of pottery, to the design elements and technical mastery found in work produced before the arrival of the railroad in 1880 (see Dauber 1993).

17. See Traugott 1999 for a recent discussion of the myths surrounding the Sikyatki Revival.

18. This, of course, would come as a great shock to thousands of aboriginal inhabitants of the Southwest who engaged daily in expressions of their culture.

19. NMAIA was renamed the Southwestern Association on Indian Affairs in 1959 (SWAIA). The NMAIA was established in 1922 as a political advocacy organization, largely in response to the Bursum bill, which threatened Pueblo land titles. Along with the Eastern Association on Indian Affairs in New York City, with which it shared some members, the association fought to protect Native Americans' rights and worked to promote economic development. SWAIA gradually focused its energies on the promotion of Native American arts and was renamed again in 1993 Southwestern Association for Indian Arts to reflect changing emphases (Bernstein 1999:69n; Penney and Roberts 1999). See Bernstein 1993b for a detailed history of SWAIA's development as sponsor of the annual Santa Fe Indian Market.

20. Thirteen articles were published in *New Mexico Magazine* between February 1936 and July 1937, including pieces by Chabot, Wittner Bynner, Franc Newcomb, Margretta Dietrich, and Kenneth Chapman.

21. This is echoed in some stories told among the Pueblos of the portal being set aside by early Spanish officials as a Pueblo-only marketplace.

Chapter 3

1. Minutes from the September 12, 1956, NMAIA board meeting note the interpueblo tensions: "Complaints about conditions under the portal of the Governors Palace were discussed. Most of them have been directed against vendors from Santo Domingo Pueblo by Indians from other pueblos, who complain of the aggressiveness and untidiness of the Santo Domingo people" (SWAIA Records, File 45A).

2. For example, Bertha Dutton (1958:63) added the sentence: "As with all other Indian articles, it is recommended that purchases be made from reputable agents such as those advertised or mentioned herein" to her revision of *Indians of the Southwest* (previously *New Mexico Indians*). A decade earlier, this had apparently not been an issue significant enough to warrant mention.

3. The loss of businesses oriented toward serving the local community is noted and bemoaned by other longtime Santa Feans besides the Portal vendors (Sarah Laughlin, pers. com. 1999).

4. The preferential treatment of Indian people is in turn supported by the special status of Indian tribes stemming from recognition of (limited) tribal sovereignty in the U.S. Constitution (Art. I, Sec. 8[3]) and from the development in the nineteenth century of what government officials perceived as a "guardian/ward" relationship between the U.S. government and Indian people.

5. Sara Livingston was also a quilt maker; the Livingstons started making jewelry because of slow quilt sales (Evans-Pritchard 1990:67). The couple also had a history of political activism, and at one point Paul Livingston told a reporter that he "[hadn't] had so much fun since the Vietnam War ended" (*Empire Magazine* of the *Denver Post*, October 14, 1979).

6. Defining what is and what is not authentic ethnic art is an issue being debated by members of indigenous communities around the world. In New Zealand, for example, the Aotearoa Maori Tourism Federation defines authentic Maori art as something that "is conceived from the mind of a Maori, executed by a Maori, and is the work of someone with Maori *tapuna* (ancestry)" (Ryan and Crotts 1997:909).

7. Brian Joyce seems to have been more an activist looking for a fight than a serious vendor. Portal Program participants have told of Joyce

attempting to sell bananas and other fruit on the portal (see also *Albuquerque Journal,* February 8, 1978). As George Ewing noted, Joyce eventually headed south to the capitol building where he took up another cause.

8. According to George Ewing, it was Assistant Attorney General Jill Cooper, counsel for the museum, who suggested that Livingston become a lawyer.

9. The New Mexico Indian Arts and Crafts Act (30-33-4(H) NMSA 1978), cited in the Portal Program rules, defines findings as "an ingredient part of the product that adapts the product for wearing or display, including silver beads used in jewelry containing Indian handmade adornments in addition to beads, leather backing, binding material, bolo tie clips, tie bar clips, tie-tac pins, earring pins, earring clips, earring screw backs, cuff link toggles, money clips, pin stems, combs and chains." German silver is also called nickel silver; it is an alloy of nickel, copper, and zinc and contains no silver.

10. Indeed, carrying and using photographic equipment is one of the identifying characteristics used by van den Berghe to locate tourists in San Cristóbal, Mexico (van den Berghe 1994:26), and Urry (1990:139) identifies the camera draped around the neck as an unequivocal symbol of the tourist.

11. There was some confusion about this change, and a total of three rule modifications were filed with the New Mexico State Records Center in the first five months of 1987. "Indian handmade," according to the New Mexico Indian Arts and Crafts Sales Act, "means any product in which the entire shaping and forming of the product from raw materials and its finishing and decoration were accomplished by Indian hand labor and manually controlled methods that permit the maker to control and vary the construction, shape, design or finish of each part of each individual product, but does not exclude the use of findings, hand tools and equipment for buffing, polishing, grinding, drilling, sawing or sewing and other processes approved by regulations adopted under the Indian Arts and Crafts Sales Act." "Household" was not defined at this time. As is discussed elsewhere, the concept of household can be complicated and the program rules have been adjusted to account for the variety of different types of households vendors reside in.

12. Francis Begay was arrested for failure to obey a lawful police order. She later pled no contest to the charge.

13. Traditional "outside-firing" with a wood fire requires considerable knowledge and skill to perform successfully and even when done correctly has a much higher failure rate than firing in an electric or gas kiln.

14. Exceptions are made to this rule in cases of extreme conflict between vendors, when it is decided by the involved vendors, the committee, and the museum administration that it is in the best interests of the program to keep vendors apart.

Chapter 4

1. The museum has always distanced itself from vendors' business. In 1978, for example, museum director George Ewing adamantly asserted that pricing was the privilege of each individual vendor (Memo, George H. Ewing to Vendors, October 12, 1978, Portal Log). Another myth that I have heard occasionally about the Portal is that vendors from particular pueblos will meet to set prices for various items. However, I have never seen any evidence of vendors consulting about pricing, except within individual households.

2. In mid-1999 there were approximately 153 Jemez vendors enrolled in the program, out of 2,588 tribal members. At the same time there were approximately 313 vendors from Santo Domingo Pueblo. The pueblo's tribal enrollment was 4,050, and the population of the village was 3,446 (tribal enrollment and village population statistics from Tiller 1996). Numbers are approximate because some vendors have multiple tribal heritages. Also, some vendors are more closely linked economically (through domestic partnership or marriage) to communities outside of their tribe of enrollment (for example, a number of Navajos and people from other tribes have married into Santo Domingo), and this limits the significance of identifying all vendors by tribe of enrollment for purposes of gauging economic impact on communities.

3. Picuris Pueblo, south of Taos, is the only federally recognized New Mexican Native American community not represented under the portal at the time of this writing.

4. This generalization does not apply to the very limited number of artists

who produce work that is the most highly valued in the market and who show and sell their work through fine art galleries or to artists producing commissioned works.

5. For example, see Lange 1993:231. This is a common first perception of the Portal, one that I have heard voiced on a number of occasions in conversations with people who have visited Santa Fe once or twice but have not gained an understanding of the program.

6. I conducted an informal experiment along these lines in Nogales, Sonora, Mexico. During one visit, I bargained for and eventually purchased a tin-framed mirror from a shopkeeper in the Nogales tourist district. About a month later I took a friend to Nogales, and he bargained with the same salesman for an identical mirror. The final negotiated price was the same on each occasion. The salesman refused all lower offers each time, demonstrating that he had a clear minimum selling price in mind and also exposing the artificiality of "bargaining" in such marketplaces. Incidentally, we later found the same mirrors for less in a store with set prices.

Chapter 5

1. Sometimes a "big, dysfunctional family."

2. Of course, such communities move far beyond such simple consolidation in the face of adversity. As Eileen Luna and Susan Lobo made clear in a recent dinner conversation (1999) regarding their experiences with the Intertribal Friendship House in Oakland, California, communities develop their own internal dynamics that often have little to do with outside pressures.

3. In the case of cyber-communities, one could argue that physical geographic boundedness is replaced by a virtual boundary shaped by listservs, chat rooms, and other electronically created forums of interaction.

4. For discussion of urban Native American communities based on tribal identity—in fact, being satellite villages of Laguna Pueblo—see Peters 1994, 1995.

5. Because of the large representation of Santo Domingo Pueblo and the Navajo Nation among the vendors, a significant proportion of committee members come from these two cultural groups each year.

6. Lillian Garcia, though Navajo, married into and lives at Santo Domingo. The 2001–2 Portal Chair, Mavis Garcia, is of Goshute heritage but is likewise married into and resident at Santo Domingo.
7. Transcript from videotape of Native American Vendors Program Annual Meeting, April 22, 1999. Videotape in Portal Program collections.
8. James has gained considerable celebrity and has been pictured on television and in books selling newspapers on Palace Avenue. Concern for his own safety led him to find a way to watch both westbound and eastbound traffic. He has elaborated his watching into a distinctive dance that he often performs as he sells papers to passing motorists.
9. These concerns are echoed by the museum shop staff and other museum personnel who worry about the close proximity of the food to the shop inventory and the museum's collections.

Chapter 6

1. Transcript from videotape of Native American Vendors Program Annual Meeting, April 22, 1999. Videotape in Portal Program collections.
2. The term "living exhibit" was used to distinguish displays that incorporated living people from the more common static displays. The idea that museum exhibits can be greatly enhanced by the attendance of indigenous people as subjects and interpreters continues to be very popular among museum professionals and is limited primarily by the unavailability of funding to pay indigenous participants.
3. Ettawageshik (1999) notes a similar process in northern lower Michigan where the sale through curio shops of Odawa products such as quill-decorated boxes has helped to preserve and even rejuvenate traditional artistic production.
4. Thomas Chávez, videotaped interview, 1997.
5. I am indebted to several museum professionals who discussed these issues with me at length following my presentation of a paper entitled "Making a Market: Native American Vendors Under the Palace Portal" at the 1999 Native American Art Studies Association meeting in Victoria, B.C., Canada, in which I presented some of the issues considered here.
6. An August 8, 1997, *Albuquerque Tribune* article estimated that while artists earn between $4 million and $6 million through Market sales,

some $140 million in revenue comes into the Santa Fe economy during Market weekend.

7. There are a number of institutions that support Native art that were created by and are run by and for Native artists. A prime example is the Institute of American Indian Arts, located a block from the portal in Santa Fe. Another is the 'Ksan Indian Cultural Centre at Hazelton, B.C., Canada (Graburn 1993).

Chapter 7

1. This is certainly not limited to the devaluation of indigenous art. As Plattner (1996:78) notes, even in Western fine arts worlds, artists who produce popular (i.e., readily marketable) work or who are amateur artists are labeled "sellouts," "hack artists," or "Sunday painters" by "real" artists.

2. Here I include Navajo sandpaintings. However, as Parezo (1990:571) notes, such work is usually categorized by dealers and collectors as "craft" because of the materials used—an example of the devaluation of media outside the canon of "fine" art.

3. Formal institutional efforts have also been made to train young Native artists working in the media of Western, "fine" art, specifically, painting. Foremost among these is "the Studio School" of the Santa Fe Indian School established by Dorothy Dunn in 1932 (Berlo and Phillips 1998:217) and its successor, the Institute of American Indian Arts, which was established in 1962 in Santa Fe (Bernstein 1999:66; see also Brody 1971).

4. The material was available on the Internet at http://vh1149.infi.net /indianartnw/index.html. The show was discontinued after its second year but is planned again for 2002 in conjunction with a music festival later in the year.

5. This is just one of many strategies used to give indigenous art meaning for consumers. For example, see Steiner 1995 for a discussion of how middlemen create value in African art. Also see Littrell 1990 on how tourists impart meaning to textile crafts.

6. This is not a new discussion. At the first NAASA meeting in 1979, a very similar discussion was held (Nancy Parezo, pers. com. 2000).

7. See Rule 12A in Appendix.

8. It has been suggested that vendors be allowed to set up tables to sell from, but this has been rejected by participants because it would further limit the number of vendors who could sell each day.

9. Mary Eustace's "ear twirl" is a patented earring design. Instead of a post or hook, the ear wire is an integral part of the design, making a full twist around the body of the earring so that it cannot fall out of the ear and be accidentally lost.

10. It is widely acknowledged among artists in ethnic art markets that larger, more expensive pieces can be made in less time and with less effort than smaller pieces but that not as many of the larger pieces can be sold (Graburn 1976:15).

11. A large percentage of the low-priced Kachina-style carvings on the market are made by Diné (Navajo) people for sale. Because Kachina dolls, and more important the spiritual Katsinam from which the dolls are drawn, are of Puebloan origin, there is considerable controversy surrounding the production of dolls by non-Pueblo (or more specifically, non-Hopi) people.

Chapter 8

1. Poem © Mary Eustace, used with permission of the author.

2. Though I have heard no reports of carpal tunnel syndrome from Native American artists, repetitive motion injuries could affect producers over time. One of the last living White Mountain Apache makers of coiled baskets has stopped working in recent years because of the pain of arthritis in her hands.

Bibliography

Annie H., ed.
  1916 "The Journal of John Greiner." *Old Santa Fe* 3(2):189–243.

Ablon, Joan
  1964 "Relocated American Indians in the San Francisco Bay Area: Social Interaction and Indian Identity." *Human Organization* 23:296–304.

Adair, John
  1944 *The Navajo and Pueblo Silversmiths.* Norman: University of Oklahoma Press.

Adams, Eleanor B., and Fray Angélico Chávez
  1956 *The Missions of New Mexico, 1776: A Description by Fray Francisco Dominquez.* Albuquerque: University of New Mexico Press.

Adams, Kathleen M.
  1997 "Ethnic Tourism and the Renegotiation of Tradition in Tana Toraja (Sulawesi, Indonesia)." *Ethnology* 36(4):309–20.

Adams, Vincanne
  1996 *Tigers of the Snow and Other Virtual Sherpas: An Ethnography of Himalayan Encounters.* Princeton: Princeton University Press.

Allison, W. H. H.
  1914 "Santa Fe as It Appeared during the Winter of the Years 1837 and 1838." *Old Santa Fe* 2(2):170–83.

Anderson, Clinton P.
  1944 "The Adobe Palace." *New Mexico Historical Review* 19(2):97–122.

Appadurai, Arjun
  1990 "Disjuncture and Difference in the Global Cultural Economy." *Public Culture* 2(2):1–24.

Archambault, JoAllyn
  1999 "Art and Craft—The Perennial Dialogue as Seen by Modern Plains Indians, Some of Whom Create ART." Paper presented in session, Yes, There Is a Word for It: Educating the Educators about American Indian Art and Culture, 12th Biennial Native American Art Studies Association Conference, October 14–16, Victoria, B.C., Canada.

Arnold, Carrie Forman
1984   "The Museum's Adobe Palace." *El Palacio* 90(2):36–45.

Arrillaga, Pauline
2000   "Jewelry Fraud Plagues Tribes." *Arizona Daily Star,*
January 16 (Associated Press).

Atencio, Juanita
1996   Interview with Sarah Laughlin and Tom McCarthy
for Portal Program Oral History Archive.

Bancroft, Hubert H.
1967   *History of Arizona and New Mexico: 1530–1888.*
New York: McGraw-Hill.

Barsh, Russel Lawrence
1996   "Puget Sound Indian Demography, 1900–1920: Migration
and Economic Integration." *Ethnohistory* 43(1):65–97.

Barstow, David
1999   "Guiliani Ordered to Restore Funds for Art Museum."
New York Times, November 2.

Basso, Keith H.
1979   *Portraits of "The Whiteman": Linguistic Play and Cultural
Symbols Among the Western Apache.* Cambridge: Cambridge
University Press.

Baumann, Gustave
1989   "Concerning a Small Untroubled World." In *Window on the
West: The Collector's El Palacio,* 125–40. Santa Fe: Museum of
New Mexico Foundation.

Becker, Howard Saul
1982   *Art Worlds.* Berkeley: University of California Press.

Benedict, Burton
1983   *The Anthropology of World's Fairs: San Francisco's Panama
Pacific International Exposition of 1915.* London and
Berkeley: Lowie Museum of Anthropology in association
with Scolar Press.

1994   "Rituals of Representation: Ethnic Stereotypes and
Colonized Peoples at World's Fairs." In *Fair Representations:
World's Fairs and the Modern World,* edited by Robert W. Rydell
and Nancy Gwinn, 28–61. Amsterdam: VU University Press.

Berlo, Janet Catherine, and Ruth B. Phillips
1998   *Native North American Art.* Oxford: Oxford University Press.

Bernstein, Bruce David
1993a   "From Indian Fair to Indian Market." *El Palacio*
        98(3):14–18, 47–54.

1993b   "The Marketing of Culture: Pottery and Santa Fe's Indian
        Market." Ph.D. dissertation, University of New Mexico.

1999   "Contexts for the Growth and Development of the Indian Art
        World in the 1960s and 1970s." In *Native American Art in
        the Twentieth Century,* edited by W. Jackson Rushing III,
        57–71. London: Routledge.

Bloom, Lansing B.
1913   "New Mexico under Mexican Administration, 1821–1846."
        Old Santa Fe 1(1–4):3–49, 131–75, 235–87, 347–68.

1914   "New Mexico under Mexican Administration, 1821–1846."
        Old Santa Fe 2(1–4):3–56, 119–69, 223–77, 351–80.

1929   "Ynstruccion a Peralta Por Vi-Rey." English translation
        by Ireneo L. Chaves. *New Mexico Historical Review*
        4(2):178–87.

Boissevain, Jeremy
1996   "Introduction." In *Coping with Tourists: European Reactions
        of Mass Tourism,* edited by Jeremy Boissevain, 1–26.
        Providence, R.I.: Berghahn Books.

Boorstin, Daniel
1961   *The Image: A Guide to Pseudo-Events in America.* New York:
        Harper & Row.

Boxberger, Daniel L.
1988   "In and Out of the Labor Force: The Lummi Indians and the
        Development of the Commercial Salmon Fishery of North
        Puget Sound, 1880–1900." *Ethnohistory* 35:161–90.

Boyd, E. (Elizabeth)
1974   *Popular Arts of Spanish New Mexico.* Santa Fe: Museum of
        New Mexico Press.

Brevoort, Elias
1884   "Santa Fe Trail in 1884." Manuscript, P-E8, Bancroft Library,
        University of California, Berkeley.

Brody, J. J.
  1971   *Indian Artists & White Patrons.* Albuquerque: University
          of New Mexico Press.

Bunting, Bainbridge
  1970   "Take a Trip with NMA: An Architectural Guide to Northern
          New Mexico." *New Mexico Architecture* 12(9–10):13–51.

Bunting, Bainbridge, and John P. Conron
  1966   "The Architecture of Northern New Mexico." *New
          Mexico Architecture* 8(9–10):14–50.

Burrows, James K.
  1986   "'A Much-Needed Class of Labour': The Economy and
          Income of the Southern Interior Plateau Indians,
          1897–1910." *British Columbia Studies* 71:27–46.

Burton, Henrietta K.
  [1936] 1975   *The Re-establishment of the Indians in Their Pueblo
          Life Through the Revival of Their Traditional Crafts
          a Study in Home Extension Education.* Millwood,
          N.Y.: Kraus Reprint Co.

Calloway, Larry
  1969   "The Plaza at the End of the Trail." *New Mexico Magazine*
          47(8):22–23.

Chabot, Maria
  N.d.   Report on the Saturday Indian Markets held under the
          portal of the Old Governor's Palace during the Months
          of July and August, 1936. Typescript, Southwestern
          Association on Indian Affairs Records. State Records
          Center and Archives, Santa Fe, New Mexico.

Chauvenet, Beatrice
  1983   *Hewett and Friends: A Biography of Santa Fe's Vibrant Era.*
          Santa Fe: Museum of New Mexico Press.

Chávez, Fray Angélico
  1953   "The First Santa Fe Fiesta Council." *New Mexico Historical
          Review* 28:183–91.

Chávez, Thomas E.
  1985   "Santa Fe's Own: A History of Fiesta." In *¡Vivan Las Fiestas!*
          edited by Donna Pierce, 6–17. Santa Fe: Museum of New
          Mexico Press.

1997   Interview with Karl A. Hoerig and Sarah Laughlin for Portal
        Program Oral History Archive.

Clifford, James
    1986   "Introduction: Partial Truths." In *Writing Culture: The
            Poetics and Politics of Ethnography,* edited by James Clifford
            and George E. Marcus, 1–26. Berkeley: University of
            California Press.

Cohen, Felix
    1982   *Handbook of Federal Indian Law.* Albuquerque: University of
            New Mexico Press.

Collections Archives
    N.d.   Palace of the Governors. Santa Fe, New Mexico.

Crick, Malcolm
    1989   "Representations of International Tourism in the Social
            Sciences: Sun, Sex, Sights, Savings, and Servility." *Annual
            Review of Anthropology* 18:307–44.

Crouch, Dora P., Daniel J. Garr, and Axel I. Mundigo
    1982   *Spanish City Planning in North America.* Cambridge,
            Mass.: MIT Press.

Dauber, Kenneth Wayne
    1993   "Shaping the Clay: Pueblo Pottery, Cultural Sponsorship
            and Regional Identity in New Mexico." Ph.D. dissertation,
            University of Arizona.

Davis, W. W. H.
    [1857] 1982 *El Gringo: New Mexico and Her People.* Lincoln:
            University of Nebraska Press.

Deloria, Vine, Jr.
    1969   *Custer Died for Your Sins.* New York: Macmillan.

Dietrich, Margretta
    1952   "The History of Indian Market." SWAIA Papers, file #106,
            New Mexico Records Center Archives, Santa Fe. [Published
            in *Santa Fe New Mexican,* August 29, 1952, "Indian Fair
            Has Been Built Up Over Span of 30 Years."]

Dubin, Margaret
    2001   *Native America Collected: The Culture of an Art World.*
            Albuquerque: University of New Mexico Press.

Dutton, Bertha P.
  1948   *New Mexico Indians.* Santa Fe: New Mexico Association for
         Indian Affairs.

  1958   *Indians of the Southwest.* Santa Fe: New Mexico Association
         for Indian Affairs. [Revision of 1948 *New Mexico Indians.*]

Edell, Marsha
  1998   "Replacing Community: Establishing Linkages for Women
         Living with HIV/AIDS—A Group Work Approach." *Social
         Work with Groups* 21(3):49–62.

Erisman, M.
  1983   "Tourism and Cultural Dependency in the West Indies."
         Annals of Tourism Research 10:337–62.

Espinosa, J. Manuel
  1942   *Crusaders of the Rio Grande: The Story of don Diego de Vargas
         and the Reconquest and Refounding of New Mexico.* Chicago:
         Institute of Jesuit History.

Espinosa, J. Manuel, trans. and ed.
  1940   *First Expedition of Vargas into New Mexico, 1692.*
         Albuquerque: University of New Mexico Press.

Ettawageshik, Frank
  1999   "My Father's Business." In *Unpacking Culture: Art and
         Commodity in Colonial and Postcolonial Worlds,* edited by
         Ruth B. Phillips and Christopher B. Steiner, 20–29. Berkeley:
         University of California Press.

Evans-Pritchard, Dierdre
  1987   "The Portal Case: Authenticity, Tourism, Traditions, and the
         Law." *Journal of American Folklore* 100:287–96.

  1990   "Tradition on Trial: How the American Legal System Handles
         the Concept of Tradition." Ph.D. dissertation, University of
         California, Los Angeles.

Ewing, George
  1998   Interview with Karl A. Hoerig and Sarah Laughlin for Portal
         Program Oral History Archive.

Feld, Stephen
  1990   *Sound and Sentiment: Birds, Weeping, Poetics, and Song in
         Kaluli Expression,* 2d ed. Philadelphia: University of
         Pennsylvania Press.

The Fiesta of Santa Fe
  1919   Fiesta program, Hewett Papers, Box 54, Museum of New
          Mexico Fray Angélico Chávez History Library.

Finger, John R.
  1991   *Cherokee Americans: The Eastern Band of the Cherokees
          in the Twentieth Century.* Lincoln: University of
          Nebraska Press.

Fowler, Catherine S.
  1999   "Willows with Beads: Weaving Contemporary Washoe and
          Northern Paiute Beaded Baskets." Paper presented at
          12th Biennial Native American Art Studies Association
          Conference, October 14–16, Victoria, B.C., Canada.

Gomez, Penny
  1997   Interview with Karl A. Hoerig for Portal Program Oral
          History Archive.

Gordon, Gary L.
  1996   "A Qualitative Study of the Meaning of Work and
          Workplace Experiences among Native Americans in Upstate
          New York." Ph.D. dissertation, Syracuse University.

Graburn, Nelson H. H.
  1976   "Introduction: The Arts of the Fourth World." In *Ethnic and
          Tourist Arts: Cultural Expressions from the Fourth World,* edited
          by Nelson H. H. Graburn, 1–32. Berkeley: University of
          California Press.

  1977   "Tourism: The Sacred Journey." In *Hosts and Guests: The
          Anthropology of Tourism,* edited by Valene Smith, 17–31.
          Philadelphia: University of Pennsylvania Press.

  1993   "Ethnic Arts of the Fourth World: The View from Canada." In
          *Imagery & Creativity: Ethnoaesthetics and Art Worlds in the
          Americas,* edited by Dorothea S. Whitten and Norman E.
          Whitten Jr., 171–204. Tucson: University of Arizona Press.

Greenwood, Davydd J.
  1977   "Culture by the Pound: An Anthropological Perspective
          on Tourism as Cultural Commoditization." In *Hosts
          and Guests: The Anthropology of Tourism,* edited by
          Valene Smith, 129–38. Philadelphia: University of
          Pennsylvania Press.

BIBLIOGRAPHY

Gregg, Josiah
[1844] 1967 *The Commerce of the Prairies.* Lincoln: University of
Nebraska Press.

Grimes, Ronald L.
1992 *Symbol and Conquest: Public Ritual and Drama in Santa Fe.*
Albuquerque: University of New Mexico Press.

Hackett, Charles Wilson, ed.
1923 *Historical Documents Relating to New Mexico, Nueva Vizcaya,
and Approaches Thereto, to 1773.* Vol. 1. Washington, D.C.:
Carnegie Institution of Washington.

1942 *Revolt of the Pueblo Indians of New Mexico and Otermin's
Attempted Reconquest 1680–1682.* Vols. 1 and 2.
Albuquerque: University of New Mexico Press.

Hannerz, Ulf
1980 *Exploring the City: Inquiries toward an Urban Anthropology.*
New York: Columbia University Press.

Hanson, J. W.
1904 *The Official History of the Fair, St. Louis, 1904.* Chicago:
Monarch Book Co.

Harris, Marvin
1968 *The Rise of Anthropological Theory.* New York: Crowell.

Hazan, Haim
1990 *A Paradoxical Community: The Emergence of a Social World in
an Urban Setting.* Greenwich, Conn.: JAI Press.

Hewett, Edgar Lee
N.d. Collection. Museum of New Mexico Palace of the Governors,
Fray Angélico Chávez History Library.

Hesuse, Lorraine (Lori)
1997 Interview with Karl A. Hoerig and Sarah Laughlin for Portal
Program Oral History Archive.

Historic Santa Fe Foundation
1972 *Old Santa Fe Today.* 2d ed. Albuquerque: Historic Santa Fe
Foundation/University of New Mexico Press.

Hoikkala, Paivi Helena
1995 "Native American Women and Community Work in
Phoenix, 1965–1980." Ph.D. dissertation, Arizona
State University.

Hordes, Stanley M.
  1990 "The History of the Santa Fe Plaza, 1610–1720." In *Santa
        Fe Historic Plaza Study*, edited by Linda Tigges, 3–36. Santa
        Fe, New Mex.: City Planning Department.

Horgan, Paul
  1956 *The Centuries of Santa Fe*. New York: E. P. Dutton.

Hoxie, Frederick
  1984 *A Final Promise*. Lincoln: University of Nebraska Press.

Hyer, Sally
  1990 *One House, One Voice, One Heart: Native American
        Education at the Santa Fe Indian School*. Santa Fe:
        Museum of New Mexico Press.

James, Mike
  1963 "Indian Market." *New Mexico Magazine* 41(8):22–23.

James, Thomas
  [1846] 1962 *Three Years among the Mexicans and Indians*.
        Chicago: Rio Grande Press.

Jules-Rosette, Bennetta
  1984 *The Messages of Tourist Art: An African Semiotic System in
        Comparative Perspective*. New York: Plenum Press.

Kawulich, Barbara Bussell
  1998 "Muscogee (Creek) Women's Perceptions of Work." Ph.D.
        dissertation, Georgia State University.

Keil, Linda
  1997 "Organizational Empowerment: Perceptions of Native
        Americans and Non-Native Americans." Ph.D. dissertation,
        Union Institute.

Kenneson, Susan Reyner
  1978 "Through the Looking-Glass: A History of Anglo-American
        Attitudes towards the Spanish-Americans and Indians of
        New Mexico." Ph.D. dissertation, Yale University.

Kessell, John L.
  1987 *Kiva, Cross, and Crown: The Pecos Indians and New Mexico,
        1540–1840*. Albuquerque: University of New Mexico Press.

Kessell, John L., and Rick Hendricks, eds.
  1992 *By Force of Arms: The Journals of don Diego de Vargas,
        New Mexico, 1691–93*. Albuquerque: University of
        New Mexico Press.

Kessell, John L., Rick Hendricks, and Meredith Dodge, eds.
  1995   *The Royal Crown Restored: The Journals of don Diego de Vargas, New Mexico, 1692–94.* Albuquerque: University of New Mexico Press.

  1998   *Blood on the Boulders: The Journals of Don Diego de Vargas, New Mexico, 1694–97.* 2 vols. Albuquerque: University of New Mexico Press.

La Farge, Oliver, ed.
  1959   *Santa Fe: The Autobiography of a Southwestern Town.* Norman: University of Oklahoma Press.

Lange, Patricia Fogelman
  1993   "Pueblo Pottery Figurines: Art as Social Criticism." Ph.D. dissertation, New York University.

Las Casas, Bartolomé de
  1971   *History of the Indies.* Translated and edited by Andrée Collard. New York: Harper & Row.

Lavie, Smadar
  1990   *The Poetics of Military Occupation: Mzeina Allegories of Bedouin Identity under Israeli and Egyptian Rule.* Berkeley: University of California Press.

Layard, John
  1942   *Stone Men of Malekula.* London: Chatto & Windus.

Lee, Molly
  1999   "Tourism and Taste Cultures: Collecting Native Art in Alaska at the Turn of the Twentieth Century." In *Unpacking Culture: Art and Commodity in Colonial and Postcolonial Worlds,* edited by Ruth B. Phillips and Christopher B. Steiner, 267–81. Berkeley: University of California Press.

Lippard, Lucy R.
  1999   *On the Beaten Track: Tourism, Art, and Place.* New York: New Press.

Littrell, Mary Ann
  1990   "Symbolic Significance of Textile Crafts for Tourists." *Annals of Tourism Research* 17:228–45.

Littrell, Mary Ann, Luella F. Anderson, and Pamela J. Brown
  1993   "What Makes a Craft Souvenir Authentic?" *Annuals of Tourism Research* 20:197–215.

Littlefield, Alice, and Martha C. Knack, eds.
1996   *Native Americans and Wage Labor: Ethnohistorical Perspectives.*
Norman: University of Oklahoma Press.

Lomawaima, K. Tsianina
1994   *They Called It Prairie Light: The Story of Chilocco Indian
School.* Lincoln: University of Nebraska Press.

Loyola, Sister Mary
1939   *The American Occupation of New Mexico 1821–1852.*
Historical Society of New Mexico Publications in History,
vol. 8. Albuquerque: University of New Mexico Press.

MacCannell, Dean
[1976] 1999 *The Tourist: A New Theory of the Leisure Class.* Berkeley:
University of California Press.

Marcus, George E.
1998   *Ethnography through Thick and Thin.* Princeton: Princeton
University Press.

Marcus, George E., and Michael M. J. Fischer
1986   *Anthropology as Cultural Critique: An Experimental
Moment in the Human Sciences.* Chicago: University of
Chicago Press.

Marcus, George E., and Fred R. Myers
1995   "The Traffic in Art and Culture: An Introduction." In *The
Traffic in Culture: Refiguring Art and Anthropology,* edited by
George E. Marcus and Fred R. Myers, 1–51. Berkeley:
University of California Press.

McAllister, Dorothy
"The Santa Fe Fiesta." *El Palacio* 11(6):78–83.

McCrossen, Helen Cramp
1931   "Native Crafts in New Mexico." *School Arts Magazine*
30(7):456–58.

McKean, Philip Frick
1977   "Towards a Theoretical Analysis of Tourism: Economic
Dualism and Cultural Involution in Bali." In *Hosts
and Guests: The Anthropology of Tourism,* edited by
Valene Smith, 93–107. Philadelphia: University of
Pennsylvania Press.

Medicine, Beatrice
1999   "Lakota Expression of Art." Paper presented in session, Yes,
        There Is a Word for It: Educating the Educators About
        American Indian Art and Culture, 12th Biennial Native
        American Art Studies Association Conference, October
        14–16, Victoria, B.C., Canada.

Miller, Daniel
1991   "Primitive Art and the Necessity of Primitivism to Art." In
        The Myth of Primitivism: Perspectives on Art, edited by Susan
        Hiller, 50–71. London: Routledge.

Mills, Barbara J.
1995   "Gender and the Reorganization of Historic Zuni Craft
        Production: Implications for Archaeological Interpretation."
        Journal of Anthropological Research 51:149–72.

Mitchell, Nancy Marie
1993   "Why Do Indians Make Art? Role and Restriction in
        Santa Fe." Paper presented at the joint meetings of the
        American Ethnological Society and the Council for Museum
        Anthropology, April 16, Santa Fe, New Mex.

Mobley-Martinez, T. D.
1997   "The Man in the Middle [and related stories]." *Albuquerque
        Tribune,* August 8.

Morinis, E. Alan
1982   "'Getting Straight': Behavioral Patterns in a Skid Row Indian
        Community." *Urban Anthropology* 11(2):193–212.

Moses, L. G.
1996   *Wild West Shows and the Images of American Indians,
        1883–1933.* Albuquerque: University of New
        Mexico Press.

Muccigrosso, Robert
1993   *Celebrating the New World: Chicago's Columbian Exposition
        of 1893.* Chicago: Ivan R. Dee.

Mucha, Janusz
1983   "From Prairie to the City: Transformation of Chicago's
        American Indian Community." *Urban Anthropology*
        12(3–4):337–71.

Mullin, Molly H.
1993   "Consuming the American Southwest: Culture, Art, and
        Difference." Ph.D. dissertation, Duke University.

1995   "The Patronage of Difference: Making Indian Art 'Art, Not
           Ethnology.'" In *The Traffic in Culture: Refiguring Art and
           Anthropology*, edited by George E. Marcus and Fred R. Myers,
           166–98. Berkeley: University of California Press. First pub-
           lished in *Cultural Anthropology* 7, no. 4 (November 1992).

Murdock, George Peter
    1949   *Social Structure*. New York: Macmillan.

Museum of New Mexico
    1991   Rules and Regulations Governing the Portal Program at the
            Palace of the Governors (Adopted 7/18/1991). Santa Fe. On
            file at State Records Center.

Museum of New Mexico Board of Regents
    N.d.   MNMBOR meeting notes and related documents. On file at
            MNM administrative office, Santa Fe.

Norcini, Marilyn Jane
    1995   "Edward P. Dozier: A History of Native American Discourse
            in Anthropology." Ph.D. dissertation, University of Arizona.

Naylor, Thomas H., William H. Willimon, and Rolf Österberg
    1996   "The Search for Community in the Workplace." *Business and
            Society Review*, no. 97:42–47.

Nestor, Sarah
    1978   *The Native Market of the Spanish New Mexican Craftsmen:
            Santa Fe, 1933–1940*. Santa Fe: Colonial New Mexico
            Historical Foundation.

Official Souvenir Program
    1922   Official Souvenir Program of the 210th Santa Fe Fiesta and
            the First Annual Southwest Indian Fair and Arts and Crafts
            Exhibition. Hewett Collection, Box 54, Museum of New
            Mexico Palace of the Governors, Fray Angélico Chávez
            History Library.

    1923   Official Souvenir Program of the 211th Anniversary of the
            Santa Fe Fiesta and the Second Annual Southwest Indian Fair.
            Hewett Collection, Box 54, Museum of New Mexico Palace
            of the Governors, Fray Angélico Chávez History Library.

Oldenquist, Andrew
    1991   "Community and De-alienization." In *Alienation,
            Community, and Work*, edited by Andrew Oldenquist and
            Menachem Rosner, 91–108. New York: Greenwood Press.

O'Rourke, Dennis
1987   *Cannibal Tours.* VHS, 77 min. Los Angeles: Direct Cinema.

Ostler, Jim
1991   "The Making of Zuni Crafts: The Economics of Specialists." In *Zuni History: Victories in the 1990s,* edited by E. R. Hart and T. J. Ferguson, sec. 2, pt. 4, p. 21. Seattle: Institute of the North American West.

El Palacio
1919   "The Santa Fe Fiesta." 7(5–6):97–132.

1922a "Prizes for Indian Handicraft." 12(6):81.

1922b "Indian Arts Exhibit." 12(11):148.

1922c "The Southwest Indian Fair." 13(8):93–97.

1923a "Southwest Indian Fair and Crafts Exhibition." 15(2):23, 25–27.

1923b "Santa Fe Fiesta and Indian Fair." 15(6)100–104.

1924   "Southwest Indian Fair and Crafts Exhibition." 16(7):109–13.

1925   "The 1925 Fiesta." 19(5)88–117.

1926   "Southwest Indian Fair 1926." 20(10):204–12.

1927   "The Indian Fair." 23(13)343–46.

Paredes, Américo
1978   "On Ethnographic Work among Minority Groups: A Folklorist's Perspective." In *New Directions in Chicano Scholarship,* edited by Ricardo Romo and Raymund Paredes, 1–32. La Jolla: Chicano Studies Program, University of California, San Diego.

Parezo, Nancy J.
1983   *Navajo Sandpainting: From Religious Act to Commercial Art.* Tucson: University of Arizona Press.

1990   "A Multitude of Markets." *Journal of the Southwest* 32(4):563–75.

Parezo, Nancy J., and Karl A. Hoerig
   1999   "Collecting to Educate: Ernest Thompson Seton and
          Mary Cabot Wheelwright." In *Collecting Native America,*
          1870–1960, edited by Shepard Krech and Barbara Hail,
          203–31. Washington, D.C.: Smithsonian Institution Press.

Parsley, Jon Keith
   1993   "Regulation of Counterfeit Indian Arts and Crafts: An
          Analysis of the Indian Arts and Crafts Act of 1990." Student
          Comment. *American Indian Law Review* 18:487–514.

Penney, David W., and Lisa Roberts
   1999   "America's Pueblo Artists: Encounters on the Borderlands."
          In *Native American Art in the Twentieth Century,* edited by
          W. Jackson Rushing III, 21–38. London: Routledge.

Peters, Kurt
   1994   "Watering the Flower: The Laguna Pueblo and the Atchison,
          Topeka, and Santa Fe Railroad, 1880–1980." Ph.D. disserta-
          tion, University of California, Berkeley.

   1995   "Santa Fe Indian Camp, House 21, Richmond, California:
          Persistence of Identity among Laguna Pueblo Railroad
          Laborers, 1945–1982." *American Indian Culture and*
          Research Journal 19(3):33–70.

Phillips, David
   1998   Interview with Karl A. Hoerig and Sarah Laughlin for Portal
          Program Oral History Archive.

Plattner, Stuart
   1996   *High Art Down Home: An Economic Ethnography of a Local*
          Art Market. Chicago: University of Chicago Press.

Portal Log
   N.d.   Notes, newspaper clippings, and other materials.
          On file in Native American Vendors Program office,
          Palace of the Governors.

Powers, Marcella
   1967   "The Mud Palace." *New Mexico Magazine*
          45(3):22–25, 36.

Price, Richard, and Sally Price
1994 *On the Mall: Presenting Maroon Tradition-Bearers at the 1992 FAF.* Special Publications of the Folklore Institute No. 4. Bloomington: Indiana University.

Prucha, Frances Paul
1984 *The Great Father.* 2 vols. Lincoln: University of Nebraska Press.

Read, Benjamin M.
1927 "In Santa Fe during Mexican Regime." *New Mexico Historical Review* 2(1):90–97.

Reddin, Paul
1999 *Wild West Shows.* Urbana: University of Illinois Press.

Reiter, Rayna Rapp
1977 "The Politics of Tourism in a French Alpine Community." In *Hosts and Guests: The Anthropology of Tourism,* edited by Valene Smith, 139–47. Philadelphia: University of Pennsylvania Press.

Romero, Orlando
1997 Interview with Karl A. Hoerig and Sarah Laughlin for Portal Program Oral History Archive.

Rothman, Hal K.
1998 *Devil's Bargain: Tourism in the Twentieth-Century American West.* Lawrence: University of Kansas Press.

Russell, Marion
1954 *Land of Enchantment: Memoirs of Marian Russell Along the Santa Fé Trail.* As dictated to Mrs. Hal Russell. Evanston, Ill.: Branding Iron Press.

Ryan, Chris, and John Crotts
1997 "Carving and Tourism: A Maori Perspective." *Annals of Tourism Research* 24(4):898–918.

Sahlins, Marshall
1999 "What Is Anthropological Enlightenment? Some Lessons of the Twentieth Century." *Annual Review of Anthropology* 28:i–xxiii.

Salodof, Jane
1998 "Indian Market People." *Indian Market Magazine.*56–71.

Scholes, France V.
  1937   *Church and State in New Mexico, 1610–1650.* Historical
        Society of New Mexico Publications in History, vol. 7.
        Albuquerque: University of New Mexico Press.

Schrader, Robert Fay
  1983   *The Indian Arts & Crafts Board: An Aspect of New
        Deal Indian Policy.* Albuquerque: University of New
        Mexico Press.

Schroeder, Albert H.
  1979   "Pueblos Abandoned in Historic Times." In *Handbook
        of North American Indians,* vol. 9, *Southwest,* edited by
        Alfonso Ortiz, 236–54. Washington, D.C.: Smithsonian
        Institution Press.

Seifert, Donna J.
  1979   "Archaeological Excavations at the Palace of the Governors,
        Santa Fe, New Mexico: 1974 and 1975." MSS, Collections,
        Palace of the Governors.

Seton, Ernest Thompson
  N.d.   "The Seton Institute." *Backlog* [ca. 1940]:9–15.

Sheppard, Carl D.
  1988   *Creator of the Santa Fe Style: Isaac Hamilton Rapp, Architect.*
        Albuquerque: University of New Mexico Press.

Shibutani, Tomatsu
  1955   "Reference Groups as Perspectives." *American Journal of
        Sociology* 60:562–69.

Shiffman, John
  1998   "$1 Billion Industry Reeling as Faux Crafts Flood Market."
        USA Today, April 8.

Shishkin, J. K.
  1972   *The Palace of the Governors.* Santa Fe: Museum of
        New Mexico.

  N.d.   The Unquiet Centuries: A Biography of the Palace of the
        Governors. MSS. Museum of New Mexico Palace of the
        Governors, Fray Angélico Chávez History Library.

Simmons, Marc
  1977   *New Mexico: A Bicentennial History.* New York: Norton.

  1990   *Spanish Government in New Mexico.* 2d ed. Albuquerque:
        University of New Mexico Press.

BIBLIOGRAPHY

Singletary, Otis A.
1960   *The Mexican War.* Chicago: University of Chicago Press.

Slim, Marvin
1998   Interview with Karl A. Hoerig and Sarah Laughlin for Portal
       Program Oral History Archive.

Smith, Marc A., and Peter Kollock, eds.
1999   *Communities in Cyberspace.* London: Routledge.

Smith, Pamela
1997   Interview with Karl A. Hoerig for Portal Program
       Oral History Archive.

Snow, Cordelia Thomas
1974   "A Brief History of the Palace of the Governors &
       a Preliminary Report on the 1974 Excavation."
       El Palacio 80(3):1–22.

1993   "A Living Artifact. The Palace of the Governors:
       Archaeological Excavations from 1884 to 1987, and a Review
       of the History of the Building from 1610 to 1846." Report
       prepared for the Getty Grant Program Project Identification
       Grant. MSS., Collections, Palace of
       the Governors.

Steiner, Christopher B.
1995   "The Art of the Trade: On the Creation of Value and
       Authenticity in the African Art Market." In *The Traffic
       in Culture: Refiguring Art and Anthropology,* edited by George
       E. Marcus and Fred R. Myers, 151–65. Berkeley: University
       of California Press.

Striffler, Steve
1999   "Wedded to Work: Class Struggles and Gendered Identities in
       the Restructuring of the Ecuadorian Banana Industry."
       Identities 6(1):91–120.

SWAIA Records
N.d.   Southwestern Association on Indian Affairs Records.
       Collection 9684, State Records Center and Archives,
       Santa Fe, New Mex.

Swain, Margaret Byrne
1977   "Cuna Women and Ethnic Tourism: A Way to Persist
       and an Avenue to Change." In *Hosts and Guests: The
       Anthropology of Tourism,* edited by Valene Smith, 71–81.
       Philadelphia: University of Pennsylvania Press.

Swentzell, Rina
   1987   "The Process of Culture—The Indian Perspective."
          El Palacio 93(1):3–5.

Sze, Corinne P., and Beverley Spears
   1988   *Santa Fe Historic Neighborhood Study.* Santa Fe, New Mex.:
          City of Santa Fe.

Tanner, Clara Lee
   1960   "The Influence of the White Man on Southwest Indian Art."
          Ethnohistory 7:137–50.

Taylor, Benjamin F.
   [1847] 1936 *Short Ravelings from a Long Yarn, or, Camp and
          March Sketches of the Santa Fe Trail.* From the notes of
          Richard L. Wilson. Santa Ana, Calif.: Fine Arts Press.

Tigges, Linda, ed.
   1990   *Santa Fe Historic Plaza Study.* Santa Fe, New Mex.:
          City Planning Department.

Tiller, Veronica E. Velarde
   1996   *Tiller's Guide to Indian Country: Economic Profiles
          of American Indian Reservations.* Albuquerque:
          BowArrow Publishing Co.

Tilley, Christopher
   1997   "Performing Culture in the Global Village." *Critique
          of Anthropology* 17(1):67–89.

Tönnies, Ferdinand
   [1957] 1988 *Community and Society (Gemeinschaft und Gesellschaft).*
          Tranlated by Charles P. Loomis. Reprint, New Brunswick,
          N.J.: Transaction Books.

Traugott, Joseph
   1999   "Fewkes and Nampeyo: Clarifying a Myth-Understanding."
          In *Native American Art in the Twentieth Century,* edited
          by W. Jackson Rushing III, 7–20. London: Routledge.

Turner, Victor
   1974   *Dramas, Fields, and Metaphors.* Ithaca: Cornell
          University Press.

   [1969] 1995 *The Ritual Process: Structure and Anti-Structure.*
          New York: Aldine de Gruyter.

Twitchell, Ralph Emerson
   1924   *The Palace of the Governors: The City of Santa Fe, Its Museums and Monuments.* Historical Society of New Mexico Publications no. 29. Santa Fe: Historical Society of New Mexico.

   [1925] 1963 *Old Santa Fe: The Story of New Mexico's Ancient Capital.* Chicago: Rio Grande Press.

Underhill, Ruth
   [1944] 1979 *Pueblo Crafts.* Palmer Lake, Colo.: Filter Press.

Unruh, David R.
   1983   *Invisible Lives: Social Worlds of the Aged.* Beverly Hills, Calif.: Sage.

Urbanowicz, C. F.
   1989   "Tourism in Tonga Revisited: Continued Troubled Times?" In *Hosts and Guests: The Anthropology of Tourism,* 2d ed, edited by Valene Smith, 105–18. Philadelphia: University of Pennsylvania Press.

Urry, John
   1990   *The Tourist Gaze: Leisure and Travel in Contemporary Societies.* London: Sage.

USA Today
   1998   "A 1990 Federal Law Has Never Been Used to Catch Counterfeiters." April 8, 1998, p. 2A.

U.S. House
   1992   Committee on Interior and Insular Affairs. To Expand the Powers of the Indian Arts and Crafts Board. 101st Cong. Washington, D.C.: Government Printing Office.

van den Berghe, Pierre
   1980   "Tourism as Ethnic Relations: A Case Study of Cuzco, Peru." *Ethnic and Racial Studies* 3(4):375–92.

   1994   *The Quest for the Other: Ethnic Tourism in San Cristóbal, Mexico.* Seattle: University of Washington Press.

Wade, Edwin L.
   1976   "The History of the Southwest Indian Ethnic Art Market." Ph.D. dissertation, University of Washington.

1985 "The Ethnic Art Market in the American Southwest, 1880–1980." In *Objects and Others: Essays on Museums and Material Culture, History of Anthropology,* vol. 3, edited by George W. W. Stocking, 167–91. Madison: University of Wisconsin Press.

Walter, Paul A. F.
1915 "New Mexico's Contributions to the Panama-California Exposition." *El Palacio* 3(1):3–16.

1920 "The Fiesta of Santa Fe." *Art & Archaeology* 9:15–23.

Weibel, Joan
1978 "Native Americans in Los Angeles: A Cross-Cultural Comparison of Assistance Patterns in an Urban Environment." *Anthropology UCLA* 9(1–2):81–100.

Weibel-Orlando, Joan
1991 *Indian Country, L.A.: Maintaining Ethnic Community in Complex Society.* Urbana: University of Illinois Press.

Weiner, Carolyn L.
1981 *The Politics of Alcoholism: Building an Arena around a Social Problem.* New Brunswick, N.J.: Transaction Books.

Wellman, Barry, Janet Salaff, Dimitrian Dimitrova, Laura Garton, Milena Gulia, and Caroline Haythornthwaite
1996 "Computer Networks as Social Networks: Collaborative Work, Telework, and Virtual Community." *Annual Review of Sociology* 22:213–38.

Wenzel, George W.
1983 "The Integration of 'Remote' Site Labour into the Inuit Economy of Clyde River, N.W.T." *Arctic Anthropology* 20(2):79–92.

Williams, Raymond
Culture and Society, 1780–1950. New York: Harper & Row.

Williams, Raymond, ed.
1983 *Keywords.* London: Fontana.

Wilson, Christopher M.
1997 *The Myth of Santa Fe: Creating a Modern Regional Tradition.* Albuquerque: University of New Mexico Press.

1981   "The Santa Fe, New Mexico Plaza: An Architectural and Cultural History, 1610–1921." M.A. thesis, University of New Mexico.

Wilson, Olive
  1915   "The Survival of an Ancient Art." *Art & Archaeology* 9(1):24–29.

Wyatt, Victoria
  1987   "Alaskan Indian Wage Earners in the 19th Century." *Pacific Northwest Quarterly* 78(1–2):43–49.

Index